AF600068

THE CATHOLIC UNIVERSITY OF AMERICA
CANON LAW STUDIES
No. 186

PRIVILEGES OF REGULARS TO ABSOLVE AND DISPENSE

AN HISTORICAL CONSPECTUS AND COMMENTARY

BY THE

REV. RALPH VINCENT SHUHLER, O.S.A., J.C.L.
Priest of the Province of St. Thomas of Villanova

A DISSERTATION

Submitted to the Faculty of the School of Canon Law of the Catholic University of America, in Partial Fulfillment of the Requirements for the Degree of Doctor of Canon Law

THE CATHOLIC UNIVERSITY OF AMERICA PRESS
WASHINGTON, D. C.
1943

Nihil Obstat:

HENRICUS A. CAFFREY, O.S.A.,

Censor Deputatus.

Imprimi Potest:

JOANNES T. SHEEHAN, O.S.A., J.C.D.,

Prior Provincialis.

Villanova, Pa., die 3 Maii, 1943.

Nihil Obstat:

EDUARDUS G. ROELKER, S.T.D., J.C.D.,

Censor Deputatus.

Washingtonii, D. C., die 10 Maii, 1943.

Imprimatur:

✠ MICHAEL J. CURLEY, D.D.,

Archiepiscopus Baltimorensis-Washingtoniensis.

Baltimorae, Md., die 10 Maii, 1943.

COPYRIGHT, 1943
THE CATHOLIC UNIVERSITY OF AMERICA PRESS

Printed by
THE PAULIST PRESS
New York, N. Y.
51

TABLE OF CONTENTS

FOREWORD

The Church, despite its zeal for uniformity of discipline, is not unmindful of the reward to be given for special service. This reward for extraordinary merit takes the form of ecclesiastical honors and favors. Emanating from the competent ecclesiastical superiors, such concessions permit the recipient of the honors and favors to exercise functions and powers possibly beyond and contrary to the limits established by the common law. In ages past, the Roman Pontiffs, out of gratitude for the marvelous fruits of sanctification wrought in the faithful by Religious institutes, rewarded them with special privileges not usually granted to diocesan clergy. Many of these privileges have remained until the present day; others, however, have fallen into desuetude.

This dissertation is not an exhaustive study of all the privileges granted to Religious institutes during their many centuries of existence. Rather, the work is limited to a study of privileges shared in common by religious who are known as *Regulars*. Specifically, only those Apostolic privileges are treated which grant special powers of absolving and dispensing in relation to the Sacrament of Penance. The writer has a twofold purpose in the development of the dissertation: the determination of the extent of powers granted by the Roman Pontiffs by a critical analysis of available historical documents; and the determination of the present status of such privileges by a canonical study of their relation to the present Code of Canon Law.

The writer takes this occasion to express his sincere gratitude to the superiors of the Order of Hermits of St. Augustine, and especially to the Very Rev. John T. Sheehan, O.S.A., the Provincial of the Province of St. Thomas of Villanova, for the opportunity of pursuing advanced study in Canon Law; to the Faculty of the School of Canon Law of the Catholic University of America for their assistance and guidance, and to all who have generously given of their time and energy in the preparation of this dissertation.

INTRODUCTION

A PRIVILEGE is commonly defined as a constitution of the supreme ruler, granting a special favor.[1] From its etymological derivation (*privata lex*) privilege may be defined as a concession to a particular person, or group of persons, whether moral or physical, of some special favor. As opposed to law,[2] a privilege is not established immediately for the common good of the community. It is a grant or favor to a person; and in so far as it is contrary to the common law, it removes that person from subjection to the common law. A privilege, therefore, derogates from the common law when it conflicts with that law, unless the law has a clause specifically abrogating privileges contrary to it. A privilege, then, is more accurately defined as *a private law conferring upon some person a special favor contrary to or outside of the common law.*[3]

Privileges may be variously divided. In the present work, wherein privileges of Regulars regarding absolution and dispensation in relation to the Sacrament of Penance are considered, one division will suffice: *communicated* privileges and *non-communicated* privileges. A privilege is communicated when its scope is enlarged under a provision by which the legislator expressly permits a privilege already granted directly to one person to be extended to another; otherwise it is non-communicated, or a direct concession. Communicability in a privilege is that quality which denotes its capacity to be shared by or extended to another person.

Communication may be of two kinds: communication *in forma aequiprincipali,* and *in forma accessoria.*[4] The distinction between

[1] Privilegium . . . est supremi principis constitutio specialem favorem concedens.—Ferraris, *Prompta Bibliotheca, Canonica, Moralis, Theologica, necnon Ascetica, Polemica, Rubricistica, Historica* (9 vols., Romae, 1885-1899), s.v. "Privilegium," art. 1, n. 1.

[2] Lex est ordinatio rationis ad bonum commune, et ab eo, qui curam habet communitatis, promulgata.—St. Thomas Aquinas, *Summa Theologica,* Ia, IIae, q. 90, a. 4, c.

[3] Cf. A. Cicognani, *Canon Law,* Authorized English version by J. O'Hara and F. Brennan (2. ed., Philadelphia: Dolphin Press, 1935), p. 779. "Privilegium dici solet lex privata, contra vel praeter ius, aliquid concedens."—Ferraris, *loc. cit.*

[4] Cf. Piat, *Praelectiones Iuris Regularis* (3. ed., 2 vols., Tornaci, 1906), II, Qu. 140-143.

these forms of communication is based upon the relative stability of the privileges once they have been acquired. A privilege obtained *in forma accessoria* has only a dependent existence. It is dependent upon the privilege from which communication has originated in such a way, that, if the original privilege is increased, diminished, or lost, the communicated privilege is likewise increased, diminished, or lost. A privilege obtained *in forma aequiprincipali* has independent existence. Although such a privilege is dependent upon the original privilege for its acquisition, it is thereafter entirely independent of it; so that, once acquired, it remains intact, even though the original privilege is diminished, or lost entirely. Briefly, then, privileges *in forma aequiprincipali* are communicated absolutely; privileges *in forma accessoria,* relatively.

In examining the terms of the title of the present work one meets the word *Regulars.* What is its meaning? The term *Regulars* is derived from the Latin *regula,* a rule. The term was used to designate those persons who followed a Rule of life. The Regular life originated in the earliest centuries of the Church, when men and women by the thousands withdrew from the cities into the deserts and into monasteries to live under the rule of life established by some saintly man. Thus one finds in early history the Rule of St. Pachomius (286-346), of St. Basil (329-379), of St. Augustine (354-430), and of St. Benedict (480-543). These Rules of life in time received the official approval of the Church, and form today the foundation of that manner of life known as the religious life under its various aspects: monastic, Regular, etc. Those Orders which were approved during the Middle Ages and fused the monastic with the active life came to be known as Regular Orders. In the present canon law Regulars are those who make profession of temporary or solemn vows in a religious institute of solemn vows.[5]

The terms *Regular* and *Mendicant* will be used frequently in this study, oftentimes interchangeably. They are not synonymous however. Mendicants are those who according to their institute and in virtue of their primitive constitution are radically incapable of possessing property in common. Such were the followers of St. Francis (1182-1226), united in an Order in 1209, and approved by Pope

[5] Cf. canon 488, § 2.

Honorius III (1216-1227) in 1223. Since they had no means of sustenance other than by begging, they were given the name *Mendicantes,* beggars; whence the name Mendicant.

The privilege of begging for their sustenance wherever they happened to reside was given to these religious by the Roman Pontiff, so that, lay authorities and local Ordinaries could not interfere. In time, however, other religious institutes were given the same privilege, even though their members were permitted to possess property in common. These Orders were likewise called Mendicants.[6]

All those religious Orders which obtained the privilege of begging were called Mendicants. By the time of the V general Lateran Council (1512-1517), at least six great religious Orders shared in the privileges of Mendicants: the Order of Friars Minor (approved in 1223); the Order of Friars Preachers (approved in 1216); the Order of Hermits of St. Augustine (united in 1256); the Order of Carmel (approved in 1274); the Servites (approved in 1303); and the Order of Minims of St. Francis of Paula (rule first approved in 1474; revised and finally approved in 1506).[7]

The title of this present work includes the words *dispense and absolve.* These words imply the use of jurisdiction. A dispensation is a relaxation of a law in a particular case;[8] in order that one dispenses validly, jurisdiction from the legitimate ecclesiastical authority is demanded. Absolution is the remission of a sin or penalty imparted by one who has the requisite authority; jurisdiction is also required for valid absolution. The present study treats the powers of dispensing and absolving in relation to the Sacrament of Penance.

[6] Nomine Mendicantium, stricto sensu, veniunt illi Ordines, qui, vi primaevae institutionis, quam adhuc servant, ne in communi quidem possunt bona possidere ut propria; sensu vero latiori, etiam illi, qui, ex relaxatione vel dispensatione Pontificia nunc in communi bona possident.—Wernz, *Ius Decretalium* (6 vols., Romae, 1905-1913), III, tit. 24, n. 597.

[7] Cf. Leo X, const. *Dudum per nos,* 10 dec. 1519.—*Bullarum Diplomatum et Privilegiorum Sanctorum Romanorum Pontificum Taurinensis editio* (25 vols., Augustae Taurinorum, 1857-1872), V, 733. This work will be cited as *Bull. Rom.*

[8] Cf. canon 80.

CHAPTER I

GENERAL HISTORICAL EVOLUTION OF CONFESSIONAL PRIVILEGES AMONG RELIGIOUS

Article 1. Confessional Privileges from their Origins to the Rise of the Mendicant Orders

The Roman Catholic Church in its divine constitution exercises a twofold parallel authority over the faithful: the authority of the Roman Pontiff, and the authority of the bishops in communion with the Holy See. The Roman Pontiff, as Pastor of the Universal Church, has direct, immediate and ordinary power over each soul cleansed by the waters of baptism.[1] The bishops, each in his own diocese, have divinely given, immediate and ordinary power over the flocks committed to their charge.[2]

This power of ruling the faithful is called the power of jurisdiction. Authors define it as the public power of ruling subjects for the purpose of achieving the aim of a perfect society.[3] This power is exercised freely by one who has ordinary power. It may be delegated in whole or in part to anyone capable of exercising jurisdiction, unless the law of the superior authority forbids such delegation.[4] As a matter of historical fact, this power of jurisdiction has been delegated to others in every age from the earliest days of the Church. Its recipients, almost without exception, were the clerics of the various dioceses, to whom, as assistants to the bishops, was entrusted a large portion of the sacred ministry. Priests and deacons by reason of their sacred ordination were especially suited to be helpers of the

[1] Cf. canon 218, § 2.

[2] Cf. canon 329.

[3] Iurisdictio est potestas regendi subditos in ordine ad finem societatis perfectae consequendum.—Coronata, Matthaeus, Conte a, *Institutiones Iuris Canonici* (5 vols., vols. I-II, 2. ed., 1939; vols. III-V, 1. ed., 1933-1936; Taurini: Marietti), I, n. 275.

[4] Cf. canons 198; 199, § 1.

bishop. The conducting of the sacred ceremonies, the preaching of the word of God, and the absolving from sins, were frequently committed to priests. After the fifth century, the delegation of jurisdiction to priests to hear the confessions of all the faithful and to absolve from sins became general. Only a few of the public and more heinous sins were reserved to the bishop or to the pope for absolution.

In the early centuries of the Church, and continuing almost to the time of the Council of Trent (1545-1563), little provision by statutory enactment was made for the training and education of young men for the priesthood. Youths were trained by being taken into the household of the bishop, and were ordained by him after they were schooled sufficiently in the sacred sciences. Naturally this was a slow process, and the number thus trained was entirely inadequate to fill the needs of a rapidly spreading faith. Bishops therefore turned to the faithful in search of men whose learning and holy lives could be turned to usefulness in supplementing the number of the clergy. To no better place could they turn for scholarly, well-trained candidates, than to the monasteries of religious men whose holy lives were an example and inspiration to the faithful everywhere.

The practice of ordaining monks to the priesthood dates from very early times. A document written about the year 385 and ascribed to Pope Siricius (384-398) attests to the fact that it was not only the practice of the Church at that time but also the will of the Supreme Pontiffs that monks be ordained priests.[5] St. Augustine (354-430)[6] and St. Jerome (342-420)[7] bear witness to the same practice. In Africa one monastery founded by St. Augustine at Tagaste in 387 furnished the African Church with many bishops and priests.[8] In the Oriental Church the burden of hearing the confes-

[5] Cf. c. 29, C. XVI, q. 1; Jaffé, *Regesta Pontificum Romanorum ab condita Ecclesia ad annum post Christum natum MCXCVIII* (editionem secundam correctam et auctam auspiciis Gulielmi Wattenback curaverunt S. Loewenfeld, F. Kaltenbrunner, P. Ewald, 2 vols. in 1, Lipsiae, 1885-1888), n. 255. This work will be cited as **JK, JE, JL.**

[6] Cf. ep. 48—Migne, *Patrologiae Cursus Completus, Series Latina* (221 vols., Parisiis, 1858-1864), XXXIII, 168; c. 30, C. XVI, q. 1; ep. 60—Migne, *ibid.*, 228; c. 36, C. XVI, q. 1. Migne's work will be cited as *MPL.*

[7] Cf. ep. 125—*MPL*, XXII, 1082; c. 26, C. XVI, q. 1.

[8] Cf. Possidius, *Vita S. Aurelii Augustini*, c. 5—*MPL*, XXXII, 37, 38.

sions of the faithful and of preaching the Gospel fell mainly upon the monks. This is abundantly substantiated by the findings of Christianus Lupus (1612-1681) [9] and of the Bollandists.[10]

Within the monastery the right to administer the sacraments pertained in the first place to the abbot or monastic superior. He could delegate his powers to others of his subjects. The original status of the monastic superior's jurisdictional powers is not entirely clear. A study of his powers, however, reveals the fact that most probably his jurisdiction derived from the bishop of the diocese in which the monastery was located.[11] There is a possibility, however, that such superiors exercised their jurisdiction by reason of the monastic rule itself, independent of any delegation from the bishop. Since the notion of jurisdictional authority was not developed at that time as it was later developed under the Scholastics, it seems correct to infer that the monastic priests received from the ordaining bishop at the time of ordination the necessary jurisdiction to administer the sacraments. The lawful exercise of such jurisdiction was dependent upon the permission of the monastic superior. Gratian, in a *dictum* to one of the decretals,[12] seems to imply the same:

> His omnibus auctoritatibus perspicue monstratur, monachos posse poenitentiam dare, baptizare, et caetera sacerdotalia officia licite administrare. Quod vero populi electione, episcoporum institutione, et abbatis consensu potestatem exequi valeant, Hieronymi, Gelasii, et Gregorii auctoritate probatur.

The abbot of the monastery exercised quasi-parochial rights by reason of his office even over the laity who were engaged in the service

[9] Cf. *Synodorum Generalium ac Provincialium Decreta et Canones* (12 vols. in 6, Venetiis, 1723-1729), tom. 3, pars 3, c. 10, a. 9, p. 391; *Exhibitio Sacrorum Canonum circa Ius Regularium Ecclesiarum quoad Praedicationem Divini Verbi* (opuscula posthuma, Venetiis, 1729), cc. 2, 3.

[10] They relate: . . . ab antiquissimis temporibus, monachos in Ecclesia Orientali solos fere adhibitos ad excipiendas poenitentium confessiones.—*Examen Historicum et Canonicum Libri M. Verhoeven* (Bruxellis, 1847), p. 256.

[11] Cf. Schiewietz, "Pachomianische Klöster im vierten Jahrhunderte," *Archiv für katholisches Kirchenrecht,* LXXXII (1902), 454. This work will be cited as *AKKR*.

[12] Cf. c. 25, C. XVI, q. 1.

of the monastery. This was especially true in the monasteries of England and Ireland, where there was "a government of abbots with the bishops as subordinate officers discharging episcopal functions, but without jurisdiction." [13]

For the Oriental Church, St. Jerome [14] testifies that in one monastery there were five monks who exercised the right of conferring the sacrament of baptism upon the faithful, though this right was usually reserved to the bishops.

The monastic life spread rapidly throughout the West. Its form of organization differed somewhat from that of the East. While the East maintained separate independent monasteries, the West introduced the method of establishing filial houses apart from the parent monastery but connected with it for its discipline and jurisdictional powers. Throughout Ireland, France and Italy, the central monasteries established filial houses in the neighboring dioceses. The Benedictine Congregation of Monte Cassino in the seventh and eighth centuries was an example of this type of monastic organization. Such filial houses looked to the parent monastery for their legislation, and their jurisdiction came from the archabbot. But since the early monastic foundations did not enjoy exemption from the local Ordinaries, it was only natural that no uniformity of discipline could exist throughout the parent and filial monasteries because of the individual statutes of the different dioceses where their houses were located. The monks sought to secure uniformity. About the year 524 a large group of abbots in the monasteries of Africa devised a plan whereby the monasteries of the African Church might obtain a uniform discipline. At the Synod of Carthage (c. 525) they laid their proposal before the assembled bishops in which they asked to be exempted from the jurisdiction of all the African bishops, except the Primate of Africa. They asked that the Primate alone be allowed to legislate for them. This exemption was granted them.[15] It provided that

[13] Haddon and Stubbs, *Councils and Ecclesiastical Documents Relating to Great Britain and Ireland* (3 vols. in 4, Oxford, 1869-1873), I, 142.

[14] Cf. *Liber contra Joannem Hierosolymitanum*, c. 42—*MPL*, XXIII, 393.

[15] Mansi, *Sacrorum Conciliorum Nova et Amplissima Collectio* (53 vols. in 60, Parisiis, 1901-1927), VIII, 635-650; Harduinus, *Acta Conciliorum et Epistolae Decretales ac Constitutiones Summorum Pontificum* (ed. Regia, 12 vols.; Parisiis, 1715).

thenceforth no bishop of Africa other than the Primate could exercise jurisdiction over, or interfere in the discipline of their monasteries.

Once the privilege of monastic exemption came into existence it spread quickly throughout the Western Church. Various popes from the time of Gregory the Great (590-604), who was a Benedictine monk himself, granted partial exemption to individual monasteries.[16] Complete papal exemption was granted for the first time in the year 628 when Pope Honorius I (625-638) placed the monastery of Bobbio, founded by St. Columbanus (c. 545-615), directly under the jurisdiction of the Roman Pontiff, thereby exempting it from the jurisdiction of all local Ordinaries.[17] During the succeeding centuries there was a gradual extension of withdrawal of monasteries from the jurisdiction of the bishops. By the time of Pope Urban II (1088-1099), the *libertas Romana* was looked upon as complete exemption of a monastery from the jurisdiction of the local Ordinary in all that pertained to its internal discipline. Thus, the abbot did not require jurisdiction from the bishop to hear the confessions of his subjects; he, with his whole community, was exempt from such jurisdiction. His jurisdiction came directly from the Roman Pontiff.[18] The choice of the superiors of the monastery pertained now directly to the subjects of the monastery, without reference to, or intervention from, the local Ordinary.[19] So also was the choice of candidates for the priesthood determined according to the rules of the monastery.[20] And in the eleventh and twelfth centuries monasteries generally possessed the privilege of sending their candidates for the priesthood to any bishop in communion with the Holy See for their ordination.[21]

[16] Cf. Montalembert, *Monks of the West* (2 vols., Boston, 1872), I, 397, 398.

[17] Cf. Montalembert, *ibid.*, I, 583; JE, n. 2017.

[18] Cf. Hüfner, "Das Rechtsinstitut der klösterlichen Exemtion in der abendländishen Kirche"—*AKKR,* LXXXVI (1906), 648-650; Reilly, *The Visitation of Religious* (Catholic University of America Canon Law Studies, n. 112, Washington, D. C.: Catholic University of America Press, 1938), pp. 41-45.

[19] Cf. *Benedicti Regula Monachorum,* c. 64—*MPL,* LXVI, 879.

[20] Cf. Harduinus, *op. cit.,* II, 1065. See also c. 4, C. XVIII, q. 2; JK, n. 645.

[21] Cf. Knowles, *Monastic Orders in England* (Cambridge University Press, 1940), p. 585.

Monastic exemption pertained only to the subjects of the monastic superior. Over the rest of the faithful the local Ordinary exercised complete jurisdiction. Consequently, when priests from the monasteries assisted in hearing the confessions of the faithful outside the monastery, or in preaching and catechizing, they needed special permission and jurisdiction from the bishop. However, here again, one finds exceptions in history. With the permission of the Roman Pontiff, St. Equitius (died c. 540) preached the Gospel wherever he went without permission from the local Ordinaries, according to the testimony of Gratian.[22] Bede the Venerable (673-735) relates that St. Fursey (died c. 648) preached throughout England, and that St. Wilfrid (634-709) built a monastery for religious whose duty it was to preach the Gospel throughout the land.[23] Pope Gregory IV (828-844) granted Rabanus Maurus (c. 784-856) the privilege of preaching the Gospel throughout France.[24] The abbot of Corbie in France was given the same privilege in 833.[25] That this papal privilege of preaching carried with it the jurisdiction to hear the confessions of those who attended the sermons is indicated from a constitution of Pope Innocent IV (1243-1254).[26]

St. Walter (died 1070) received directly from Pope Victor II (1055-1057) jurisdiction to hear the confessions of all who approached him to confess.[27] A similar privilege was granted St. Aybert (died 1140) by popes Pascal II (1099-1118) and Innocent II (1130-1143).[28] St. Hugh (1024-1109), abbot of the monastery at Cluny received from Pope Alexander II (1061-1073) the privilege of choosing from his monastery suitable priests, who should absolve the sins

[22] C. 40, C. XVI, q. 1, *in fine*.

[23] Cf. *Historia Ecclesiastica Gentis Anglorum* (2 vols., ed. Plummer, London, 1896), I, lib. 3, cc. 19, 26; lib. 4, cc. 14, 27.

[24] JE, n. 257, ad annum 828.

[25] JE, n. 2577, 2578.

[26] Const. *Quoniam*, 24 mart. 1244—Th. Ripoll, *Bullarium Praedicatorum* (8 vols., Romae, 1729), I, 137. This work will hereafter be cited as *Bull. Praed.*

[27] Cf. *Acta Sanctorum* (ed. Bollandus et Henschenius) ad diem 11 maii, II, c. 3, n. 13, p. 703.

[28] Cf. *Acta Sanctorum*, ad diem 7 aprilis, I, c. 3, n. 18, p. 675.

of any of the faithful who presented themselves at the monastery for absolution.[29] This privilege which was obtained by the abbot of Cluny only in the eleventh century (c. 1066) seems to have been in use in the Irish foundations centuries previously. Whether it had been obtained by custom, or by a specific concession of the popes, of which there is no record, is not certain. At least, all lay persons who came to the monastery as students, or servants, were regarded as belonging to the monastic family, and under the jurisdiction of the abbot. St. Columbanus (c. 545-615) brought this practice into France and Germany, but met with widespread opposition from the diocesan clergy. Watkins[30] states that:

> It was with such a *clientela* [sic], at once within and without the monastery enclosure, that Columbanus had to deal; and he dealt with it as an Irish abbot was wont to deal. He would ask no outside authority. His was the "Nation of the Monks." Those who come to him accept his jurisdiction. And once within his bounds, his jurisdiction goes unquestioned.

In lands where no diocesan organization was had, the Roman Pontiff exercised exclusive jurisdiction. Missionaries sent to convert those lands were dependent entirely upon the Pope for jurisdiction to minister the sacraments to converts to the Faith. For such apostolic labors, the Roman Pontiffs called upon monastic priests for the greater part. Thus, we have the example of St. Augustine (died c. 604), Prior of the monastery of St. Andrew on the Coelian Hill at Rome, who, with a large group of his Benedictine monks, was sent to England. These missionaries received papal jurisdiction to minister the sacraments wherever they went, despite the fact that there were some bishops in residence there.[31]

[29] Cf. *Bull. Rom.*, II, 28. See also the privileges of the Abbey of Cluny in JL, n. 5372.

[30] Cf. *A History of Penance* (2 vols., London: Longmans, Green & Co., 1920), II, 614.

[31] Gregory I, *ep.* 57, 58—*MPL,* LXXVII, 841, 842; Mabillon, *Annales Ordinis Sancti Benedicti* (6 vols., Lucae, 1739-1745), lib. 9, n. 13, t. 1, p. 224; Knowles, *Monastic Orders in England,* pp. 19, 20.

Article 2. The Mendicant Orders and Pontifical Concessions before the Council of Trent

The student of history will notice that the monastic form of the religious life prevailed during the first millennium of the Church. Outside of the few scattered communities of hermits, the Benedictine religious discipline predominated until the thirteenth century. Monasteries formed a haven for those who preferred to consecrate their lives to prayer and contemplation within the security of cloistral walls. Intent upon their own salvation, they were little concerned with advancement to priestly Orders and to the active ministry among the faithful living in the world. Indeed, it was only in the eleventh and twelfth centuries that greater numbers of them aspired to Holy Orders. And one discovers that it was precisely in these centuries that the Roman Pontiffs granted them more extensive privileges regarding exemption from episcopal jurisdiction, and regarding the administration of the sacraments to those living outside the monastery.

The thirteenth century, however, witnessed the inauguration of a new form of religious life: the *mixed form.* This form of religious life, the object of which was to blend harmoniously the monastic ideals with the pressing needs of the Church, had its origin at the beginning of the thirteenth century. It found its first great organized community in the establishment of the Order of Preachers by St. Dominic (1170-1221). The Order was approved in 1216 by Pope Honorius III; its approval was soon followed by the approval in 1223 of a similar Order, that of the Friars Minor. In the new foundations greater numbers aspired to the holy priesthood, for it was only as priests that they could carry out the duties connected with the active ministry. From a consideration of the fact of exemption from the jurisdiction of the local Ordinary which they possessed, and of the fact that these Orders were established to take a very active part in the work of the dioceses, one would naturally expect to find more papal privileges regarding the administration of the sacraments to the faithful during this period than previously. And since the labors of the diocesan clergy and of the religious clergy frequently overlapped, it is logical to suppose that this period was marked by controversies over their respective rights and privileges.

The period lends itself to division into two sections: Section A. The period of direct concessions of privileges; Section B. The period of general communication of privileges.

Section A. The Period of Direct Concessions of Privileges (1216-1474)

The Dominican Order was the first to receive special privileges from the Holy See for the administration of the sacraments. Founded for the purpose of preaching the word of God, from which the Order received its name of Friars Preachers, its members traveled throughout the dioceses of Europe teaching and converting the people. Their work was only half accomplished, however, if they simply moved people to repentance without also absolving their sins. In order that this work might not be hampered, Pope Gregory IX (1227-1241), by special Apostolic privilege, granted to those religious who were chosen by their superiors for the office of preaching, the right to absolve the sins of all lay people who confessed to them. This grant of the pope as contained in the Constitution *Quoniam* of the year 1227 was to be presented to the Ordinaries of the dioceses where the Friars were to preach. It informed the Ordinaries that the Friars were to be received kindly and that they were not to be molested in their labors, since they preached and absolved with the permission of the Pope himself:

> . . . cum auctoritate nostra liceat confessiones audire, ac poenitentias iniungere.[32]

The tenor of this constitution indicates that already serious disputes had been in progress between the friars and the secular clergy. Bishops in some instances had refused to let the religious preach. They were frequently loaded with reproaches by the diocesan clergy who resented interference in their parochial work. For these reasons the pope, from the plentitude of his ordinary power over all the

[32] Const. *Quoniam,* 10 maii 1227—*Bull. Praed.,* I, 19; Potthast, *Regesta Pontificum Romanorum inde ab anno post Christum natum MCXCVIII ad annum MCCCIV* (2 vols., Berolini, 1874-1875), n. 7896. This work will be hereafter cited as Potth.

faithful, granted them the right to preach and absolve without first having received jurisdiction from the local Ordinary.

A study of the privilege reveals two noteworthy provisions. In the first place, the papal jurisdiction was not granted to all the priests of the Order indiscriminately; it was limited to those who were chosen for the office of preaching. Secondly, some form of presentation of the priests chosen had to be made to the local Ordinary. This is implied in the opening words of the letter which was directed to the bishops of the places where the Friars happened to preach. The Pope commanded them to receive the religious kindly *(ut benigne recipiatis)*. The religious therefore had to present themselves to the bishop before the Apostolic privilege became operative. In the whole history of papal privileges regarding administration of the sacraments to lay people, some form of presentation to the local Ordinary was a prerequisite for the valid use of papal jurisdiction. This rule suffered only one exception for a brief period of a few years which will be pointed out later. In the appointment of a religious priest to a parish entrusted to an Order the bishop always had the right to accept or reject the priest presented by the religious superior. This is abundantly clear from a constitution of Pope Honorius III, issued to the Dominicans in 1216:

> In parochialibus vero ecclesiis quas habetis, liceat vobis sacerdotes eligere, et dioecesano episcopo praesentare, quibus, si idonei, episcopus animarum curam committit.[33]

This constitution seems to indicate that it was the bishop who bestowed the power to administer the sacraments. It must be remembered that this constitution was issued prior to any explicit grant of Apostolic jurisdiction to religious Orders.

Meanwhile the Order of Friars Minor had received similar privileges. The use of such privileges, however, was tempered by the Rule of St. Francis who refused to permit his subjects to enter a diocese against the wishes of the local Ordinary.[34] Gregory IX, in a

[33] Const. *Religiosam vitam*, 22 dec. 1216—*Bull. Rom.*, III, 309; Potth., n. 5403. Pope Urban III (1185-1187) expressly commanded monastery churches to be provided for and ruled over by a chaplain appointed by the bishop after consultation with the monks—cf. c. 1, X, *de capellis monachorum*, III, 37.

[34] Cf. c. 3, *de verborum significatione*, V, 12, in VI°, *post medium*.

letter of 1233, strongly urged the bishops not to refuse the Franciscans the right to preach in their dioceses.[35] In the same year the Pope gave them jurisdiction to hear the confessions of the faithful in the lands of the infidels, especially in the Near East. Penitents in these lands could be absolved by Franciscan Friars from all excommunications, even those reserved in any way to the Holy See.[36]

The special privileges granted by the Roman Pontiffs to Regulars caused a very tempest of protests and jealousies among the diocesan clergy. Despite the real religious revival begun by the friars, the parish priests, awakened out of their lethargy, too often found time only to criticize and calumniate their holy labors. Pope Innocent IV (1243-1254) was forced to issue a strong rebuke to those who molested them.[37] The attacks against the Orders became very bitter. From the chairs of theology in the great universities professors taught that absolution of sins by reason of pontifical jurisdiction was invalid. William of St. Amour (died 1272), canon theologian at the University of Paris, published two pamphlets [38] attacking the very foundation of the mendicant religious life. He attempted to show that religious, who should be spiritually dead to the world, incur eternal damnation by laboring in the active ministry. He was ably refuted by St. Bonaventure (1221-1274)[39] and by St. Thomas Aquinas (1226-1274).[40] Pope Alexander IV (1254-1261) ordered the works of William to be burned and retractation of his errors to be made. This pope also vindicated the papal privileges of Regulars in his Bull *Non sine*

[35] Const. *Quia potestatem*, 4 ian. 1233—Sbaralea, *Bullarium Franciscanum* (4 vols., Romae, 1759-1768), I, 90; Potth., n. 9064.

[36] Const. *Animarum salute*, 24 mart. 1233—*Bull. Francisc.*, I, 100; Potth., n. 9130; const. *Cum messis*, 8 apr. 1233—*Bull. Francisc., loc. cit.;* Potth., n. 9139. See also Potth., nn. 9184, 9196, 9197.

[37] Nec impediatis, quominus illi, qui ad eorum (Praedicatorum) praedicationem accesserint, tunc eorum sacerdotibus valeant confiteri.—const. *Quoniam*, 24 mart. 1244—*Bull. Praed.*, I, 137; Potth., n. 11299.

[38] 1. *De Periculis Novissimorum Temporum* (1256); 2. *Liber de Anti-Christo* (c. 1266). Cf. *Encyclopedia Italiana* (36 vols., 1929-1938), s. v. "Guiglielmo de Saint Amour."

[39] *De Paupertate* (1256)—*Opera Omnia* (7 vols., Ad Claras Aquas, 1895), V, pp. 124-165.

[40] *Contra Impugnantes Dei Cultum et Religionem*—*Opuscula Selecta* (4 vols., Parisiis, 1881), tom. III, Pars XIV, pp. 59-253.

of October 19, 1256.[41] It was all to no avail. The disputes raged on at the University of Paris.[42] Again Pope Alexander IV rebuked severely those diocesan priests who demanded that the permission of the pastor be secured before penitents could be validly absolved by a priest of a religious institute.[43]

Meantime the Order of Hermits of St. Augustine (Augustinians) had been formed into a union in 1256 from many separated communities living under the Rule of St. Augustine.[44] The communities, united under a Prior General by Pope Alexander IV, took their place at the side of the Franciscans and Dominicans as a Mendicant Order. In 1294 the Order received a very extensive privilege from Pope Celestine V.[45] The pope granted to all the priests of the Order, if they were approved for preaching and hearing confessions in their provincial chapters, the privilege of absolving sins and preaching everywhere by Apostolic authority.[46]

Boniface VIII (1294-1303), ascending the papal throne after Celestine's resignation, sought to end the scandalous disputes raging between the Regular and secular clergy over confessional jurisdiction. In the year 1300 he issued the famous Constitution *Super cathedram* which outlined the procedure to be followed by religious superiors in the presentation of their own priests to the local Ordinaries.[47] The superior was to choose suitable priests from his community and

[41] Fratres Praedicatorum et Minorum, de licentia et commissione vel concessione Romani Pontificis, seu legatorum eius, vel Ordinariorum locorum, licite possint praedicare populis et confessiones audire, ac poenitentias iniungere salutares—*Bull. Praed.*, I, 320; Potth., n. 16588.

[42] For documents concerning these disputes, cf. H. Denifle, *Chartularium Universitatis Parisiensis* (5 vols., Parisiis, 1899-1907), I, nn. 317-344.

[43] Const. *Cum olim*, 18 ian. 1259—*Bull. Praed.*, I, 369; Potth., n. 17452.

[44] Alexander IV, const. *Licet Ecclesiae*, 9 apr. 1256—L. Empoli, *Bullarium Ordinis Eremitarum S. Augustini* (Romae, 1628), p. 18. This work will be cited hereafter as *Bull. O. E. S. A.*

[45] Pope Celestine, a Benedictine monk, was pope for a very brief period, resigning from the papal chair in 1294. He died in 1296. Cf. *Catholic Encyclopedia*, s. v. "Celestine V."

[46] Cf. const. *Ad fructus uberes*, 27 nov. 1294—*Bull. O. E. S. A.*, p. 103; Potth., n. 24016.

[47] Const. *Super cathedram*, 18 febr. 1300, as found in c. 2, *de sepulturis*, III, 7, in Clem.; Potth., n. 24913.

present them to the local Ordinary for approbation. If the selected priests were rejected by the bishop, then others were to be presented. If these too were rejected and permission to hear confessions was refused, then by Apostolic authority the decision of the bishop was nullified, and all the presented priests could lawfully hear the confessions of all the faithful in that diocese. The text is given:

> Praefati ministri, priores, provinciales (Regulares) . . . eligere studeant personas idoneas, quas representent vel faciant representari Praelatis . . . Et si idem Praelati petitam licentiam confessionum huiusmodi audiendarum concesserint . . . cum gratiarum recipiant actione . . . Quod si quemquam ex dictis fratribus praesentatis . . . non ducerent admittendum, eo amoto, debeat alius surrogari. Si vero iidem Praelati praefatis fratribus ad confessiones audiendas electis, huiusmodi exhibere licentiam recusarint, Nos, ex nunc, ipsis, ut confessiones sibi confiteri volentium libere, liciteque audire valeant . . . gratiose concedimus de plenitudine apostolicae potestatis.

The provisions of this decree were extremely important, since the constitution became the prevailing law until the time of the Council of Trent. Pope John XXII (1316-1334) inserted it into the Clementine Decretals. A study of its provisions reveals the fact that the superior could choose from his community only such priests as were suitable *(idonei)* to hear confessions. The priests selected could not be examined by the local Ordinary concerning their knowledge of theology. The law demanded that the superior present his subjects either personally or through a legitimate representative. And finally, the bishop was free to reject the first group presented. If he chose to do this, other priests had to be presented. It was only after these were refused approbation that the Apostolic jurisdiction was granted to all the priests that were presented.

It will be noticed that, according to the constitution of Boniface VIII, the bishop did not delegate jurisdiction to hear confessions. Jurisdiction came in every instance from the Roman Pontiff through the religious superior. It is implied in the provision that only suitable priests be presented by the superior. This is clear from the whole history of papal privileges up to the time of Boniface VIII, especially from a constitution of Celestine V, which granted to the Celestinians the power to absolve by Apostolic authority.[48] The provisions of the decree of Boniface VIII, therefore, were conditions for the valid use of the papal privileges in the hearing of the confessions of the faithful. Their use was conditioned moreover upon the permission of the religious superior, for the unanimous teaching of all commentators upon papal privileges regarding confessional jurisdiction was that the use of the privileges against the wishes of the superior rendered the confessional absolution invalid and illicit. Schmalzgrueber[49] expresses this teaching succinctly:

> Hoc privilegium non immediate religiosis particularibus, sed ipsis ordinibus religiosis, horumque superioribus datur . . . Non possunt religiosi particulares muneri audiendi confessiones fidelium sese sponte ingerere; sed debent ad hoc habere consensum superiorum suorum: alias, collatae ab ipsis absolutiones erunt invalidae, quia hoc privilegium datum est dependenter a voluntate superiorum, ut hi communicare hoc possint iis, quos ad sacramenta istud administrandum idoneos iudicarint; consequenter, antequam communicetur, religiosi particulares carent iurisdictione.

The provisions of Boniface VIII had little effect upon the disputes raging between the religious and secular clergy. Benedict XI (1303-1304), ascending the papal throne upon Boniface's death, determined to solve these disputes by removing all limitations to the use of the papal privileges. In the Constitution *Inter cunctas,* issued in the first year of his pontificate,[50] all priests religious, who had been adjudged suitable for hearing confessions by their religious superiors, were permitted to hear the confessions of the faithful everywhere without presentation to, or permission of the local Ordinaries. This is the only instance in the history of papal confessional privileges in which some form of presentation of the religious priests to the local Ordinary was not necessary. The constitution remained in effect only a short

[48] Cf. const. *Etsi cunctos,* 1294. The text is given by Augustinus a Virgine Maria, *Privilegia Omnium Religiosorum* (Lugduni, 1661), p. 118. This work will be cited as *Comp. Privileg.*

[49] *Ius Ecclesiasticum Universum* (5 vols. in 12, Romae, 1843-1845), lib. V, tit. 38, n. 44.

[50] C. 1, *de privilegiis,* V, 7, in Extravag. com.

time. It was abrogated by Clement V in the Council of Vienne (1311-1312), and the constitution of Boniface VIII was restored.[51]

The Mendicant Friars were not entirely guiltless in the disputes. The diocesan clergy had sufficient cause for just complaints. They not only abused their privileges, but often assumed complete parochial rights. Many of the friars assisted at marriages without proper permission of the pastors; others administered the sacraments to the sick and dying even when the pastor was able and willing to perform his duties. Some went even further by enticing people away from the parochial churches with their preaching at the time when parochial functions were scheduled. Clement V determined to put an end to such flagrant abuses. In the Council of Vienne he placed under excommunication all religious who should dare to administer Holy Communion, or the Last Sacraments, or to assist at marriage, without the previous permission of the proper pastor. Religious who detracted the pastor in their sermons, or attempted to entice people away from parochial functions, were likewise placed under censure reserved to the Holy See. Those who presumed to absolve from reserved cases were excommunicated *ipso facto*.[52]

The measures taken by Clement V had some effect, but disputes broke out sporadically with extreme bitterness during the succeeding centuries. During the pontificate of John XXII, John de Polliaco (died after 1322), Master of Theology at the University of Paris, had the audacity to maintain that neither the Roman Pontiff, nor God, could dispense the faithful from making their Easter confession to the parish priest, as commanded in the IV general Lateran Council (1215).[53] The friars by reason of their privileges had been hearing confessions regularly during the Easter season, and many of the faithful had approached them for absolution. De Polliaco taught that such confessions were entirely invalid, and that the sins thus confessed had to be resubmitted to the pastor for absolution. John

[51] Cf. const. *Dudum*, as found in c. 2, *de sepulturis*, III, 7, in Clem.

[52] Cf. c. 1, *de privilegiis et excessibus privilegiatorum*, V, 7, in Clem. The exact date of this constitution is not certain. It was certainly not promulgated before it appeared in the Clementine Decretals during the pontificate of John XXII.

[53] Cf. c. 12, X, *de poenitentiis et remissionibus*, V, 38.

XXII condemned this opinion in 1321 as erroneous, false, and contrary to the Catholic Faith.[54] The condemnation of the proposition was reaffirmed by Pope Eugene IV (1431-1447) [55] and renewed by Callistus III (1455-1458).[56]

Pope John XXII extended *pariformiter* to the Order of Carmel all the privileges previously granted to the Mendicant Orders by popes Clement V and Boniface VIII.[57] The following year he extended the same privileges to all the Mendicant Orders.[58]

The final privilege of this period regarding the confessions of the faithful to religious was granted to the Order of Friars Minor by Pope Boniface IX (1389-1404).[59] According to this privilege, all Franciscan priests who had been presented to the local Ordinary and were refused, or whose petition had been neglected, could validly and licitly hear confessions in that diocese. Those who had been chosen for the office of confessor and were presented to the bishop *nominatim et in scriptis,* and accepted, were permitted to hear the confessions of the faithful everywhere, even outside the diocese, without further approval. Priests once approved needed no new approval anywhere, nor was presentation necessary.

The right to administer the sacraments to lay people living within the monastery as servants was never questioned as a privilege of the Regular Orders; it was taken over from the Benedictine monasteries. The position in law of these lay residents of the monasteries will be treated in a later chaper; it will suffice here to recall that a special papal confirmation of the practice was given as early as 1244.[60] Superiors were later granted the right to absolve those seeking entrance to the religious life from all censures, except a few which were specially

[54] Const. *Vas electionis* as found in c. 2, *de haereticis,* V, 3, in Extravag. com. Cf. Denzinger-Bannwart-Umberg, *Enchiridion Symbolorum, Definitionum, Declarationum de Rebus Fidei et Morum* (22-23 ed., Friburgi-Brisgoviae: Herder, 1937) n. 492.

[55] Const. *Gregis nobis,* 16 ian. 1446—*Bull. Praed.*, III, 207.

[56] Const. *Inter caetera,* 22 mart. 1456—*Comp. Privileg.*, p. 135.

[57] Const. *Inter caeteros,* 21 nov. 1326—Mollat, *Jean XXII: Lettres Communes* (14 vols., Paris, 1904-1935), n. 27104.

[58] Const. *Frequentes* as found in c. *un., de iudiciis,* II, 1, in Extravag. com.

[59] Const. *Ad fructus uberes,* 1402—*Comp. Privileg.*, pp. 125-128.

[60] Cf. const. *Qui Deum,* 5 febr. 1244—*Bull. Praed.*, I, 131; Potth., n. 11240.

reserved to the Roman Pontiff.[61] Not only religious, but also all lay persons residing in the monastery as servants, were declared immune from episcopal censures in certain cases. An explicit grant of this privilege is traceable in a constitution of Pope Innocent VI (1352-1362) issued to the Augustinan Order.[62] Furthermore, special privileges for absolving lay people from censures of the common law and from episcopal reservations existed from the very earliest years. This is evidenced by a constitution of Pope Urban IV (1261-1264) which granted to the Carmelites the right to absolve from all censures, except a few reserved to the Roman Pontiff.[63] These privileges will be treated in later chapters.

Section B. The Period of General Communication of Privileges (1474-1563)

The study of the privileges obtained by Regulars during the first two and a half centuries reveals the fact that papal concessions were made directly to particular Religious Orders. The Pontificate of Sixtus IV (1471-1484), however, marks the beginning of a new era in the evolution of privileges. This period which extends from 1474 to the close of the Council of Trent (1545-1563) may be styled the "Age of General Communication" among religious institutes.

It is well to note, however, that this period does not deal exclusively with communicated privileges; nor does the earlier period deal exclusively with direct concessions. Indeed, during the period of direct concessions one finds evidence of a form of communication between the First, Second, and Third Orders within the one religious Order.[64] This communication was *in forma accessoria*. In reality

[61] Cf. Clemens IV, const. *Virtute conspicuos*, 21 iul. 1265—*Bull. Rom.*, III, 735; Potth., n. 19280.

[62] Const. *Religionis favor*, 16 ian. 1353—*Bull. O. E. S. A.*, p. 185.

[63] Const. *Vobis ad hoc*, 1262, in Mari Magno Carmelitarum—Potth., n. 18306.

[64] The Mendicant Orders usually have a threefold grouping of persons in their internal structure: the First Order Regular consists of men religious, mendicants properly so-called; the Second Order is composed of women religious with solemn vows, and are properly called *moniales;* the Third Order includes lay and religious men and women who, according to their state of life, imitate the Rule and spirit of the First Order Regular.

it was the extension of the privileges, granted to the First Order Regular, to the Second and Third Orders in so far as these were capable of enjoying them. An example of this communication is found in a constitution of Boniface IX in which he approved the Second Order of Hermits of St. Augustine:

> (Hae religiosae) gaudeant et gaudere possint . . . tam exemptionis privilegio, quam omnibus immunitatibus, libertatibus, indulgentiis, ac aliis privilegiis quibuscumque praefato Ordini Eremitarum, eiusque Fratribus . . . per Apostolicam Sedem iam concessis, et quae in posterum concedentur, quatenus . . . competunt.[65]

Since the Second and Third Orders were incapable of enjoying any privileges regarding the administration of the sacraments, this form of communication will not be considered here.

Again, many new direct concessions of privileges were made during the period of general communication. But there was this difference between the direct concessions of the two periods: in the earlier period one could safely maintain that a privilege granted to one Order could not be enjoyed by another, unless that second Order was mentioned explicitly in the concession; in the later period a privilege granted directly to one Order was enjoyed immediately by all other Orders which had a participated communication in the privileges of that Order, unless explicit prohibition of communication was made in the privilege itself, or unless the privilege by its nature was limited to that Order. Therefore one cannot speak of direct concessions of privileges in the later period without adverting at once to the fact that the same privileges were enjoyed by other Orders by reason of the special institute of law known as communication.

Sixtus IV granted the first general communication of privileges between the Religious Orders in 1474. On February 7 of that year he made the Augustinian Order participant of all the privileges possessed in the past by the Orders of Preachers and Friars Minor; furthermore, participated communication in all privileges which should accrue to those Orders in the future was granted to it. The constitution is found in the *Mare Magnum* of the Augustinian Order:

[65] Const. *In sinu sedis,* 7 nov. 1401—*Bull. O. E. S. A.*, p. 53.

> Cum praedictorum (Fratrum O.E.S.A.), sicut Praedicatorum et Minorum Fratrum Ordinum professores, pro fidei . . . dilatatione continue indefesse laborent . . . ac propterea fuerint variis . . . privilegiis decorati, ut quos labor, pariaque merita coniungunt privilegia et favores; eisdem Fratrum Eremitarum professoribus, ut concessis eisdem Fratribus Praedicatoribus et Minoribus privilegiis, indulgentiis, . . . a praedictis, et aliis Romanis Pontificibus praedecessoribus nostris . . . quae omnia, *ac si nominatim exprimerentur,* haberi hic volumus pro expressis; . . . ac decernimus robur perpetuae firmitatis obtinere . . . et debeant perpetuis futuris temporibus *in omnibus . . . prorsus et sine ulla differentia,* perinde ac si . . . Ordini Eremitarum . . . *nominatim concessa fuissent,* aut concederentur in futurum.[66]

That this communication of privileges was *in forma aequiprincipali* is easily seen in the examination of the terms: *ac si nominatim exprimerentur, sine ulla differentia,* and *ac si nominatim concessa.*[67]

On May 27 of the same year, the Order of Minims, founded by St. Francis of Paula, received a general communication in the privileges of all Mendicants.[68] Several months later, on August 31, Sixtus IV issued the famous Constitution *Regimini universalis,* which brought complete and mutual communication of all privileges enjoyed by the Dominican and Franciscan Orders. The constitution is especially noteworthy since it effected for the first time a mutual intercommunication of privileges; it made common to both Orders the privileges of each. This mutuality of communication distinguishes it from the communication granted to the Augustinians earlier in the year, for while the Constitution *Dum fructus uberes* granted to the Augustinians the privileges of the other two Orders, it was not reciprocal. It was only in the *Bulla Aurea* of 1479 that the Franciscans and Dominicans participated in the special privileges of the Augustinians. The difference between the two kinds of communication is manifest from the following words of the Constitution *Regimini universalis:*

[66] Const. *Dum fructus uberes,* 7 febr. 1474—*Bull. O. E. S. A.*, p. 347.

[67] Concerning the canonical effects of communication *in forma aequiprincipali,* cf. Appeltern, *Compendium Praelectionum Iuris Regularis* (2. ed., Parisiis: Casterman, 1913), QQ. 590-595.

[68] Cf. Sixtus IV, const. *Sedes Apostolica,* 27 maii 1474—*Bull. Rom.,* V, 212.

> . . . quae omnia (privilegia, etc.), ac si nominatim exprimerentur, haberi volumus pro expressis . . . ac . . . robur perpetuae firmitatis obtinere . . . debeant sine ulla differentia, proinde ac si, *quae uni Ordinibus praedictis sunt concessa, utrique simul nominatim concessa fuissent,* aut concederentur in posterum.[69]

It was by such grants as these that the *Mare Magnum* of privileges of the Religious Orders was established. The Carmelites received communication with the Dominicans, Franciscans, and Augustinians in 1476; and in 1530, a special confirmation of the privileges implied in this communicaton.[70] The Servites had received a participated communication of privileges with the Augustinians in 1392 from Boniface IX.[71] They, therefore, shared in all the privileges communicated to the Augustinians in 1474. The Order of Minims received special confirmation of their *Mare Magnum* of privileges from Julius II (1503-1513) in 1506.[72] The Augustinians received a similar confirmation from the same pope in 1508.[73] So thorough was the intercommunication of privileges among the Orders that Pope Leo X (1513-1521) could state that the Dominicans, Franciscans, Augustinians, Carmelites, Servites and Minims held all their privileges in common.[74] Subsequently the Jesuati,[75] the Benedictines,[76] Jesuits [77] and Trinitarians [78] received communication in all the privileges of

[69] Sixtus IV, const. *Regimini universalis,* 31 aug. 1474—*Bull. Rom.,* V, 217-223.

[70] *Mare Magnum Carmelitarum,* 1476—*Comp. Privileg.,* p. 90; Clemens VII, const. *Ex clementi,* 12 aug. 1530—*Bull. Rom.,* VI, 144.

[71] Const. *Sacra vestra,* 1392—*Comp. Privileg.,* p. 89.

[72] Const. *Dudum ad sacrum,* 28 iul. 1506—*Bull. Rom.,* V, 421.

[73] Cf. const. *Etsi ad benemerendum,* 17 iun. 1508—*Bull. Rom.,* V, 471; *Bull. O. E. S. A.,* p. 207.

[74] Const. *Dudum per nos,* 10 dec. 1519: "Illaque omnia et singula inter dictorum Ordinum personas pariformiter communia fuisse et esse volumus, prout in singulis literis praedictis plenius continetur."—*Bull Rom.,* V, 733.

[75] Clemens VII, const. *Sacrae religionis,* 1532—*Comp. Privileg.,* p. 97. The Jesuati received confirmation as a Mendicant Order from Pius V; cf. const. *Romanus Pontifex privilegia,* 18 nov. 1567—*Bull. Rom.,* VII, 636.

[76] Cf. Pius V, const. *Ex supernae,* 16 aug. 1567—*Bull. Rom.,* VII, 584.

[77] Cf. Pius V, const. *Dum indefessae,* 7 iul. 1571—*Bull. Rom.,* VII, 923.

[78] Cf. Paul V, const. *Ecclesiae catholicae,* 15 dec. 1609—*Bull. Rom.,* XI, 608.

the Mendicant Orders. All of these could claim the confessional privileges granted to anyone of them, with the exception of: (1) the privileges granted to a particular convent or place; (2) the special and extraordinary privileges granted to an Order for a particular reason; (3) the privileges containing a clause prohibiting communication; (4) the privileges which were inconsistent with the statutes or Rule of a particular Order.[79]

The purpose of such complete communication of privileges is indicated in the constitutions which granted it. It was: (a) a reward for those Orders which labored tirelessly and equally in the vineyard of Christ; equal labor merited equal recompense.[80] It was: (b) a means of removing the suspicion that certain popes were favoring a particular Order unduly; it showed their equal rank among the religious institutes.[81] It was: (c) a means of obviating difficulties and complaints among the religious institutes regarding the relative merits of their privileges.[82]

New privileges were also granted during the period of communication. In the Constitution *Regimini universalis* of Sixtus IV [83] Regulars were granted the privilege of absolving their own subjects from all reservations (and to dispense where necessary) except four, which were specially reserved to the Holy See, namely, the reservations touching relapsed heretics, schismatics, falsifiers of papal documents, and those who carried forbidden weapons to the infidels for making war against the Christians:

> . . . declaramus haereticos relapsos, schismaticos, et qui literas apostolicas falsificassent, aut ad infideles prohibita detulissent, dumtaxat, esse ad Sedem Apostolicam merito destinandos.

[79] For a fuller treatment of this matter cf. A Vasto, *De Communicatione Privilegiorum praesertim inter Religiones* (Aquilae, 1936), n. 87, pp. 55-58; Ellis, "De Communicatione Privilegiorum inter Religiones"—*Periodica,* XXVII (1938), 157-162.

[80] Cf. Sixtus IV, const. *Regimini universalis,* 31 aug. 1474—*Bull. Rom.,* V, 217.

[81] Cf. Sixtus IV, const. *Sacri Praedicatorum et Minorum,* 26 iul. 1479—*Bull. Rom.,* V, 278.

[82] For a fuller treatment, cf. Pignatelli, *Consultationes Canonicae* (10 vols., Coloniae, 1717-1719), X, *consult.* 1, n. 26.

[83] Cf. *Bull. Rom.,* V, 217-223.

The same constitution permitted Regulars to administer the Holy Eucharist and Extreme Unction to any of the faithful, provided that these had been refused the sacraments without a reasonable cause by the pastor of the place. Superiors were likewise granted the privilege of dispensing their own subjects from irregularities. These privileges will be discussed in a special chapter.

The Fifth general Lateran Council (1512-1517) brought profound modifications in the law of Boniface VIII regarding the approbation necessary for the hearing of the confessions of the faithful. The old disputes between the Regular and diocesan clergy had been smoldering throughout the previous century. When the *agenda* of the Council were in process of preparation, a very determined element among the bishops demanded that all confessional privileges of Regulars be abrogated; that Regulars be made subject once again to the requirements of the common law under the jurisdiction of the local Ordinaries. During the four years immediately preceding the Council a bitter fight was waged between the partisans favoring the continuance of the Regulars' privileges and their opponents.[84]

In the Council the following regulations were issued: (1) priests Religious, chosen for the office of confessor by the superior, must be presented to the bishop personally, if the bishop demands such presentation; or, if the bishop is absent for two or more days, presentation must be made to the Vicar General, who will approve them. (2) The bishop may examine the priests proposed, but only on matter concerning the sacrament of penance. (3) On condition that the priest has been approved, or has been denied approbation *unjustly*, he can licitly and validly absolve the faithful of the diocese, even during the Easter season. (4) No priest Religious may absolve *ab homine* reservations without special faculties from the local Ordinary. (5) Regulars are forbidden to administer to the sick and dying, even after these have been refused by the pastor, unless there is a just cause, sworn to by a notary or two witnesses. (6) The admin-

[84] A graphic summary of this dispute has been left us by Aegidius of Viterbo (c. 1469-1532), in a letter written to the convents of the Augustinian Order of which he was Prior General at the time. He was one of the principal defenders of the privileges. Cf. Bollandistae, *Examen Historicum et Canonicum Libri M. Verhoeven*, pp. 274, 275.

istration of the sacraments to lay people serving in convents or monasteries of Regulars is limited to the time when they are actually under the obedience of the religious superior.[85]

Thus, at the time of the Council of Trent, one finds the common law stressing the need of approbation from the local Ordinary before the hearing of confessions may be undertaken. In only one instance could a Regular hear confessions of the faithful without this approbation, namely, when approbation was unjustly denied to him. But it will be discovered that new restrictions were enacted by the Council of Trent.

[85] Cf. Leo X, const. *Dum intra,* 19 dec. 1516—*Fontes Codicis Iuris Canonici cura Emi. Petri Card. Gasparri editi* (9 vols., Romae-Civitate Vaticana: Typis Polyglottis Vaticanis, 1923-1939; vols. VII-VIII-IX, ed. cura et studio Emi Iustiniani Card. Seredi), n. 72. This work will be cited as *Fontes.*

CHAPTER II

HISTORY OF CONFESSIONAL JURISDICTION OF REGULARS FROM THE COUNCIL OF TRENT TO THE PRESENT TIME

Article 1. Legislation from the Council of Trent to the Code

The Council of Trent (1545-1563) inaugurated a much needed reform of the Church from within. The Council, which was convened by order of Pope Paul III (1534-1549), had the reorganization of the Church's disciplinary system as one of its primary objectives. The Church, which like a productive tree throughout the centuries had yielded rich and manifold fruits of sanctity, was in need of revitalization that could come only through a spiritual process of pruning away the old obnoxious growths and of engrafting new elements of life. Within the membership of the Church there existed political schemes which jeopardized the Church's continued vitality; outside of it there were the attacks of heresy and the encroachments of excessive nationalism, which made it imperative for the Church to reorganize her spiritual forces to meet the impending onslaught. There were stains upon her moral beauty, too; for that beauty had become tainted with the factors occasioned by a careless and insufficiently disciplined clergy. Doctrines needed clarification, abuses had to be eradicated, and points of friction required for their alleviation a greater harmony in mutual effort and co-operation. Among these latter elements, the problem of harmonizing the privileges of Regulars with the demands of the common law was not the least of the problems that confronted the Fathers assembled at Trent for the opening session on December 13, 1545.

The history of the Council as given by Pallavicini (1607-1667)[1] is very revealing to the student of the history of religious privileges.

[1] *Vera Concilii Tridentini Historia* (24 books in 3 vols., Antwerp, 1670), lib. VII, cc. 4, 5; lib. XII, cc. 12-14; lib. XXIV, cc. 3-6.

The bitterest disputes of the Council were waged over the respective jurisdictional rights of pastors and of the Regular clergy and concerning the necessity of approbation for the hearing of confessions. But when the last session of the Council came to an end on December 4, 1563, clear and definite legislation had been enacted on a majority of the disputed points. The evolution of papal privileges regarding confessional jurisdiction was almost complete. It remained for canonists and theologians of the succeeding years to clarify and crystallize the work accomplished in the Council.

On the point of previous approbation by the local Ordinary as a prerequisite for the hearing of the confessions of the faithful, the Council issued the following decree:

> Although priests receive by ordination the power of absolving from sins, nevertheless the holy council decrees that no one, even though a regular, can hear the confessions of seculars, even priests, and that he is not to be regarded as qualified thereto, unless he either holds a parochial benefice, or is by the bishops, after an examination, if they deem it necessary, or in some other manner, judged competent and has obtained their approval, which shall be given gratuitously; any privileges and customs whatsoever, even immemorial, notwithstanding.[2]

Whatever disputes there may have been after the Council over the status of privileges contrary to the Tridentine decrees which did not specifically incorporate an abrogating clause,[3] the above quoted decree certainly effected the abrogation of all privileges contrary to it, for the decree was fortified with an explicit abrogating clause. A comparison of this decree with that of Boniface VIII concerning the presentation and approbation of priests religious by the local Ordinary reveals the changes in the law. No longer could such priests

[2] Sess. XXIII, *de ref.*, c. 15—*Canons and Decrees of the Council of Trent* (English translation by Schroeder, St. Louis: Herder, 1941), p. 173.

[3] Reiffenstuel (*Ius Canonicum Universum,* lib. V, tit. 33, n. 138) and Suarez (*De Legibus,* lib. VIII, c. 18) held with the common opinion that only two classes of privileges of Regulars were abrogated by the Council: (1) those which had an express abrogating clause; (2) those which were contained in sess. XXV, *de regularibus*. A few authors, including Donatus (I, 1, 2, q. 15, 4), held that all privileges contrary to any decrees of the Council were abrogated.

validly and licitly absolve the faithful of the diocese if the local Ordinary refused approbation. The provision of the V general Council of the Lateran (1512-1517) which permitted a Regular to hear the confessions of the faithful, provided he had been examined by the bishop and had been refused approbation unjustly, was likewise abrogated by this decree. Henceforth, the emphasis was not on the presentation of the religious to the local Ordinary by the religious superior, but on the *approbation* given by the local Ordinary.

Approbation on the part of the local Ordinary for the confessions of the faithful was a prerequisite for valid absolution of sins. The decree stated that "no one can hear confessions . . . without approbation." No exception was made, as the Sacred Congregation of the Council very clearly indicated in a response of 1648: no Regulars—not even Jesuits—could absolve lay people without the previous approval of the bishop.[4] The force of the decree was such that, even after examination by the local Ordinary and a most *unjust* refusal of approbation, a priest could not validly absolve the sins of the faithful of the diocese. There were a few authors after the Council of Trent who maintained the contrary opinion. The opinion was implicitly condemned by Alexander VII (1655-1667) in 1665 in the condemned proposition that "one satisfies the precept of annual confession by confessing to a Regular who has been presented to the bishop, but has been unjustly refused approbation." [5]

While the Council of Trent made no explicit demand that the superior present the priest religious to the local Ordinary, such a procedure is implied in the decree. The judgment concerning the priest's knowledge of theology pertained to the bishop, but the testimony concerning his moral fitness pertained to the superior who presented him. This presentation could be insisted upon by the bishop, for the Sacred Congregation of the Council decreed that the bishop, if he chose to do so, could demand personal presentation of the priest by his superior.[6]

[4] S. C. C., *Angelopolitana,* 14 maii 1648—Pallottini, *Collectio Omnium Conclusionum et Resolutionum Congregationis Concilii ab anno 1564 ad annum 1860* (18 vols., Romae, 1868-1893), s. v. "Sacramentum Poenitentiae," n. 131.

[5] Cf. Denzinger-Bannwart-Umberg, *Enchiridion,* n. 1113.

[6] Cf. S. C. C., *Olomucen.,* 11 iul. 1665—Pallottini, *ibid.,* n. 127.

Since the approbation of the local Ordinary was so important that without it the absolution of sins was invalid, one may ask what was the precise nature of approbation as demanded by the Council of Trent? The decree required of everyone who had not received a parochial benefice that he obtain approbation. It is clear that a priest who was a pastor by reason of a parochial benefice absolved in virtue of ordinary power of jurisdiction. All others, whether secular or religious, absolved by reason of delegated jurisdiction. Whence came this jurisdiction? For the diocesan clergy the jurisdiction came from the local Ordinary; they had no other source. Regulars, however, had claimed jurisdiction over all the faithful in virtue of papal privileges which were granted them from the first years of this foundations.[7] The use of these privileges was conditioned by the need of previous presentation and approbation of the bishop of the place where they were to hear confessions. Were such privileges abrogated, so that now the local Ordinary granted jurisdiction directly for the hearing of confessions when he granted his approbation? The decree did not distinguish between the approbation granted to diocesan priests, and that granted to priests religious. A literal understanding of the text would indicate that the local Ordinary bestowed jurisdiction on both Regular and secular clergy alike.

However, the common teaching of canonists and theologians from the Council of Trent to the advent of the Code was that Regulars absolved in virtue of their papal privileges; the approbation of the local Ordinary was not an implicit grant of jurisdiction, but only a condition demanded by the law without which absolution of sins was invalid. The reasons for the common teaching were summed up concisely by Ferraris (died c. 1763),[8] who based it upon the distinction that exists between the concepts of *jurisdiction* and *approbation*. Approbation is the authentic judgment or declaration on the part of the bishop concerning the knowledge and fitness of the priest to hear confessions. The granting of approbation connotes essentially an act of the intellect. Jurisdiction, on the other hand, connotes a positive act of the will whereby the power to absolve is actually

[7] Cf. *Supra,* chap. 1, art. 2, sect. A.

[8] *Bibliotheca,* s. v. "approbatio," art. 1, nn. 1-3; cf. also Lehmkuhl, *Theologia Moralis* (12. ed., 2 vols., Friburgi-Brisgoviae, 1914), II, n. 483.

granted to the priest. The approbation given by the local Ordinary according to the requirements of the Council of Trent did not therefore necessarily include the grant of jurisdiction; this power was already possessed by Regulars in virtue of papal privilege.

Added strength was given to the common teaching, according to the authors, by the words of Pope Innocent X (1644-1655) [9] who decreed that "Regulars *who have Apostolic faculties* cannot be restrained from hearing confessions, etc." Special confirmation of the doctrine is implied by the fact that the Sacred Congregation of Bishops and Regulars in various decisions held that bishops could not *restrict at will* the faculties of Regulars.[10] If it is assumed that jurisdiction of Regular confessors emanated solely from the local Ordinary, it is logical to suppose that he could restrict that jurisdiction according to his own good pleasure with respect to time, place or persons over whom the jurisdiction was exercised. The decisions of the Holy See which denied this right to the local Ordinary argue for the fact that he was not the source (at least not the only source) of the jurisdictional power of Regular confessors. Therefore, papal jurisdiction must be presumed to have been still in existence.

Evidences of this restriction as placed upon bishops are numerous. Pope St. Pius V (1566-1572) decreed that, once a Regular priest has been approved and admitted into the diocese, his approbation must be considered permanent; he could not be reexamined by the same bishop without a grave justifying cause.[11] Furthermore, a Regular who had been approved after an examination could not be restricted in the use of his faculties to a period of time less than a year.[12] If the examination was personally conducted by the bishop and the needed approval was given, the Regular confessor had to be admitted into the diocese *simplicter et absque ulla temporis prae-*

[9] Cf. const. *Exponi nobis,* 7 febr. 1645—*Bull. Rom.,* XV, 362; cf. also, S. C. C., *Senonen.,* 28 febr. 1654—Pallottini, *ibid.,* n. 34.

[10] Cf. S. C. Ep. et Reg., *Pisauren.,* 22 sept. 1645—*Fontes,* n. 1774; *Collectanea in Usum Secretariae Sacrae Congregationis Episcoporum et Regularium* (2. ed., Bizzarri, Romae, 1885), p. 27. Cf. also S. C. Ep. et Reg., 13 sept. 1641 —*Fontes,* n. 1765; Bizzarri, *ibid.,* pp. 25, 26.

[11] Const. *Etsi Mendicantium,* 16 maii 1567—*Fontes,* n. 121. Cf. also S. C. C., *Patavina,* 17 ian. 1654—Pallottini, *ibid.,* n. 139.

[12] Cf. S. C. C., *Pisauren.,* 1 dec. 1646—Pallottini, *ibid.,* n. 144.

finitione. No time limit could be placed on the use of his faculties; nor could his jurisdiction be restricted to a particular group of the faithful,[13] except that which touched the hearing of the confessions of nuns.[14] However, if the bishop did not personally conduct the examination, the priest could be re-examined if there was a reasonable cause. The successor to the bishop who had approved such a priest could examine him even without a cause.[15]

Authors adduce a further confirmatory argument for the common teaching from the constant and lawfully authorized practice of Regular confessors in absolving penitents coming from dioceses other than those in which they were approved. This practice is sanctioned by Clement X in the seventh paragraph of the Constitution *Superna.* The pope stated that all Regular confessors who had been approved by the local Ordinary could hear the confessions of penitents coming from other dioceses and absolve them from sins and censures reserved in that diocese, unless they knew that such penitents had come to them *in fraudem legis.*[16]

This argument may seem to lack validity for the student who has consulted only the present legislation. The Code permits all confessors with diocesan faculties to hear the confessions of penitents from other dioceses and to absolve them from reservations of that diocese.[17] The pre-Code legislation did not grant such powers to diocesan priests. While customary law permitted pastors to absolve all penitents residing in other parishes within the diocese, the power over *peregrini* from other dioceses was greatly restricted especially in regard to reserved cases. It was only in the nineteenth century that customary law sanctioned absolution from such extra-diocesan

[13] Cf. Clemens X, const. *Superna,* 21 iun. 1670—*Fontes,* n. 246; S. C. C., *Patavina,* 17 ian. 1654—Pallottini, *ibid.,* n. 139.

[14] For hearing the confessions of Sisters (*moniales*), Clement X decreed that special deputation must be had from the local Ordinary in each instance. Cf. const. *Superna,* § 4—*Fontes,* n. 246.

[15] Cf. S. C. C., *Mediolanen.,* anno 1586—Pallottini, *ibid.,* n. 144; S. C. C., *Neapolitana,* anno 1593—Pallottini, *loc. cit.*

[16] *Fontes,* n. 246.

[17] Cf. canons 88, § 1; 900, § 3; 2247, § 2.

reservations. From this, authors argued that Regular confessors exercised their more extensive powers in virtue of papal jurisdiction.[18]

Regular confessors, however, followed the territorial restrictions of the diocese for which they were approved. When they were outside the diocese they could not validly hear the confessions of anyone, except in a case of danger of death, not even the confessions of subjects of the bishop in whose diocese they were approved. Thus, Father Jones, a priest religious approved in diocese A, is sojourning in another diocese. James Paul who has his residence in diocese A approaches Father Jones for absolution. Father Jones cannot validly absolve James Paul because he (Father Jones) is outside the diocese for which he has been approved. The Constitution *Superna* makes explicit reference to this territoriality of approbation;[19] several decisions of the Sacred Congregation of the Council confirmed it.[20]

Although authors commonly held that Regulars absolved in virtue of Apostolic jurisdiction, it must not be assumed that local Ordinaries could not delegate jurisdiction to Regulars. By reason of their ordinary powers, local Ordinaries, if they wished to do so, could grant faculties to any priest to hear the confessions of their subjects, even though the latter was not presented by his religious superior. It is probable that they frequently did so. In such an event, the Regular confessor absolved in virtue of a twofold source, namely, in consequence of papal privilege and as a result of his episcopal delegation. The former was more extensive, but its use was dependent upon the superior's permission. The latter could be used validly even against the wishes of the superior. Thus, if a religious superior suspended his subject from hearing confessions, this subject could no longer absolve validly in virtue of his papal jurisdiction. But, if he had received jurisdiction from the local Ordinary, he could validly absolve the sins of the faithful of that diocese, even though he would be acting gravely illicitly because of his disobedience to his religious superior. All doubts among canonists concerning this point were settled in 1866 by a decision of the Sacred Congregation of Bishops

[18] Cf. Lehmkuhl, *Theologia Moralis,* II, nn. 497-500.

[19] Paragraph 4—*Fontes,* n. 246.

[20] S. C. C., *Valentina,* mense oct. 1586—Pallottini, *ibid.,* n. 123; S. C. C., *Viterbien.,* 22 nov. 1721—Pallottini, *ibid.,* n. 126.

and Regulars.[21] The following case was proposed: a Regular confessor who had been suspended by his superior received approval and jurisdiction from a local Ordinary to hear the confessions of the faithful. He actually absolved in virtue of diocesan faculties. The Sacred Congregation was asked whether a religious, if not approved by his superior, or if approved against the will of the superior by the local Ordinary, could absolve the faithful from their sins validly with only the faculty of the bishop? The decision was in the affirmative. It was also asked whether the Regular confessor could absolve validly if he was suspended by his superior? The answer was again in the affirmative; but the confessor would be acting illicitly.

Cappello [22] states that in the time just previous to the Code the approbation of the local Ordinary was looked upon as an actual grant of jurisdiction. If this statement is true, then Regular confessors, at least within the last century before the Code, absolved sins in virtue of a twofold source, by papal privilege and by episcopal delegation.

Article 2. The Privileges of Regulars and the Code

When Pope Pius X (1903-1914) issued the motu proprio *Arduum sane munus,*[23] which set in motion the process of codifying the common law of the Church, he fulfilled the fondest hopes of canonists and moralists. Agitation for such a codification had been long felt; scholars everywhere were confused by the maze of contradictory and unharmonized laws in existence. Pius IX (1846-1878) had recognized the need of a code of laws on *latae sententiae* censures in 1869, when he issued the Constitution *Apostolicae Sedis.*[24] Leo XIII (1878-1903) undertook in 1897 a much needed reform in the matter dealing with the previous censure and prohibition of books.[25] The Constitution *Conditae a Christo,*[26] the Decree *Ne temere* [27] and many

[21] S. C. Ep. et Reg., *Ordinis Praedicatorum,* 2 mart. 1866—*Fontes,* n. 1996; *Acta Sanctae Sedis,* I (1865-1866), 683. This work will be cited as *ASS.*

[22] *De Poenitentia* (Romae: Marietti, 1938), n. 405. Cf. also Lehmkuhl, *Theologia Moralis,* II, n. 483.

[23] 19 mart. 1904—*ASS,* XXXVI (1904), 549.

[24] 12 oct. 1869—*Fontes,* n. 552.

[25] Const. *Officiorum et munerum,* 25 ian. 1897—*Fontes,* n. 632.

[26] 8 dec. 1900—*Fontes,* n. 644.

[27] 2 aug. 1907—*Fontes,* n. 4340.

other smaller codifications of a similar nature fulfilled vital needs of a Church that was overburdened with laws which had become outmoded or which had fallen into disuse.

The purpose of the Commission appointed by Pius X was not only to codify a portion of the law but to collect into one handy volume all the common law of the Church. Laws, some of which dated from the earlier centuries of the Church, had to be sifted if one was to find those which were still in force; contradictory legislation had to be harmonized; new laws had to be fashioned according to the needs of the Church, so that the result would be an exclusive collection, which alone would have the force of universal law.[28]

It was not the purpose of the Commission to reduce into a Code all the particular and customary laws prevailing throughout the world. The best it could hope to do was to present general norms by which these particular laws could be related to the common law. These general norms form the first six canons of the Code.[29]

Besides determining the binding force of written particular legislation prevailing at the time of the promulgation of the Code, these general norms treat the status of concordats entered into by the Holy See with national states, of past customary laws, and of acquired rights, indults and privileges acquired in the past from the Holy See. The confessional privileges of Regulars fall into the last category. For this reason, unless they have been reduced to the status of common law, their continued post-Code existence, or their abrogation by the Code, must be determined by the fact of whether they were still in unrecalled use when the Code became law and took no action to repeal them, or whether, despite their continued legitimate use up to the time of the present codification, the Code actually recalled them by its present law.

The preliminary norms of the Code regulate the relation of these privileges to the common law whenever they have not been incorporated into the common law. A casual study of that section of the Code which legislates for Religious Orders and Congregations[30] reveals the fact that many privileges were reduced to common law.

[28] Cf. *Preface* to the Code.

[29] Cf. canons 1-6.

[30] Canons 487-681.

For example, canon 514 grants to local superiors of clerical religious institutes the right to administer the sacraments to lay persons residing within the religious house. This was formerly a special privilege granted to Regulars by the Holy See. Canons 613-625 incorporate into the law privileges once possessed by Regulars. There are many other canons [81] which either confirm or abrogate privileges possessed by a special grant of the Holy See.

On the other hand, many privileges were not touched by the Code. These privileges must be regulated by the general norms set forth in canon 4:

> . . . privilegia . . . quae, ab Apostolica Sede ad haec usque tempora personis sive physicis sive moralibus concessa, in usu adhuc sunt nec revocata, integra manent, nisi huius Codicis canonibus expresse revocentur.

This canon governs the fate of all privileges granted by the Supreme Pontiffs either directly by forthright concession, or indirectly by means of communication up to the time of the Code.

Four conditions must be verified before a privilege granted previous to the Code can be said to exist with certainty in the present legislation: (1) it must be a concession of the Holy See to some moral or physical person. The privileges granted to Regulars were grants to moral persons. (2) It must never have been revoked. The study of specific privileges will discover many past revocations of privileges acquired from the Roman Pontiffs. (3) It must have been still in use at the time of the Code. There were many temporary grants of privileges in the past which lapsed with time; other privileges often fell into disuse and are therefore outlawed by new legislation. (4) It must not have been expressly revoked by any canon of the Code. Express revocation is had when the canon itself states that all contrary privileges are abrogated. For example, canon 519 states that a religious may lawfully approach any confessor approved by the local Ordinary for hearing confessions to obtain absolution for the peace of his conscience; all privileges militating against the full lawfulness and validity of a confession thus made are revoked.[82] If a

[81] Cf. *e.g.*, canons 519; 567, § 1; 875; 876.

[82] Canon 519: . . . si religiosus . . . ad suae conscientiae quietem, confes-

privilege fulfills all the conditions demanded in canon 4 it is still in force even though it be contrary to the common law.[83]

The Code, when treating explicitly of the privileges of religious,[84] has more specific regulations regarding communicated privileges. Canon 613, § 1, rules that each religious institute enjoys only those privileges which are contained in the Code, or which are granted to it directly by the Holy See. For the future all communication of privileges between religious institutes is precluded.[85] The interpretation of this canon has been a subject of bitter dispute. All commentators, however, are agreed on one point: no privilege obtained by a religious institute directly from the Holy See after the promulgation of the Code can be shared in by other institutes by means of a participating communication. The only participating communication which obtains after 1918 is that which takes place between the First and Second Orders Regular within a religious institute. The common law permits the Second Order to share in the privileges of the First Order in so far as it is capable of enjoying such privileges.[86]

The disputes concerned the status of privileges which were obtained in the past by way of a participating communication, and which were still in use at the time when the Code became law. They were based mainly upon differences in the translation and meaning of canon 613, and its relation to canon 4. The study of canon 4 reveals that privileges enjoyed prior to the Code by means of a participated communication are still operative unless an express abrogation of them is effected in the law itself. Is canon 613, § 1, restric-

sarium adeat ab Ordinario loci approbatum . . . confessio, revocato quolibet contrario privilegio, valida et licita est.

[83] Cf. Van Hove, "De Privilegiis et Indultis ad Canonem 4"—*Jus Pontificium,* IX (1929), 290-295. This author disproves the opinion of a few authors (*e. g.*, Toso, *Commentaria Minora ad Codicem Iuris Canonici* [Romae, 1921], p. 8), who would restrict the operative norm of canon 4 to privileges *praeter legem.* Cf. also, G. Michiels, *Normae Generales* (2 vols., Lublin, 1929), I, 71, note 2.

[84] Canons 613-625.

[85] Canon 613, § 1—Quaelibet religio iis tantum privilegiis gaudet, quae vel hoc in Codice continentur, vel a Sede Apostolica directe eidem concessa fuerint, exclusa in posterum qualibet communicatione.

[86] Cf. canon 613, § 2.

tive of the general norms contained in canon 4? Authors were in disagreement; they supported divergent views according to the divergent meaning which they connected with the phrases *"iis tantum privilegiis gaudet," "concessa fuerint,"* and *"exclusa in posterum qualibet communicatione"* of canon 613.

Opinions at first were about equally divided. Gradually, however, the milder opinion prevailed, namely, that the privileges possessed by religious institutes through a participated communication with other institutes were not abrogated by the provisions of canon 613. This proved to be the correct interpretation. The Pontifical Commission for the authentic interpretation of the Code decreed that the words *"exclusa in posterum qualibet communicatione,"* refer only to post-Code, and not to pre-Code, communicated privileges.[37]

The disputes were carried on in various periodicals.[38] For the purpose of an historical synopsis there will be subjoined here a brief outline of the principal arguments presented on both sides. For the strict interpretation:

1. The sense of the law must be understood from a study of the words in its text and context.[39] A careful reading of the text will show that only one conclusion is possible, namely, that all participated communications of privileges possessed before the promulgation of the Code are now abrogated. The word *"tantum"* indicates that the legislator wished canon 613 to constitute an exclusive enumeration of all the privileges of religious. Therefore the only privileges recognized by the legislator are those which are either contained in the Code, or which were granted by a direct concession of the

[37] P. C. I., 30 dec. 1937: "An verba canonis 613, § 1, *exclusa in posterum qualibet communicatione*, ita intelligenda sint ut revocata fuerint privilegia a religionibus ante Codicem iuris canonici per communicationem legitime acquisita et pacifice possessa. R. Negative—*AAS*, XXX (1938), 73.

[38] For more detailed study, cf. A Vasto, *De Communicatione Privilegiorum praesertim inter Religiones* (Aquilae, 1936), pp. 74-94; H. Tatjer, "De Communicatione Privilegiorum inter Religiones,"—*Apollinaris*, V (1932), 458-486; A. Ellis, "De Communicatione Privilegiorum inter Religiones"—*Periodica*, XXVII (1938), 157-162; A. Larraona, "Pontificia Commissio ad Codicem authentice Interpretandum"—*Commentarium pro Religiosis*, XIX (1938), 247-251. This latter work will be cited as *CpR*.

[39] Cf. canon 18.

Holy See. Blat, in his commentary on canon 613, § 1,[40] expresses his interpretation thus:

> Idcirco revocantur expresse per verbum *tantum* omnia alia, quae forsitan hucusque possederit unaquaeque religio, et quae privilegia in sequentibus canonis clausulis non reservantur saltem implicite.

The second part of canon 613 is confirmatory of the interpretation of the first. Lest there be any doubt concerning the possibility of future communicated participations of privileges, the legislator expressly stated that such a manner of sharing privileges among the religious institutes is precluded for the future. The term *"qualibet"* excludes all forms of participating communication, whether these be *ad instar* or *in forma accessoria,* except for the special provisions made in canon 613, § 2.[41]

2. Canon 4 states that all privileges which are expressly abrogated by the canons of the Code are effectively revoked. But from the interpretation of canon 613, it is clear that the legislator wished to abrogate specifically all such communicated privileges which existed before the Code. This opinion is confirmed by canon 489 which decrees that the Rules and particular constitutions of a religious institute are abrogated if they are contrary to the canons of the Code. Now the privileges here in question are opposed to the present legislation. Furthermore, the Sacred Congregation for the Administration of Religious Affairs ordered the constitutions of religious Orders to be brought into harmony with the canons of the Code.[42]

For the milder opinion:

1. From the general principles found in the First Book of the Code one finds abundant evidence for the continuance of communicated privileges if these were possessed and in use before the advent of the Code. Canon 10 states that the laws of the Code are not to

[40] *Commentarium Textus Codicis Iuris Canonici* (6 vols., Romae, 1919-1927), II, 601.

[41] "Privilegia quibus gaudet Ordo regularis, competunt quoque monialibus eiusdem Ordinis, quatenus eorum sint capaces."

[42] S. C. de Rel., De regulis et constitutionibus religiosorum ad normam canonis 489 Codicis Iuris Canonici reformandis, 26 iun. 1918—*AAS,* X (1918), 290.

be considered retroactive unless mention of that fact is made expressly *(nominatim)* in the canons.[43] It cannot be said that canon 613, § 1, contains an express provision for the retroactivity of its law. On the contrary, the very meaning of the law is obscure: the verbal phrase *"concessa fuerint"* could possibly have reference to the past, but far more probably it refers to the future only, since the use of the future perfect tense is syntactically indicated in the structure of the sentence. The more natural rendering of the phrase thus contemplates only such privileges as shall have been granted after the advent of the Code; it abstracts from the question of privileges which were granted prior to the Code, and thus leaves room for the application of the norm contained in canon 4. Similarly by way of parallel structure, the clause *"exclusa in posterum qualibet communicatione"* abstracts from the privileges acquired by way of a participating communication prior to the Code and implies thereby the need of following the norm of canon 4 regarding their continuance or abrogation when the Code became law. At any rate, the revocation of pre-Code privileges acquired in this manner remains extremely doubtful. But it is certain that a law of doubtful meaning and import cannot effectively abrogate a juridical status which follows from a general principle of law as stated in canon 10.

2. Canon 4 states that acquired rights and privileges remain intact unless the Code expressly revokes them. Canon 613, § 1, makes no such specific revocation as is to be found in many other canons of the Code.[44] The fact of revocation is stated explicitly. Frequently these canons employ the phrase *"revocato quolibet privilegio contrario"* which leaves no doubt as to the intent of the law. Canon 613, § 1, does not employ a phrase that even approximates in meaning that which is found in express revocation. This opinion is confirmed from a study of the various *schemata* proposed to the Commission for Codification. The first draft, which was rejected, evidently intended to imply an abrogation of all communicated privileges, as is evident from the use of the perfect tense in the verb form, and the omission of the phrase *"in posterum"*:

[43] "Leges respiciunt futura, non praeterita, nisi nominatim in eis de praeteritis caveatur."

[44] Cf. *e.g.*, canons 343, § 2; 413; 519; 522; 544, § 2; 654.

> Quodlibet institutum religiosum iis tantum privilegiis gaudet, quae vel a Sede Apostolica directe concessa *fuerunt,* vel in Codice continentur, *exclusa qualibet communicatione.*[45]

The fact that such a proposal was rejected argues for the fact that the codifiers did not intend to reject past communicated privileges.

More recently the mind of the Holy See was manifested more clearly with regard to such privileges. In 1933 the Holy See approved the constitutions of the Society of Jesus which contained many privileges obtained by that Order in the past by a participated communication.[46]

Finally, the legal principle "*odiosa restringi, et favores convenit ampliari*" [47] furnishes a workable basis for the milder interpretation of canon 613, § 1. In the abrogation of privileges the legislator is not presumed to have revoked his favors, unless he makes the fact evidently clear. The decision of the Pontifical Commission for the Authentic Interpretation of the Code [48] has simply recognized these principles of law.

[45] This *schema* is given by A Vasto, *op. cit.*, p. 85.

[46] Brief, *Paterna claritas,* 12 mart. 1933—*AAS,* XXV (1933), 245.

[47] Reg. 15, R. J., in VI°.

[48] Cf. *AAS,* XXX (1938), 73.

CHAPTER III

THE CONFESSIONS OF THE SUBJECTS OF THE REGULAR SUPERIOR

Article 1. Discipline of the Present Code

Religious Orders have always been recognized by the Church as true ecclesiastical societies. Their members, united by the common bond of religious obedience, strive toward the goal of religious perfection through the observance of the vows of obedience, chastity, and poverty.[1] As religious societies, the members of which harmonize the contemplative with the active life in accordance with the spirit of their founders, Religious Orders have the further purpose of laboring for the salvation of people living in the world. This purpose is accomplished through parochial and missionary activity, by preaching and by teaching the word of God.

Clerical Religious Orders are endowed with all the powers which accrue to subordinate societies within the Church. Through the Church's recognition they possess legislative, judicial and executive powers, the representation and exercise of which are vested in legitimate superiors. These superiors as a result can exercise not only dominative but also jurisdictional authority over their subjects.[2] The power of jurisdiction is not equal in all superiors. It reflects a graduated scale of authority similar in many respects to that which obtains in the Universal Church. For, just as the Supreme Pontiff, the local Ordinaries and the pastors of parishes, have ordinary jurisdiction over the subjects residing within their territories in relation to the sacrament of penance,[3] so also the supreme moderators, the provincials and the local superiors, according to each clerical Order's particular statutes, exercise an ordinary jurisdiction over their subjects. This doctrine is admirably expressed in a response of the

[1] Cf. canon 487.

[2] Cf. canon 501, § 1.

[3] Canon 873, § 1.

Sacred Congregation of Bishops and Regulars to a case presented to it in 1864:

> (Consultor istius Congregationis dicit) certum omnino esse Praelatos Regulares iurisdictionem quasi Episcopalem in suos subjectos habere: triplicis autem generis esse huiusmodi Praelatos, scilicet, *infimos, medios,* et *supremos* secundum superioritatis gradum, quem obtinent: quapropter Moderatores generales esse *praelatos supremos,* Provinciales *medios,* et Superiores Conventuales *infimos.*[4]

The quasi-episcopal nature of the offices of the supreme Moderator and the Provincial was never doubted since the time of the papal grants of exemption from the jurisdiction of the local Ordinaries. Before the Council of Trent the exact nature of the local superior's jurisdictional powers was disputed. Later commentators, however, were almost unanimous in teaching that the local superior in the hearing of the confessions of his subjects exercised an ordinary jurisdiction.[5] This power is now granted in the Code to all local superiors of exempt clerical religious institutes according to the norms of the particular constitutions.[6]

Since Regular superiors exercise an ordinary power of jurisdiction in the administration of the sacrament of penance for their subjects, they can delegate their power to other priests. Canon 875, § 1, expressly permits them to pick confessors for their subjects from priests of the secular clergy, or of other religious institutes. The common law does not demand that the priests thus chosen have previous approbation from the local Ordinary; individual constitutions, however, may demand that only priests with previous approval from the local ordinary be chosen. For a valid delegation of jurisdiction to hear the confessions of his subjects, the Code demands only that the superior delegate one who is a priest. That the delegation be licit, the superior must determine the priest's fitness either through an

[4] S. C. Ep. et Reg., *Piscien. seu Ordinis Eremitarum S. Augustini,* 3 iun. 1864—*Fontes,* n. 1992.

[5] Cf. *e.g.,* Fagnanus, *Commentaria Super Quinque Libros Decretalium* (4 vols., Venetiis, 1679), lib. V, tit. 31, c. 3; St. Alphonsus, *Theologia Moralis,* lib. VI, n. 593.

[6] Cf. canons 873, § 2; 875, § 1.

examination or in some other way.[7] The superior would act licitly if, without further examination, he delegated a priest whom he knows to have faculties in some diocese to hear the confessions of the faithful.

The Church has been ever insistent that members of a religious community confess regularly to priests specially deputed for that purpose by the religious superior. The Code legislates for this in canons 518 and 519. The nature of the religious life damands a uniform direction of the spiritual life of the community—a direction which can be effected best by one or, at most, a few confessors who are well trained in the direction of souls. It is not the mind of the Church that religious be permitted to approach any confessor according to their inclinations. Such a procedure might open the way to serious abuses. A very definite example of the Church's wisdom in securing uniform direction is seen in the law which permits only one ordinary confessor for each community of women religious.[8] That is why some commentators [9] in treating canon 519 maintain that a religious, making use of the special concession of the law to confess for the peace of his conscience to any confessor approved by the local Ordinary, has not thereby fulfilled his obligation of confessing according to the prescriptions of the constitutions.[10]

The legislator in the discipline of the present Code has made special provision to protect the liberty of a religious to approach for the peace of his conscience a confessor outside the Order. Should a reli-

[7] Canon 877, § 1.

[8] Canon 520, § 1. The Church shows its prudence, too, in securing the freedom of conscience by permitting a woman religious to be given a special confessor for any righteous cause; cf. canon 520, § 2.

[9] Cf. *e. g.*, Génicot-Salsmans, *Theologia Moralis* (9. ed., 2 vols., Bruxellis, 1921), II, n. 337; Van Acken, "Abusus libertatis religiosis pro confessione concessae"—*CpR*, VII (1926), 255-260.

[10] This opinion seems to the author to be too severe. While the wording of the law seems to indicate that confession at the stated times is in order for all the members of the community, it does not seem that the legislator intends that one who has made use of the privilege be bound by a twofold obligation. The better opinion seems to be that which allows the religious on occasion, but not habitually, to omit confessing at the stated times after making use of the privilege granted him in canon 519. Cf. A Coronata, *Institutiones Iuris Canonici*, I, n. 544, p. 676, note 4.

gious in such circumstances confess to a priest approved by the local Ordinary his confession and the absolution would be valid and licit. It would be valid, since canon 874, § 1, expressly states that the local Ordinary grants jurisdiction to hear the confessions of both religious and lay persons within his territory. It is licit, for canon 519 permits a religious to confess to any priest approved by the local Ordinary, provided the confession is made for the peace of his conscience. Any provisions of particular constitutions which run counter to this privilege are revoked by the law itself.

This freedom of choosing confessors permitted in canon 519 is a recent innovation in the penitential discipline of religious institutes. It dates from the decree *In audientia* of the Sacred Congregation of Religious on August 5, 1913.[11] Previous to that decree religious had very little freedom of choice. They were required to confess to the confessors designated by the superior. To understand the gradual evolution of this law, and to discover whether special privileges were granted to Regulars in this regard, an analysis of the historical background must be made.

Article 2. Pre-Clementine Legislation

The penitential discipline of the Religious Orders, modeled upon that of the Benedictine monasteries, took its origin in the privilege of exemption. A community of Regulars within the diocese became juridically a community apart, withdrawn completely from episcopal jurisdiction in the discipline of the administration and reception of the sacraments. Over such a community the local superior, in subjection to his own higher superiors, exercised quasi-episcopal powers, the exercise of which was limited to the persons subject to his obedience. This personal character of his jurisdiction distinguished his powers from those of the bishops; the latter's powers were considered to be both personal and territorial.[12]

The restriction of episcopal jurisdiction over Regulars by papal exemption withdrew them from subjection to the bishop. Because of this non-subjection the bishop could not grant any priest the juris-

[11] *AAS,* V (1913), 431.

[12] Cf. Boudinhon, "La Confession des Religieux"—*Le Canoniste Contemporain,* XXXVI (1913), 698-700; A Coronata, *op. cit.,* I, n. 280.

diction to hear the confessions of members of a Regular community; the power of jurisdiction can be exercised directly only upon subjects.[13] The ancient discipline, otherwise than the present law,[14] did not grant to local Ordinaries the power to delegate jurisdiction for hearing the confessions of religious within his diocese. Since the religious superior exercised ordinary jurisdiction over his subjects, it was within his province to delegate jurisdiction for hearing their confessions to any priest, whether religious or diocesan, whom he considered suitable for hearing confessions. If such delegation was not received, then the absolution from sins confessed by a religious, when given by a priest with solely diocesan faculties, was both illicit and invalid.

In the first centuries of the Religious Orders it was most rare for a religious to confess to a priest outside his own Order. Indeed, the superior claimed exclusive right to hear the confessions of his subjects.[15] His powers over the confessions of his subjects were regarded as similar to those of the pastor in his parish. According to the law promulgated in the IV General Lateran Council (1215),[16] pastors were granted the exclusive right to hear the confessions of their parishioners in the fulfillment of the precept of annual confession. According to many authors of that time, the precept was not fulfilled unless the confession was made to one's proper pastor; confession of sins made contrary to this decree made the absolution invalid, and the penitent was required to repeat the confession to the pastor.[17]

Pope Innocent IV (1243-1254)[18] explained the wisdom of the law which demanded periodic confession to one's own pastor. It is

[13] Cf. canon 201, § 1.

[14] Canon 874, § 1.

[15] Cf. Piat, *Praelectiones Iuris Regularis,* I, Q. 431.

[16] C. 12, X, *de poenitentiis et remissionibus,* V, 38.

[17] This disposition of the law regarding fulfillment of the precept of annual confession was the source of endless disputes between the diocesan and Regular clergy. The latter claimed the right to hear confessions during the Paschal season in virtue of their papal privileges. Legislation regarding this question is found as late as 1670; cf. Clemens X, const. *Superna,* 21 iun. 1670—*Fontes,* n. 246.

[18] Cf. const. *Etsi animarum,* 21 nov. 1254—Potth., n. 15562. The text is given in *CpR,* XI (1930), 360.

to be noted that confessions were not so frequent in the Middle Ages as they are today. Consequently the yearly confession of sins was often the only means within the hands of the pastor to ascertain the spiritual condition of his flock. He was responsible to God for the condition of his flock; therefore it was only right that he should have the opportunity to correct abuses, to strengthen the wavering, and to weed out the errors from his flock. Furthermore, the concomitant element of shame in the confession of his sins to a priest who knew him personally was frequently a strong deterrent for the penitent against the commission of sin.[19]

When one relates the reasons, as given by Pope Innocent IV, to the duty of the religious to confess his sins to his religious superior, one can understand why the religious subject's confession to his superior, or to a priest specially deputed by the superior, was considered so important. A practice of confessing one's sins to a priest outside of the community, apart from serious reasons for so doing, could only lead to grave abuses. Religious discipline could not exist under such conditions. For these reasons the rule of confessing to one's own superior or his delegate was recognized as law in the Universal Church. Even Pope Benedict XI,[20] who mitigated the stricter discipline of yearly confession to be made by lay people to their proper pastor, did not consider it opportune to change the law for religious.[21] The enactments of Benedict XI were shortly repealed by his successor, Clement V, in the Council of Vienne (1311-1312),[22] but there was no change made in the confessional discipline of religious.

Various Orders received specific regulations with regard to the confessions of their members. Thus, almost a half century before the law became general, Pope Clement IV (1265-1268) explicitly forbade members of the Franciscan Order to confess to a priest other

[19] Cf. Van Espen, *Ius Ecclesiasticum Universum* (5 vols., Lovanii, 1753), tom. I, pars 2, sect. 1, tit. 6, c. 8; G. Oesterle, "Clemens VIII relatio ad lib. II, C. I. C., tit. X, cap. II, de confessariis et cappellanis"—*CpR*, XI (1930), 360.

[20] Cf. *supra*, chap. 1, sect. A, p. 14.

[21] ". . . non religiosos, qui secundum statuta suorum ordinum propriis praelatis confiteri debent, aut ab eis, ne confiteantur aliis, prohibentur, absolvant."—c. 1, *de privilegiis*, V, 7, in Extravag. com.

[22] Cf. c. 2, *de sepulturis*, III, 7, in Clem.

than the superior or to those priests of the Order designated according to the Rule and statutes:

> Inhibemus insuper universis Fratribus, ne aliquis eorum, nisi necessitatis urgente periculo, aliis quam Praelatis suis sua peccata confiteri praesumant, vel aliis eiusdem Ordinis sacerdotibus, secundum Regulam et ipsius Ordinis instituta.[23]

In accordance with this decree there was no possibility for a Franciscan to make his confession to anyone other than a Franciscan, except in a case of urgent necessity. A case of urgent danger could occur if the religious were away from his monastery and happened to be stricken with a dangerous illness. If no brother-priest were in attendance, universal custom permitted any priest to absolve him. It is interesting to note that as late as 1742 Capuchins were forbidden by their statutes to confess to any priest except a fellow-religious of the Order, even when they were on a journey far from their monastery.[24]

Jurisdiction to hear the confessions of his subjects could be delegated by the Regular superior in two ways: (1) he could call a priest to the religious house and grant him jurisdiction directly; (2) he could authorize his subjects to choose a priest outside the Order who was suitable for hearing confessions and delegate indirectly through the religious the faculty to the priest chosen. Each of these was recognized as a legitimate means of bestowing jurisdiction.[25] In the indirect delegation of jurisdiction, however, the subject needed permission to choose the confessor, otherwise the absolution was null and void.

Excessive restrictions such as these wrought great hardships upon those members of religious communities who had to be away from the monastery for days at a time. During this period of their history great numbers were sent out among the faithful especially in the rural sections; it was difficult for such religious to return to their re-

[23] Const. *Virtute conspicuos,* 21 iul. 1265—*Bull. Rom.,* III, 736; Potth., n. 19280.

[24] Cf. Hilling, "Das Dekret, *In audientia,* über die Absolution der Ordensleute"—*AKKR,* XCIV (1913), 628; G. Oesterle, *Praelectiones Iuris Canonici* (Romae: apud Collegium S. Anselmi, 1931), I, 262.

[25] Cf. cc. 3, 6, 27, 28, X, *de officio et potestate iudicis delegati,* I, 29.

ligious brethren within a few days. Suppose that a religious placed in such circumstances should be so unfortunate as to commit grave sin which required absolution before Holy Mass could be offered. Without the express permission of his superior to choose a priest as confessor, he could not be absolved except by a priest of his own Order. Frequently these brother-religious were not at hand.

To overcome the handicaps suffered from a lack of confessors by religious who were legitimately absent from their monasteries, Pope Innocent VII (1404-1406) favored the Franciscan and Dominican Orders with a special privilege.[26] Religious of these Orders, when they were sent on a journey by their superiors, could choose any priest to hear their confessions validly and licitly, provided that (1) he were suited for hearing confessions, and (2) no other priest of their Order, likewise suited for hearing confession, were present. The constitution reads as follows:

> Nos Fratribus . . . quos itinerari et per eorum Superiores mitti contigerit, ut si aliquem presbyterorum idoneum . . . dicti Ordinis habere non possint, quemcumque alium presbyterum idoneum et discretum religiosum vel saecularem eligere valeant, qui confessiones eorum licite audire possit.

Such was the first of many papal privileges which granted to Regulars, while on a journey with the permission of their superior, the right freely to choose a priest outside the religious institute to hear their confessions licitly and validly. The words of the constitution do not indicate that any delegation from the superior was necessary. No previous permission to choose a confessor was required. Provided the conditions mentioned in the constitution were verified jurisdiction seems to have been supplied by apostolic authority; its source was the Roman Pontiff.

At the time of the general intercommunication of privileges among the Religious Orders this privilege granted to the Franciscans and Dominicans by Innocent VII was communicated in by all the Orders which shared in the privileges of Mendicants.[27] The Order of

[26] Const. *Provenit,* 17 oct. 1405—*Bull. Praed.*, II, 477; Oesterle, *op. cit.*, I, 262.

[27] C. Sixtus IV, const. *Supplicari,* 2 aug. 1479—*Bull. Praed.*, III, 592; Bouix,

Carmel received a privilege similar to that of Innocent VII directly from Pope Clement VII.[28] Other Orders also received similar direct privileges.[29]

Many authors, in commenting upon these privileges,[30] maintained that the religious on a journey could confess to either a regular or secular priest on a presumed permission from his superior. Certainly it seems beyond dispute that the legitimate permission of the superior was a necessary condition for the valid use of the papal privilege. Therefore apostates and fugitives from the monastery could not claim a legitimate use of the concession.[31] Was a grant of jurisdiction from the superior indirectly to the confessor chosen implied in the very permission to leave the monastery? An examination of the document reveals that nowhere is express delegation of the superior required. Indeed, the need of jurisdiction or delegation is not even mentioned. The sole requisite conditions were (1) that the religious was legitimately absent from the monastery, and (2) that no suitable priest of his own Order was present. St. Alphonsus [32] taught that even a tacit permission to be absent from the religious house sufficed for the lawful use of the privilege.

One may be inclined to question the opinion of those canonists who saw, in the very permission to leave the religious house, an implicit grant of jurisdiction from the superior to the priest chosen. To be sure, this was the usual manner of receiving delegation, for jurisdiction for hearing the confessions of the religious was considered to come directly from the Holy See to the religious superiors, who in turn delegated it to others.[33] It is possible that they beheld in this privilege only a mitigation of the previous discipline regarding

De Iure Regularium (2 vols., Parisiis, 1883), II, 252; Ferraris, *Bibliotheca*, s. v. "approbatio," II, 9.

28 Const. *Ex clementi*, 12 aug. 1530—*Bull. Rom.*, IV, 147.

29 Cf. E. Rodriquez, *Quaestiones Regulares* (Lugduni, 1634), Resolutio XXXII, nn. 22, 23.

30 Cf. *e. g.*, Ferraris, *loc. cit.;* Bachofen (Charles Augustine), *Compendium Iuris Regularium* (New York, 1903), pp. 242-244.

31 Cf. Appeltern, *Compendium Praelectionum Iuris Regularis* (2. ed., Parisiis, 1913), Q. 291.

32 *Theologia Moralis*, lib. VI, n. 575.

33 Cf. Schmalzgrueber, *Ius Ecclesiasticum Universum*, lib. V, tit. 38, n. 44.

an extraordinary case of need, and therefore regarded the privilege as being subject to a strict interpretation. For them the privilege represented a remedy for the continual seeking of express permission from the superior in each instance. That is probably why they taught that jurisdiction was *implicitly*, or *tacitly*, or *presumptively* delegated to any confessor chosen, by the very fact that permission was granted to the subject by the superior to leave the monastery. Perhaps a more forceful reason for this opinion may be found in an authoritative interpretation of confessional privileges by Pope Clement VIII (1592-1605).[84] This Pontiff declared that, in all that pertains to confessional privileges, it had always been the mind of the Holy See that religious use their papal privileges only in accordance with the will of their superiors. Therefore, even when a religious chose to make his confession to someone in virtue of apostolic privilege, it was understood that the permission for the use of the privilege and the jurisdiction necessary for the confessor chosen, came from the Holy See, but through the medium of the religious superior.

A study of the privilege of Innocent VII reveals further that the confession of sins by an itinerant religious did not need to be made to a priest with diocesan faculties.[85] It stated merely that the priest chosen had to be suitable, *idoneus*, for the hearing of confessions. A serious question arises in relation to the judgment of the religious on the suitability of the priest whom he chose to hear his confession. Did that judgment pertain to the individual religious? Or was there need of some public and official pronouncement? Opinions were divided. According to the norms enacted by Boniface VIII (1294-1303) to be followed in presenting religious priests to the local Ordinary for approval, the superior himself had to pass judgment upon the fitness of his subject before presentation was made.[86] This constituted an official judgment concerning the candidate's suitability for the hearing of the confessions of the faithful.

According to St. Alphonsus and most of the canonists of the post-Tridentine times, however, the word *idoneus* merely implies that the penitent know by some means that the priest he chooses is suitable

[84] Const. *Romani Pontificis*, 23 nov. 1599—*Bull. Rom.*, X, 549.

[85] This was the *sententia communior;* cf. Bachofen, *loc. cit.*

[86] Cf. c. 2, *de sepulturis*, III, 7, in Clem.

for hearing his confession.[37] They add, moreover, that before the Council of Trent a person could confess to any simple diocesan priest even if this priest was not approved by the local Ordinary.

It may be objected that the Council of Trent abrogated the privilege of Innocent VII. The Council was very definite in its legislation demanding previous approbation by the local Ordinary for the hearing of the confessions of the faithful. The following decree on reform was issued:

> Decernit . . . nullum, etiam regularem, posse confessiones saecularium, etiam sacerdotum, audire, nec ad id idoneum reputari, nisi aut parochiale beneficium, aut ab Episcopis per examen, si illis videbitur necessarium, aut alias idoneus iudicetur, et approbationem . . . obtineat.[38]

A casual reading of this decree may leave the impression that an all-inclusive demand for approbation from the local Ordinary was made with reference to hearing the confessions of anyone, whether religious or lay. This cannot be substantiated by a close study of the law. In this instance the Council was legislating only regarding the confessions of seculars, *saecularium*. It did not touch the problem of approbation for hearing the confessions of religious. In short, the law states explicitly that no one, even though he be a priest of a religious Order, may hear the confessions of diocesan clerics and lay persons without first obtaining a parochial benefice, or some official approval from the local Ordinary. Theologians and canonists, therefore, commonly held the opinion that the privilege granted by Innocent VII was not abrogated, and that Regulars could still be validly absolved by any suitable priest, even though he was not approved according to the decree of the Council of Trent.[39]

The privilege of Innocent VII contained a very important condition to be verified before the papal jurisdiction became operative: *provided that the religious did not have available a fellow-priest of*

[37] Cf. St. Alphonsus, *Theologia Moralis*, lib. VI, n. 575; Cappello, *De Poenitentia*, n. 428.

[38] Sess. XXIII, *de ref.*, c. 15.

[39] Cf. Gury-Ballerini-Palmieri, *Compendium Theologiae Moralis* (15. ed., 2 vols., Romae, 1907), I, n. 1124, 4°.

his Order who was suited for the hearing of his confession.[40] All authors are agreed that the use of the word *idoneus* with respect to the fellow-priest of his own Order did not demand the previous official approval by the religious superior. If this priest of his Order had the requisite fitness for the office of confessor, the religious was given no choice; he had to make his confession to his fellow-priest. This provision was consonant with the whole history of the penitential discipline among religious institutes of that time. Confession of sins had to be made to a member of one's proper religious Order whenever it was possible to do so.

ARTICLE 3. CLEMENTINE LEGISLATION

The law which required religious to make their confession to the religious superior, despite its obvious good qualities, had many drawbacks. One can readily imagine how difficult it must have been for a religious of timorous conscience to make his confession to one who had the power to punish him in the external forum. St. Thomas Aquinas, himself a member of a religious Order, wrote that such a system proved a snare for many souls who concealed their faults from fear of public punishment.[41] For the superior himself the temptation to make use of confessional knowledge in the government of his community could have proven very strong. Superiors usually realized such dangers, and accordingly the practice of appointing several mature priests as regular confessors of the community became common long before the pontificate of Clement VIII (1592-1605).

This pope determined to abolish entirely a practice which could occasion the destruction of souls. In 1593 he promulgated the decree *Sanctissimus* [42] which effected a complete transformation of the existing confessional discipline of religious institutes. The provisions of this decree were as follows: (1) the religious superior was forbidden to hear the confessions of his subjects, except (a) when the penitent

[40] ". . . si aliquem presbyterum idoneum ex professoribus dicti Ordinis habere non possint."—const. *Provenit,* 17 oct. 1405.

[41] ". . . multis laqueum damnationis iniiciunt."—*Commentum in Quattuor Libros Sententiarum* (2 vols. in 3, Parmae, 1858), lib. IV, dist. 17, q. 3, a. 4.

[42] 26 maii 1593—*Fontes,* n. 177.

had committed a sin which was reserved, and (b) when the penitent willingly and freely approached the superior to make his confession; (2) in each religious house two, three or more confessors, according to the number of professed religious, had to be designated by the superior as regular confessors with the power of absolving from all non-reserved cases; each confessor might absolve even from reserved cases if he considered it imprudent to approach the superior for the necessary faculties; (3) eight sins were specifically enumerated as capable of reservation by the superiors; to these one or two others could be added if necessity required it, but only after mature discussion in and with the consent of the General Chapter of the institute.

Pope Urban VIII (1623-1644) confirmed this decree of Clement VIII in 1624,[43] and ordered all superiors to observe it scrupulously. If at any time the superior showed himself unwilling to delegate the the faculties necessary to absolve from reserved cases, the designated confessors could proceed at once to absolve both licitly and validly.

A glance at the provisions of the new legislation will reveal its revolutionary changes. The religious superior was no longer the regular confessor of his subjects. Although he still had ordinary confessional jurisdiction, his power had to be exercised through priests delegated by him, except in the two cases permitted by the law. Wider range in the choice of a confessor was accorded the penitent, so that the danger of bad confessions was lessened especially for the weaker souls. Whether the penitent was free to approach anyone of the designated confessors at will, or whether he had to make his choice of one confessor among the ones designated, and thereafter was under obligation to approach him each time he wished to confess, was open to dispute. Suarez (1548-1617)[44] maintained that the penitent was limited to the one confessor chosen by the religious once and for all. More recent authors held that the penitent was entirely free to approach any of the designated confessors.[45] The Sacred Congregation of Bishops and Regulars, in 1866, decreed that in every religious community, no matter how small, a least one con-

[43] S. C. C., decr., 21 sept. 1624—*Fontes*, n. 2454.

[44] Cf. *Opera Omnia*, tom. XVI, tr. VIII, lib. 2, c. 15, n. 7.

[45] Cf. Piat, *Praelectiones Iuris Regularis*, I, Q. 433.

fessor was to be designated by the superior for hearing the confessions of the religious.[46]

The Clementine legislation made no change in the law requiring a religious to confess to a priest designated by the religious superior. Indeed, as late as 1864 [47] the validity of the absolution given by a priest outside the religious Order was questioned, even after the religious had received express permission from his local superior to confess to such a priest. The Sacred Congregation held that, since the local superior was a prelate exercising ordinary jurisdiction, he could delegate jurisdiction to a priest outside the Order. The confession was therefore licit and valid.

The dispute among canonists concerning the approbation necessary for a priest, who, in virtue of an apostolic privilege, was chosen by a religious on a journey to hear his confession, was left unsettled. Those authors who demanded some official approbation concerning the fitness of the priest chosen sought to find new evidence for the tenableness of their opinion in a decision of the Sacred Congregation of the Council in 1769.[48] The case involved the practice of certain members of a religious Order who spent some time each year in the town of Hildesheim which was some distance removed from their monastery. While there they chose unapproved diocesan priests as their confessors, despite the fact that priests of their own Order as well as approved diocesan priests resided in that same town. The Sacred Congregation was asked whether such confessions were licit? Valid, if the local Ordinary was unaware of the practice? Were future confessions of this kind to be considered valid if they were made with the knowledge of the bishop but against his protest? [49]

The arguments proposed in the Hildesheim case are interesting since they are a summary of the contentions in favor of the opinion that the priest chosen must have official approbation. The petitioner

[46] S. C. Ep. et Reg., decr., 16 aug. 1866—Bizzarri, *op. cit.*, 916.

[47] Cf. S. C. Ep. et Reg., *Piscien. seu Ordinis Eremitarum S. Augustini,* 3 iun. 1864—*Fontes,* n. 1992.

[48] S. C. C., *Hildeshemen.,* 16 sept., 18 nov. 1769—*Fontes,* n. 3767.

[49] The following questions were proposed: An tales confessiones licitae sint in casu? An ignorante Episcopo fuerint validae? An Episcopo sciente et contradicente, imposterum peragendae validae futurae sint? R. Negative in omnibus, et amplius.

admitted that many authors upheld the opinion that a Regular while on a journey with his superior's permission could confess to a non-approved priest. He maintained, on the contrary, that many other authors, sustained by custom and the common law previous to the Council of Trent, held the opposite opinion. This latter opinion, so the petitioner declared, was confirmed by the great importance attached by the Council of Trent to an official approbation to be obtained from the local Ordinary before a priest presumed to absolve any sins. Furthermore, the very constitutions which granted such privileges to Regulars contain the words "*presbyter idoneus et discretus,*" which words implied that an official judgment by the local Ordinary was necessary. For additional confirmation of this opinion the petitioner quoted the provisions of the Jubilee privileges relating to confession, which allowed confession of sins to be made to an approved priest only. Again, it was unreasonable to suppose that a simple unlearned religious was capable of making a sound judgment concerning the fitness of the priest whom he chose to hear his confession. On the other hand, were such a course possible, an unscrupulous religious could choose an unlearned priest as confessor in order that through his ignorance he might escape well merited correction and punishment. Finally, the petitioner alluded to the proposition condemned by Innocent XI (1676-1698) [50] that a priest could follow a probable opinion concerning the validity of the sacraments, ignoring the safer opinion.

The response of the Sacred Congregation of the Council in the case of Hildesheim, coupled with that of the Sacred Congregation of Bishops and Regulars [51] which demanded that the confessor chosen by the religious be approved by the local Ordinary, made many authors incline toward the opinion that approbation was necessary.[52] Others pointed out the fact that neither the case proposed in

[50] *Prop. damn.*: non est illicitum, in sacramentis conferendis, sequi opinionem probabilem de valore sacramenti, relicta tutiore—Denz.-Bann.-Umberg, *Enchiridion*, n. 1151.

[51] S. C. Ep. et Reg., *Piscien. seu Ordinis Eremitarum S. Augustini,* 3 iun. 1864—*Fontes*, n. 1992.

[52] Génicot, while stating that the milder opinion was probable, stated that many authors abandoned it because of these two decrees.—*Institutiones Theologiae Moralis* (5. ed., 2 vols., Lovanii, 1905), II, n. 337.

1769, nor that proposed in 1864, were cases in point. In the case of Hildesheim, priests of the same Order were present who could hear the confessions of the religious. Therefore they were not free to choose any other priest, for the privileges granted by popes Innocent VII (1404-1406) and Sixtus IV (1471-1484) permitted choice of a priest outside the Order only on condition that there was not present a priest of one's own Order who was suited for the hearing of confessions.[53]

The argument of the petitioner of Hildesheim as drawn from the interpretation of the words *"idoneus et discretus"* was stronger. However, Cappello,[54] in referring to the opinion of St. Alphonsus, notes that a priest should be considered suitable for hearing confessions if he has successfully passed his examinations in moral theology, or has been granted jurisdiction to hear confessions by any Ordinary on presentation by his superior, provided that he has not since been impeded by some infirmity of mind or body which renders him unsuitable. Before the Council of Trent a priest was considered suitable for hearing confessions if he had received permission from the pastor of the place to hear confessions. Not a few also considered a priest suitable if he was not suspended or excommunicated.[55] This latter opinion seems too lax; however, there was little foundation for the opinion which demanded official approbation from the local Ordinary before the priest chosen by the religious might absolve validly.

A study of the Constitution *Supplicari* reveals no mention of a priest who is suitable *(idoneus):*

> Ut fratres, vestra, vel aliorum praelatorum et suorum, qui pro tempore erunt, licentia, solummodo tamen cum itineraverint vel extra conventum fuerint, prout eis concedetis, confiteri possint . . . apostolica auctoritate concedimus.

It would be unreasonable, however, to presume that the pope did not demand some suitability for the hearing of confessions in the priest

[53] Cf. Gury-Ballerini-Palmieri, *Compendium Theologiae Moralis,* I, n. 1124, 4°.

[54] *De Poenitentia,* n. 428.

[55] Antoninus (1389-1459), Joannes de S. Cruz (1645-1721), and others held this opinion.—Cf. Ferraris, *op. cit.,* s. v., "approbatio," art. II, n. 27.

chosen by the itinerant religious. This fitness, according to the common opinion of authors, needed not be attested to by official approbation from the local Ordinary. It was sufficient that the religious have some knowledge concerning the fitness of the priest of his choice. The right to make such a choice was vested implicitly in the permission to make a journey.[56] Suarez added that the religious was not limited in his choice to the priests of the diocese wherein the monastery was located; he could choose any priest of the secular or religious clergy wherever he happened to be residing.

Authors who treat of the use of a probable opinion in the administration of the sacrament of penance point out that practically there does not exist any merely probable jurisdiction, for the Church supplies jurisdiction *certainly* in both common error and in positive and probable doubt.[57] The universal usage of the Church has sanctioned it.[58] The doctrine is well explained by D'Annibale (1815-1892)[59] and the Salmanticenses.[60] The latter attempt to prove the existence of a real jurisdiction in any case of probable doubt by proposing a dilemma. The confessor has either true jurisdiction when he absolves by reason of probable jurisdiction, or else such jurisdiction is entirely lacking. In the first case his absolution is both licit and valid since he absolves in virtue of true jurisdiction. In the latter instance the jurisdiction which he thinks he has is lacking, and he is in error. But since he relies upon an opinion supported by many authors, the error which he has is a common error. In such a case the Church supplies the necessary jurisdiction, and the absolution which he gives is therefore valid.

[56] Cf. Suarez, *op. cit.*, tr. VIII, lib. 2, c. 17, n. 6; Pellizarius, *Manuale Regularium*, VIII, 1, 9.

[57] Canon 209.

[58] Cf. Miaskiewicz, *Supplied Jurisdiction According to Canon 209* (Catholic University of America Canon Law Studies, n. 122, Washington, D. C.: The Catholic University of America Press, 1940), pp. 87-103.

[59] *Theologiae Moralis Summula* (4. ed., 3 vols., Romae, 1896-1897), I, nn. 79, 80.

[60] *Cursus Theologiae Completus* (20 vols., Bruxellis, 1883), XX, disp. 12, dub. 7, n. 80.

Article 4. Legislation of the Nineteenth and Early Twentieth Century

The post-Tridentine Church saw the growth of a multitude of clerical non-exempt religious congregations. The clerical members of these societies, unlike the clerical members in religious Orders, obtained their confessional jurisdiction from the local Ordinaries. Superiors of these congregations exercised no ordinary jurisdiction; superiors as well as their subjects depended upon the local Ordinary for confessional jurisdiction. This discipline was very much at variance with that of the religious Orders, and the distinction between Regulars and non-exempt religious became very important.

Non-exempt religious, because of their dependence upon jurisdiction from the local Ordinary, enjoyed greater freedom in their choice of confessors. They could be absolved validly by any confessor with diocesan faculties. Regulars, on the other hand, were still bound to the stricter discipline of confessing only to priests of their own Order, or to those specially deputed by the religious superior. It is natural that the latter should seek greater freedom, a freedom of choice similar to that of the non-exempt religious. It is possible that the popes themselves inclined to a milder discipline. At least one notices definite indications toward the confusing of the distinctive limits of episcopal and religious jurisdictions in the matter of confessions.[61] Without dispossessing the superiors of religious Orders of any of their powers, local Ordinaries began to consider themselves as having jurisdiction in confessional matters also over the subjects of the Regular superior. The beginning of this trend is noticed in the decree of the Council of Trent wherein approval of the local Ordinary was a prerequisite on the part of all priests for the hearing of the confessions of the faithful. Regulars from the earliest years of their religious foundations had claimed Apostolic jurisdiction for hearing the confessions of anyone. After the Council of Trent, even though the common opinion still sanctioned this view, the opposite opinion found many adherents. While most of the authors still claimed that the episcopal approbation was simply a necessary con-

[61] Cf. Wernz-Vidal, *Ius Canonicum* (7 vols. in 8, Romae, 1923-1938), III, n. 167, nota 5.

dition to make the use of their papal jurisdiction valid, there were other authors who held that the local Ordinary granted both jurisdiction and approbation.[62] These latter found support for their opinion in some papal writings in which the words "approbation" and "jurisdiction" were used synonymously.[63]

The controversy was finally brought to an end by a decision of the Sacred Congregation of Bishops and Regulars in 1866.[64] A case was submitted to that Sacred Congregation concerning a priest of a religious Order who had been suspended from hearing confessions by his own superior. Despite this suspension, the priest had applied for and received faculties from the local Ordinary to hear the confessions of the faithful. The Sacred Congregation was asked whether such a religious, when he is not approved by his superior according to the statutes of the institute, or when he acts against the wishes of his superior, can hear the confessions of the laity validly if he has obtained faculties merely from the local Ordinary? Whether the religous superior can suspend his subjects from hearing the confessions of the laity? The response to both queries was in the affirmative, but in the latter case, it stated, the suspended priest would act illicitly.[65]

This response struck at the very root of the dispute. For, if the Regular priest absolved in consequence of his papal privilege, then his superior could suspend his jurisdiction in such a way that he could not validly absolve any sins. But if the origin of the priest's jurisdiction rested with the local Ordinary, then no suspension inflicted by his own superior could deprive him of the valid exercise of his powers. The Sacred Congregation decided in this case that the jurisdiction of the religious priest was obtained from the local Ordinary. He could, therefore, validly absolve the subjects of the local Ordinary, even

[62] Cf. Gennari, *Consultationi Morali, Canoniche, Liturgiche* (2 vols., Romae, 1902-1904), *Consult.*, XXII.

[63] Cf. Benedictus XIV, *De Synodo Dioecesana,* lib. IX, c. 16, nn. 7, 8.

[64] S. C. Ep. et Reg., *Ordinis Praedicatorum,* 2 mart. 1866—*Fontes,* n. 1996.

[65] The questions asked were the following: An religiosus non approbatus iuxta leges proprii Ordinis a suo superiore, vel ipso invito, cum sola facultate Ordinarii, valide excipiat confessiones saecularium? An superiores Regulares . . . possint suos subditos suspendere ab audiendis confessionibus saecularium . . . ? R. Ad 1am: affirmative. Ad 2am: affirmative, ita tamen ut religiosus suspensus illicite, non tamen invalide confessiones excipiat.

though he could not exercise that jurisdiction over his own religious brothers because of his superior's suspension. He would act illicitly, since he was disobedient to the superior's mandate.

However, the response did not settle the much disputed question concerning the various juridical effects following from the possession of papal jurisdiction for the hearing of the confessions of the faithful. There was still a possibility of having jurisdiction from a twofold source, namely, from the local Ordinary and from the Holy See. The case proposed settled this fact only, that the local superior could not prevent the valid use of jurisdiction obtained from the local Ordinary.

In the latter half of the nineteenth century the local Ordinary came to be looked upon not only as actually granting to religious priests jurisdiction to hear the confessions of the faithful, but also as exercising confessional jurisdiction over the subjects of the religious superior. In a case submitted to the Sacred Penitentiary on May 14, 1902 one finds mention for the first time of a situation in which it was officially declared that a Regular was absolved not only validly but licitly in virtue solely of diocesan faculties. The case submitted was the following: a member of a Regular community approached a diocesan priest to make his confession. On being asked whether he had received the permission of his superior to choose a confessor, the religious answered that he had not had the opportunity to do so since the superior had been away for some days. The priest absolved him. The Sacred Penitentiary was asked whether the absolution in question was licit and valid? It responded:

> Si superior domus aliique confessarii tamdiu absint, saltem per unum diem, ut grave sit religioso penitenti toto eo tempore carere absolutione sacramentali, is licite et valide absolvitur ab extraneo confessario idoneo.[66]

The decision marks clearly a confirmation of the jurisdictional powers exercised by the local Ordinary relative to confessions made by Regulars within his diocese to a diocesan priest.

The final barriers were removed eleven years after this decree of

[66] Cf. Boudinhon, "La Confession des Religieux"—*Le Canoniste Contemporain*, XXXVI (1913), 702, 703; Cappello, *De Poenitentia*, n. 428, 3°.

the Sacred Penitentiary by the Sacred Congregation of Religious.[67] In February of the year 1913 Pope Pius X had issued a decree for the city of Rome permitting all religious residing in Rome to make their confessions to any priest approved by the local Ordinary. This privilege was extended to religious over the entire world on August 5 of the same year by the decree *In audientia.* Thenceforth, all religious of exempt and non-exempt religious institutes could receive absolution from their sins validly and licitly when confessing to a priest approved by the local Ordinary. The decree follows:

> Hi proinde confessarii . . . omnium Sodalium cuiuscumque Ordinis, Congregationis . . . sacramentales confessiones excipere, quin de licentia a Superiore obtenta inquirere vel petere teneantur, atque valide et licite absolutionem a peccatis in Ordine . . . etiam sub censura reservatis, impertire queant . . . constitutionibus, ordinationibus apostolicis, privilegiis qualibet efficaciori forma concessis, aliisque contrariis quibuscumque, etiam speciali atque individua mentione dignis, minime obstantibus.

In virtue of this decree Regulars could be absolved by reason of jurisdiction received either from the religious superior or from the local Ordinary. No longer could a religious superior occasion the invalidity of the confessions of his subjects through an act of withholding the grant of jurisdiction to a priest outside the Order if such a priest had received faculties for the hearing of confessions from the local Ordinary. The confessor chosen by the religious could then absolve his penitent even from the censures and sins reserved in the Order. The statutes of religious institutes which ran counter to this decree were expressly abrogated.

Article 5. Privileges of the Itinerant Regular and the Code

The Code grants to two classes of persons the privilege of choosing confessors without reference to approbation: to the cardinals, and to the bishops, regardless of whether the latter be residential or titular prelates.[68] If either a cardinal or a bishop wishes to make his con-

[67] Decr. *In audientia,* 5 aug. 1913—*AAS,* V (1913), 431.

[68] Cf. canons 239, § 1, n. 2; 349, § 1, n. 1. To the class of bishops are assimilated other *local* Ordinaries, such as abbots *nullius,* vicars and prefects apostolic, etc.; cf. canons 323, § 1; 294, § 1.

fession he need not seek for a priest who has been previously approved by the local Ordinary. The law itself grants jurisdiction to the priest chosen to absolve in such a case. But the Code nowhere grants a similar privilege to members of religious Orders; no canon of the Code grants them the right to confess to a priest who has not received previous approval either from their own religious superior or from the local Ordinary. Canon 519, to be sure, grants them the right to confess to a priest outside the Order; but it also demands that the priest chosen be approved by the local Ordinary. In such cases the law itself does not grant the jurisdiction to absolve. Absolution is given in virtue of jurisdiction received from the local Ordinary.[69]

Canon 519 is but a substantial restatement of the decree of the Sacred Congregation of Religious issued on August 5, 1913. This canon has introduced only one modification of that decree; it demands that the religious who confesses by reason of canon 519 should confess for the peace of his conscience. To abstract from this condition, especially if the confession is made against the wishes of the superior, would render the confession valid but illicit.

According to the apostolic privileges granted to many religious Orders directly [70] and extended to all the Mendicant Orders through intercommunication of their privileges, Regulars who were on a journey with the permission of the religious superior could make their confession to any priest outside the Order, provided that this priest was suited for the hearing of confessions, and provided also that no suitable priest of their own Order was present. Authors commonly taught that the priest chosen did not need the approval of the local Ordinary before being considered suited for the hearing of such a confession. Did the Code make any new provisions for the act of judging the priest's fitness? Canon 877, § 1, states that neither the local Ordinary nor the religious superior shall grant jurisdiction or permission to hear confessions, unless the priest has been found suitable *(idoneus)* through an examination or in some other way. From the wording of the canon it could seem that some *official* judgment must be made before a priest is to be considered suited. The canon does not demand, however, that the Ordinary make this

[69] Cf. canon 874, § 1.

[70] Cf. Innocentius VII, const. *Provenit,* 17 oct. 1405—*Bull. Praed.,* II, 477.

judgment personally. It states merely that jurisdiction is not to be granted to a priest unless he is found suited for the hearing of confessions; the suitability is to be judged by an examination or in some other way. Therefore, at the present time, if a priest has finished his theological studies and has passed the required examinations, there is no reason to suppose that he is not suited for the hearing of confessions, even though the Ordinary has not yet granted him faculties. Under the present discipline, a distinction between approbation, that is, the actual grant of jurisdiction, and the judgment concerning the priest's suitability for hearing of confessions is still in order. This is seen from the fact that canon 877, § 2, implies as much when it states that the bishop can subject a priest to another examination to determine his suitability, even though he already has faculties to hear confessions. The priest in question would still be approved, although he may not be suited for hearing of confessions. Granted this distinction, one can see that a Regular with apostolic privileges to choose a confessor while on a journey would not be fulfilling the conditions laid down in the privilege if he confessed to a priest who had been granted official approval by the Ordinary, but who was unsuitable for the hearing of confessions. The priest chosen according to the privilege must be suited *(idoneus)*, and there is no reason to suppose that this suitability cannot be determined by the individual religious.

The new legislation has made several important modifications of the privilege granted by Pope Innocent VII. Canon 519 has changed the previous stricter discipline which obliged a religious to confess in every instance to a brother-priest of his own Order if such a one were present. At the present time, any priest of the diocese approved by the local Ordinary may be approached if confession is made for the peace of one's conscience. Under no circumstances would he be obliged to confess to a fellow-religious, even if one or several traveled with him as his companions.[71] If several priests of a religious Order, therefore, are traveling or staying in a place away from the monastery, it is not now necessary that they confess to one another as was demanded in the constitution of Innocent VII. They may be absolved licitly and validly by any priest with diocesan faculties.

[71] Cf. Vermeersch, *Theologia Moralis* (3 vols., Romae, 1923), III, n. 479, 9°.

One may, however, suppose a case in which two priests of a religious Order are located in a place where no priests approved by the local Ordinary are available. They could not then avail themselves of the right granted to religious in canon 519. In virtue of their privileges they could, however, confess to each other, provided they were suited for the hearing of confessions, even though they were not officially approved by the religious superior. But if they were unsuited for the hearing of confessions, they could confess to a non-approved diocesan priest, provided such a priest was likewise suited for the hearing of confessions.

The following could be a very practical example: a religious brother pertaining to a religious Order is confined to a hospital where there is available only one chaplain approved by the local Ordinary. Weeks pass during which he is not visited by any priests of his Order. Priests, however, from other dioceses and from other religious institutes visit him frequently. According to the present discipline, they cannot hear his confession since they have not faculties in that diocese, even though they have faculties in other dioceses. Would it be possible for him, in virtue of his apostolic privileges, to choose from among them someone to hear his confession?

Authors like Génicot (1856-1900)[72] and Lehmkuhl (1834-1914),[73] writing just before the Code, maintained that the use of the privileges granted by Innocent VII and other popes depended upon the constitutions of each Order. The Sacred Congregation of Bishops and Regulars seems to have been of the same mind in 1864 when it responded to a case proposed at that time.[74] The query was proposed whether the Prior of a convent of the Order of St. Augustine could grant to one of his subjects the faculty to choose a priest outside the Order to absolve him from his sins. The Sacred Congregation answered: "In the affirmative, provided that the priest chosen had been approved by the local Ordinary. For other Orders, *"standum est constitutionibus et statutis."*

[72] Cf. *Institutiones Theologiae Moralis,* II, n. 337, 2°.

[73] Cf. *Theologia Moralis,* II, n. 511.

[74] Cf. S. C. Ep. et Reg., *Piscien. seu Ordinis Eremitarum S. Augustini,* 3 iun. 1864—*Fontes,* n. 1992.

Génicot, however, maintains [75] that this reply of the Sacred Congration, and that given by the Sacred Congregation of the Council to the bishop of Hildesheim in 1769,[76] were not of universal obligation since they were never formally promulgated.

An examination of the canons which treat of confessional jurisdiction and approbation in their relation to canon 4 of the Code reveals no trace of any abrogation of the apostolic privileges of Regulars when they are on a journey with the permission of their superior. In the interpretation of the privileges there is, however, one point that seems to militate against the law of the Code. It has been pointed out that authors writing before the Code held that jurisdiction was granted tacitly, implicitly, or presumptively, by the superior by the very fact that permission was given to make a journey. The Code demands that delegation of jurisdiction, in order to be valid, must be given expressly, either verbally or in writing.[77]

In the present Code, therefore, tacit or presumed jurisdiction will not suffice. A priest arriving at a parish to hear confessions, but without jurisdiction from the local Ordinary, cannot enter the confessional box and absolve on the presumption that, if the bishop would know of it, he would certainly grant him the necessary faculties. But if the priest had made application for faculties and was morally certain that the bishop had received the application and had granted the faculties, he could absolve validly. Many authors will allow such a one to hear confessions even though he has received no express notice of the grant of jurisdiction.[78]

Likewise, a pastor may invite priests of a religious institute from another diocese to give a mission in his parish. Some days later he meets his bishop and tells him, in passing, that he has made arrangements for a mission. To this the bishop consents. By that very fact the priests who give the mission cannot presume to absolve the people of the parish on the strength that the bishop has tacitly granted them faculties. A tacit concession of jurisdiction is not sufficient for the

[75] Cf. *loc. cit.*

[76] S. C. C., *Hildeshemen.*, 16 sept., 18 nov. 1769—*Fontes*, n. 3767.

[77] Canon 879, § 1—"Ad confessiones valide audiendas opus est iurisdictione scripto vel verbis expresse concessa."

[78] Cf. Vermeersch, *op. cit.*, III, n. 453; Cappello, *De Poenitentia*, n. 398, 4°.

hearing of confessions. Therefore, those authors who, according to the pre-Code discipline, maintained that a presumed or tacit delegation of jurisdiction sufficed for the hearing of confession, cannot be upheld in their opinion since the Code became law.

Those authors, however, who maintained that implicit delegation was granted by the superior in the very permission to make a journey, are entirely within the limits of the present discipline. Canon 879 states that jurisdiction must be given expressly. Express jurisdiction is twofold, either explicit or implicit. The former is had when the superior grants jurisdiction by manifest words, such as: *I delegate you.* Implicit jurisdiction is had when a priest accepts an office to which the exercise of jurisdiction is attached, or when jurisdiction is implied in the very assignment of an office. Thus a priest appointed by the bishop as curate in a parish receives implicit jurisdiction to hear the confessions of the faithful there. Again, if the bishop himself asked a priest of another diocese to give a mission in one of the parishes of his diocese, the jurisdiction to hear confessions would be implied in the very appointment to give the mission.[79]

All authors are agreed that the delegation of jurisdiction need not be made directly to the confessor. Indirect delegation suffices. Thus the Ordinary can say to a person: "I give you the permission to choose any priest you desire, and to the priest you shall choose, I grant the faculty to hear your confession." In this way even a lay person who is incapable of receiving jurisdiction can nevertheless act as an agent in the hands of the bishop to make his previously indeterminate delegation operative for a specific priest.[80] Those authors, therefore, who teach that the confessor chosen by a Regular while on a journey with the permission of his religious superior has implicit jurisdiction from the religious superior, must be understood in this sense: that the confessor receives indirect delegation through the religious subject acting as the agent for the superior. Such implicit indirect delegation is valid in the present discipline.[81]

Is it necessary, however, to interpret the privileges of the itinerant Regulars according to the canons of the Code regarding delegation

[79] Cf. Vermeersch, *op. cit.*, III, n. 453.

[80] Cf. Cappello, *De Poenitentia,* n. 394, 3°.

[81] Cf. Fanfani, *De Iure Regularium* (Taurini: Marietti, 1925), n. 127, b.

and approbation? Canon 4 states that the privileges granted by the Holy See and still in use when the Code was promulgated, remain intact, unless they are expressly revoked by the canons of the Code. Authors have shown that these privileges were still in use when the Code became law, unless individual Orders had contrary statutes. They were not expressly abrogated by the Code; therefore, in their existence and in their interpretation they should remain the same as previously. With regard to their interpretation, the most that can be said is that there is some doubt concerning the sufficiency of delegation. Applying the suppletory principle of canon 209 in cases of positive and probable doubt, one can conclude that absolution given in virtue of these privileges is certainly valid. In such a probable and positive doubt of law, most authors are agreed that no cause whatsoever is required for the licit use of supplied jurisdiction.[82]

It is well to note that the original grants of the privileges [83] make no mention whatsoever of the need of express jurisdiction. The legitimate permission of the religious superior to leave the monastery is the condition of supreme importance, not the superior's express delegation of jurisdiction. One may therefore question the correctness of Cappello's interpretation when he demands an express delegation of jurisdiction from the religious superior to the priest chosen by the religious subject, unless it is understood in the sense of an indirect delegation, implicitly contained in the very permission to leave the religious house. Cappello states:

> Si constet de iurisdictione expresse concessa, ad normam c. 879, § 1, vel a constitutionibus religiosis, vel scripto aut verbis superioris, religiosus exemptus potest in itinere, ut olim, socio confiteri; si non constet . . . non potest, quia hodie tacitus consensus superioris non sufficit.[84]

Marc (1831-1887) [85] summarizes the privileges of itinerant Regulars thus:

[82] Cf. Miaskiewicz, *Supplied Jurisdiction According to Canon 209,* p. 299.

[83] Cf. *supra,* pp. 46, 54.

[84] *De Poenitentia,* n. 429. Cf. also, Fallon, "Selection of Confessor by Exempt Religious *in Itinere*"—*Irish Ecclesiastical Record,* LVI (1940), 577-580.

[85] Cf. *Institutiones Morales* (13. ed., 2 vols., Romae, 1906), II, n. 1763.

> Si desit socius, vel alius confessarius idoneus sui Ordinis, bene possunt, ex praesumpta licentia praelati, confiteri alteri sacerdoti idoneo . . . quia . . . sufficit deputatio etiam implicita superioris, iuxta Constitutiones Ordinis vel consuetudines, neque ullo iure requiritur approbatio Ordinarii loci.

It is necessary to note likewise that individual Orders did modify these privileges for their own subjects. Thus the Capuchins limited the choice of a confessor in such a manner that the priest selected had to be among those approved by the local Ordinary.[86]

From these considerations the writer concludes that a member of a religious Order, whose constitutions do not expressly forbid the use of the apostolic privilege, may licitly choose any priest suited for the hearing of confessions, even though not approved by the local Ordinary, and be validly absolved by him, provided that he is absent from the monastery with the permission of his religious superior, and a suitable priest of his own Order is not present. With due regard for the rights granted to religious by canon 519, if a priest of his own Order suited for the hearing of confessions is present on such a journey, the religious is bound to confess to him.

[86] Cf. Benedictus XIV, const. *Quoad communi,* 30 mart. 1742; Pius IX, *Brevis,* 27 sept. 1852. Both documents are cited in Marc, *loc. cit.*

CHAPTER IV

PRIVILEGES OF REGULAR CONFESSORS IN RESERVED CASES

Article 1. General Norms of Reservation and Absolution

It has been pointed out in previous chapters that a twofold power is necessary for the valid absolution of sins in the sacrament of penance: the power of priestly ordination, and the power of jurisdiction. As long as either one is lacking, confessional absolution is impossible. The first power comes with the act of receiving the holy priesthood. The second power is obtained by appointment to an ecclesiastical office to which ordinary jurisdictional power is entrusted, or by external concession of jurisdiction by the competent ecclesiastical superior.[1] This latter power may be extended to cover all sins and persons within the competency of the one who has the right to grant the jurisdiction; it may be limited also to certain sins and to certain persons according to the will of the superior. This limitation of jurisdiction is called reservation. Reservation, therefore, with regard to sins, may be defined as the withholding or withdrawal of jurisdiction over specified cases from a lower tribunal, and placing them entirely within the competency of the superior authority.[2]

The present Code of Canon Law sets forth in canon 893, § 1, the general principles of legislative capacity to reserve cases. All persons who have the right to delegate jurisdiction to hear confessions or who can establish censures by ordinary power can likewise withdraw certain cases to their own tribunal, thus limiting the powers of inferiors to absolve. The only persons excepted are the Vicar Capitular, and also the Vicar General, unless he has a special mandate.[3] Who are those

[1] Cf. Conc. Trident., sess. XIV, c. 7; D'Annibale, *Theologiae Moralis Summula,* III, n. 318; canon 872.

[2] Cf. canon 893, §§ 1-2.

[3] Canon 893, § 1—"Qui ordinario iure possunt audiendi confessiones potestatem concedere aut ferre censuras, possunt quoque, excepto Vicario capitulari et Vicario Generali sine mandato speciali, nonnullos casus ad suum avocare iudicium, inferioribus absolvendi potestatem limitantes."

who have the right to grant jurisdiction for the hearing of confessions? Certainly the Supreme Pontiff, who has ordinary jurisdiction over all the faithful, can grant to any priest the power to hear confessions. All local Ordinaries, as defined in canon 198, § 1, can also delegate jurisdiction to hear confessions.[4] All of these, except the Vicar Capitular, and also the Vicar General when he has no special mandate, can reserve cases to themselves. Religious Superiors in a clerical exempt religious institute also possess the power to delegate jurisdiction according to their constitutions; the power to reserve cases, however, is limited to the Supreme Moderator, or, in juridically autonomous monasteries, to the abbot together with his governing Council.[5]

Canon 893, § 1, states that persons who enjoy the right to establish censures by reason of their ordinary powers can likewise reserve cases. Who then are empowered to establish censures? The Code points out that all who have the power to make laws or impose precepts, can also annex penalties to their laws or precepts.[6] Since censures are essentially penalties,[7] the reservation of censures which are attached to delicts pertains to those who have the right to make laws, or to impose precepts. According to the common law this right belongs to the Roman Pontiff, whether alone or in a General Council;[8] to the local Ordinaries, whether they legislate alone or in a synod, with the exception of the Vicar General when he is without a special mandate;[9] and exempt clerical religious superiors, according to their constitutions.[10]

The study of legislative capacity, therefore, reveals that the power

[4] This includes residential bishops, abbots, and prelates *nullius,* Apostolic administrators of dioceses, Vicars and Prefects Apostolic, and those who succeed them according to the prescripts of law. Cf. canon 374, § 1.

[5] "Inter Superiores religionis clericalis exemptae unus Superior generalis, et in monasteriis sui iuris Abbas, cum proprio cuiusque Consilio, peccata, ut supra, subditorum reservare possunt. . . ."—Canon 896.

[6] Canon 2220—"Qui pollent potestate leges ferendi vel praecepta imponendi, possunt quoque legi vel praecepto poenas adnectere."

[7] Cf. canon 2241, § 1.

[8] Cf. canons 219; 228.

[9] Cf. canons 291; 335; 362; 2220, § 2.

[10] Cf. canons 501, §§ 1 and 3; 502.

to reserve sins is not co-extensive with the power to reserve censures. The right to reserve sins is specifically limited by the number and type of sins to be reserved,[11] and by the manner in which the reservation is to be made.[12] The right to reserve censures is not limited beyond the general prescriptions of the law which demand that censures be reserved for absolution in cases only of particularly grave sins, and when the reservation has for its purpose the more efficacious control of ecclesiastical discipline and the cure of the ills of conscience for the faithful.[13]

When a case has been reserved by the legitimate authority, the jurisdiction of all inferiors over that case is suspended. Thus, if the pope reserves a case to himself, no bishop or inferior prelate can touch that reservation without express delegation from the Holy Father. Likewise, an episcopal reservation limits the powers of the priests who come under his jurisdiction; however, the bishop's superior, the pope, can absolve from such a reservation since his powers are not limited by the bishop. Therefore the Code, in treating of penalties, makes the general rule that the remission of a reserved case pertains to him who has made the reservation, to his competent superior, to his successor, and to the one to whom power over the case has been committed, either by law or by delegation.[14] This rule applies also to the absolution from reserved sins.

An examination of this rule occasions little difficulty. The competency of the superior cannot be questioned, since the superior cannot be bound by the reservations of his inferior. The successor in the office of the one who has established the reservation is juridically the same person as his predecessor, and can therefore absolve from the reservation. The law itself may commission persons with the right to absolve from certain reservations; these powers must be expressly mentioned in the law itself, and cannot be presumed. Thus canon 401, § 1, grants to the canon penitentiary the jurisdiction to absolve from all sins and censures reserved by the bishop of the diocese.

[11] Cf. canon 897.

[12] Cf. canons 895; 896; 899, § 1.

[13] Cf. canon 2246, § 1.

[14] Cf. canon 2236, § 1.

Canon 882 grants to all priests jurisdiction to absolve all sins and censures, no matter how reserved, of a penitent who is in danger of death. Outside of such definite concessions of the law itself,[15] however, no priest without special delegation from the competent authority may absolve from reserved cases.

The competent authority in all reservations, whether papal or episcopal, is the Roman Pontiff. Consequently he can grant to any priest or group of priests the jurisdiction to absolve all reserved cases. In the present legislation Cardinals have the privilege of absolving from all reservations throughout the world, except from cases reserved in a most special manner to the Holy See, and from those which constitute a revelation of the secrets of the Holy Office.[16] In the history of the privileges of Religious Orders one finds many special privileges granting jurisdiction over reserved cases. These will now be investigated.

Article 2. Privileges of Regulars in Pre-Clementine Legislation

Regular confessors in the past absolved the faithful by reason of papal jurisdiction. It has been noted that as early as 1227, Pope Gregory IX (1227-1241) [17] issued a constitution stating that confessors of the Dominican Order absolved by reason of pontifical jurisdiction. Throughout the first centuries of the existence of the Mendicant Orders this fact is brought out explicitly time after time: Regulars are not dependent in any way upon the jurisdiction of the local Ordinaries when they absolve the faithful from their sins.

The constitutions of the popes during those early years made no mention concerning any limitation of the jurisdiction of Regulars with regard to reservations which the local Ordinaries had established in their dioceses. It is quite certain that they lawfully disregarded all such reservations and absolved all the faithful who confessed to them, without any reference to the local Ordinary.

The earliest express privilege of absolving from reserved cases

[15] Cf. canons 519; 883, § 2; 899, §§ 2-3; 900; 2237, § 2; 2252; 2254, § 1.
[16] Canon 239, § 1.
[17] Cf. Const. *Quoniam*, 10 maii 1227—*Bull. Praed.*, I, 19.

was granted by Pope Gregory IX to the Order of Friars Minor in 1233.[18] Confessors appointed by the religious superiors could absolve all the faithful living in the lands of the infidels in the Near East from all excommunications, even those reserved to the Holy See. It will be seen that this privilege was very restricted in its application. However, it was not long before general faculties were granted. In 1262 Pope Urban IV (1261-1264) [19] conceded to the confessors of the Order of Carmel the privilege of absolving their own members, the personnel of their household, and any of the faithful who should confess to them, from all cases except those specially reserved to the Holy See:

> Vobis . . . concedimus, ut confratrum et familiarium, ac aliorum Christifidelium, causa devotionis ad vos recurrentium . . . confessiones audire, et eis pro commissis poenitentiam salutarem iniungere valeatis, nisi forte talia commiserint, propter quae Sedes Apostolica sit merito consulenda.

That the Religious Orders not only presumed that they had jurisdiction over episcopal reservations, but carried it also into practice, is evident from the widespread opposition to Regulars from bishops and diocesan priests. The latter were open in their denunciation of what they termed abuses of papal privileges. One can readily understand their position; the penitential discipline of the local Ordinary was greatly weakened and almost nullified by the Regular confessors, even as the penitential discipline of Religious Orders is weakened somewhat in the present legislation by the rule of canon 519. The faithful either waited to make their confession until a Regular confessor visited the parish, or obtained the permission of their pastor to make their confession to a priest of their choice, which usually was a Regular confessor. This method led to great abuses, and lessened the authority of the bishops and pastors considerably.

Pope Clement V (1305-1314) determined upon strong measures to correct prevailing abuses. In the Council of Vienne (1311-1312),

[18] Const. *Animarum salute,* 21 mart. 1233—*Bull. Fransc.,* I, 100; Potth., n. 9130. See also, Potth., nn. 9184, 9196.

[19] Const. *Vobis ad hoc,* reproduced and confirmed in the *Mare Magnum Carmelitarum,* § 14—Potth., n. 18306.

he established excommunications for all religious who should presume to absolve any of the faithful from excommunications established by the common law or by synodal and provincial legislation:

> Religiosi, qui . . . excommunicatos a canone, praeterquam in casibus a iure expressis, vel per privilegia Sedis Apostolicae concessis eisdem, vel a sententiis per statuta provincialia aut synodalia promulgatis, seu . . . a poena et culpa absolvere quemquam praesumpserint: excommunicationis incurrant sententiam ipso facto.[20]

If, however, certain Religious Orders had received special papal privileges to absolve reserved cases, they could still make use of them. It seems that this law was established to correct the false notion of many Orders that, since they had papal privileges of absolving, they were not bound by any reservations whatsoever. Some religious also claimed a participated communication in privileges at this time, so that what was granted to one Order directly could be used by all Orders. This false notion was also corrected. For all those Orders which had not received direct privileges from the Roman Pontiff to absolve reserved cases had to obtain delegated jurisdiction through the ordinary channels from the proper superior.

During this period, before the general communication in privileges took place, Pope Eugene IV (1431-1447) granted the Benedictine Congregation of St. Justina the privilege of absolving the faithful from all sins and censures, except those reserved to the Ordinary, or those specially reserved to the Holy See.[21] The same Pontiff granted to confessors of the Cistercians of the Regular Observance, who heard confessions in their own churches and monasteries, the privilege of absolving from all sins and censures, except those reserved to the Holy See.[22]

[20] C. I, *de privilegiis et excessibus privilegiatorum,* V, 7, in Clem.

[21] Const. *Regularem,* 30 iun. 1436—*Bull. Rom.,* V, 22: "Possint . . . eis beneficium absolutionis impendere ab omnibus peccatis et dispensare super omnes casus, praeter ea peccata, et eos casus, de quibus ipsis confessoribus ad eorum Ordinarios videbitur recurrendum, aut de quibus esset Sedes Apostolica merito consulenda."

[22] Const. *Commissum,* 1438—*Comp. Privileg.,* p. 132. See also, const. *Cum ad ecclesiam,* 1439—*Comp. Privileg., ibid.*

During the period of communication in privileges numerous other concessions were made to almost all religious Orders. The Salmanticenses enumerate many such grants by both Sixtus IV (1471-1484) and Julius II (1503-1513).[23] The most ample of all privileges regarding absolution from reserved cases was given to the Society of Jesus by Pope Paul III (1534-1549) in 1545. The members of the Society were granted the right to absolve all their penitents from sins, crimes, delicts, and excesses, even though reserved to the Holy See; and from any of these sins resulting in censures and ecclesiastical penalties, except those reserved in the Bull, *In Coena Domini.*[24] The constitution of Pope Paul III left no doubt concerning the absolving powers of the Regular confessor in reserved cases. Since the Society of Jesus shared in the privilege of communication with the other Mendicant Orders, this privilege was communicated to all the other Orders.[25] Regular confessors, by this concession of Paul III, obtained full powers to absolve from all episcopal and papal reservations, except from those excommunications mentioned in the list published each year on Holy Thursday, known as the Bull, *In Coena Domini.*[26] This list varied from year to year; usually there were twenty excommunications attached to grave sins against the rights of the Church.[27] To

[23] Cf. *Cursus Theologiae Moralis* (3 vols. in 2, Venetiis, 1714), I, tr. VI, c. 13, n. 51; *Comp. Privileg.*, pp. 142-150.

[24] Const. *Cum inter cunctas*, 3 iun. 1545—*Comp. Privileg.*, p. 150: "... illis ex vobis, qui presbyteri fuerint, quorumcunque utriusque sexus Christifidelium ad vos undecunque accedentium confessiones audiendi, ... et ipsos et eorum singulos ab omnibus et singulis eorum peccatis, criminibus, excessibus, et delictis, quantumcunque gravibus et enormibus, etiam Sedi Apostolicae reservatis, et a quibuscunque ex ipsis casibus resultantibus sententiis, censuris, et poenis ecclesiasticis (exceptis contentis in Bulla, quae in die Coenae Domini solita est legi) absolvendi. ..."

[25] Cf. Pius V, const. *Dum indefessae*, 7 iul. 1571—*Bull. Rom.*, VII, 923.

[26] Cf. Moriarty, *Extraordinary Absolution from Censures* (Catholic University of America Canon Law Studies, n. 113; Washington, D. C.: Catholic University of America Press, 1938), pp. 39, 40.

[27] Busembaum includes a list of these censures in his treatise on Moral Theology. The censures attached to the following delinquents:

1. Heretics and their abettors;
2. Those who appealed from the Pope to the Council; and their abettors;

confirm the fact that the privilege of absolving from episcopal censures was included in the constitution of Pope Paul III, Gregory XIII (1572-1585), in a letter written to a bishop who had taken offense at the practice of Regular confessors in absolving from such reservations, stated that such privileges had never been abrogated; and then he renewed the constitution of Paul III insofar as it need renewal.[28]

The last additional privilege of this period was granted also to the Society of Jesus. It was granted in 1552 by Pope Julius III (1550-1555). This pope gave to the Society, through its superiors, the faculty to absolve *in foro conscientiae tantum* from the sin of heresy, despite the fact that this sin was included in the lists of the

3. Pirates, and those who received goods from them;
4. Those who stole the goods of shipwrecked Christians;
5. Those who within the Papal States imposed taxes higher than those allowed by the Roman chancery, or levied new taxes;
6. Falsifiers of Apostolic letters;
7. Those who carried weapons to the Turks, and to other enemies of the Christian States;
8. Those who impeded the carriers of food and other necessities to Rome;
9. Those who came to Rome, or left Rome, for the purpose of harming official work; and those who molested members of the Curia;
10. Those who annoyed pilgrims and strangers in Rome;
11. Those who injured Cardinals and other Prelates;
12. Those who injured persons having recourse to the Roman Curia;
13. Those who appealed from the decrees of Apostolic letters to a lay power;
14. Those who impeded the execution of Apostolic letters;
15. Secular judges who forced ecclesiastical persons to appear before a lay tribunal;
16. Those who impeded prelates in the use of their jurisdiction;
17. Those who usurped the jurisdiction of the Holy See, or of any Churches, or sequestrated her goods;
18. Those who imposed tithes upon ecclesiastical persons, churches, or monasteries;
19. Secular judges who took part in criminal cases of ecclesiastical persons;
20. Those who occupied goods or lands of the Roman Church; and those who usurped her powers. Cf. *Medulla Theologiae Moralis* (2 vols., Romae, 1844), I, 664-667.

[28] Cf. Passerinus, *De Statibus Hominum* (3 vols., Lucae, 1732), Q. 187, art. 1, n. 372; *Comp. Privileg.*, p. 151.

Bull *In Coena Domini*. This concession was confirmed in 1584 by Pope Gregory XIII for all places except Spain.[29]

In the very year in which Paul III granted such extensive privileges to the Society of Jesus, the Council of Trent was convened to revise ecclesiastical discipline. Despite the strong and determined effort made by some of the Fathers of the Council to abrogate all privileges of Regulars, one finds no definite revocation of privileges with regard to reserved cases. Chapter VII of the XIV Session, on the Sacrament of Penance, summarizes the Catholic doctrine concerning the reservation of sins; outside of the hour of death, simple priests have no jurisdiction to absolve reserved cases and must send their penitents to the legitimate superiors for absolution. Canon 11 of the same Session vindicates the right of bishops to reserve certain cases, and anathematizes anyone who teaches that such reservations do not hinder a simple priest from absolving such cases. Again, Chapter VI of the XXIV Session on reform grants to bishops the faculty to dispense *in foro conscientiae,* and in occult cases only, in all cases reserved to the Holy See. This faculty can be delegated to another priest by the bishop. The final Session (XXV) in treating of the reform of Regulars states simply that Regulars must publish and observe in their churches the censures and interdicts promulgated by the bishop, if the latter requests it.[30]

There were a few authors who, in writing about the decrees of the XIV Session of the Council of Trent, maintained that the Council definitely abrogated all the privileges of Regulars in reserved cases. To a large extent they were the same authors who held that any decrees of the Council of Trent contrary to the privileges of Regulars *ipso facto* abrogated such privileges.[31] The common teaching of the authors was that these decrees of the Council did not in any way affect the privileges which Regulars possessed for absolving reserved sins.[32]

[29] Both documents are given in *Comp. Privileg.*, p. 152.

[30] Cf. Conc. Trident., Sess. XXV, *de ref.*, c. 12.

[31] Passerinus (1595-1677) cites these authors and discusses their claims; cf. *De Stat. Hom.*, Q. 189, art. 10, nn. 990, 991.

[32] Cf. Suarez, *De Legibus,* lib. VIII, c. 18, *in fine*; Reiffenstuel, *Ius Canonicum Universum,* lib. V, tit. 33, n. 138.

Article 3. Clementine Legislation

The first indications of reform in the privileges which Regulars possessed for absolving from reserved cases came shortly after the close of the Council of Trent. Three separate cases were presented to the Sacred Congregation of the Council in 1585, 1587, and 1588, which dealt with the privileges of Regulars to absolve from episcopal reservations.[33] The cases were submitted by bishops with a view to determining their rights over the Regular clergy in the matter of their own reservations. Taken by themselves, these cases represented only individual responses with local interest; but they were harbingers of future general legislation.

In the diocese of Evora, Portugal, the bishop had reserved certain sins to himself in a synod held a few years before the question was proposed to the Sacred Congregation. Mendicant friars and members of the Society of Jesus presumed to absolve from these reservations without seeking special jurisdiction from the bishop. When he asked them for justification of their practice, they answered that they absolved by reason of apostolic privileges. The Sacred Congregation was asked whether these Regulars had such a faculty. In reply, the Congregation stated that Regulars are not given by any apostolic privileges, not even the *Mare Magnum,* the power to absolve from cases reserved by the bishop to himself.[34]

In the second case, Dominican Friars contended that they could absolve all excommunications and sins reserved by the bishop, by reason of their *Mare Magnum* privileges, and by reason of special privileges given to the Society of the Holy Rosary. The Sacred Congregation of the Council gave a similar reply. The third case was a *dubium* submitted to the Sacred Congregation, namely, whether by reason of jubilee privileges, or through the *Mare Magnum* privileges, Regulars could absolve from cases which the bishop has reserved to himself. The reply was the same as that rendered in the other two

[33] S. C. C., *Eboren.,* mense maii 1585—*Fontes,* n. 2139; S. C. C., *Castellaneten.,* mense iun. 1587—*Fontes,* n. 2179; S. C. C., *Mediolanen.,* mense mart. 1588—*Fontes,* n. 2199.

[34] "Ss.mus D. N. ex sententia Congregationis respondit ex facultatibus per Mare Magnum aliave privilegia Regularibus concessis factam eis non esse potestatem absolvendi in casibus sibi ab Episcopo reservatis."—*Fontes,* n. 2139.

cases, namely, that Regulars did not possess the privilege of absolving from cases which the bishop had reserved to himself *(sibi reservaverit)*.

Pope Clement VIII (1592-1605) was an ardent reformer of the penitential discipline. It has been noted in the preceding chapter that he effected a very necessary reform in the confessional discipline of the Religious Orders by issuing the decree *Sanctissimus* in 1593.[85] Eight years later he ordered the Sacred Congregation of Bishops and Regulars to issue a decree abolishing all the special privileges which Regulars had claimed for absolving from cases reserved by the bishops to themselves. The decree is as follows:

> Sacra Congregatio . . . Episcoporum et Regularium . . . iustis et gravibus causis id exigentibus, ac de . . . Clementis Pp. VIII speciali mandato . . . sacerdotibus omnibus tam saecularibus, quam Regularibus per universam Italiam extra Urbem degentibus . . . iubet, et praecipit, ne quis eorum sub praetextu privilegiorum . . . concessorum . . . ab ullo ex casibus clare vel dubie in Bulla die Coenae Domini legi solita, contentis, vel aliis quomodocumque, Sedi Apostolicae reservatis, aut in futurum . . . in eadem Bulla, vel aliter reservandis, nec etiam a casibus, quos Ordinarii locorum hactenus reservarunt, vel in posterum sibi reservabunt, nullo casu, etiam necessitatis, vel impedimenti, nisi in mortis articulo, seu cum nova et speciali Sanctitatis Suae, . . . vel Ordinariorum, quoad casus ab ipsis tantum reservatos, respective, impetrata in scriptis licentia, . . . absolutionis beneficium de caetero impendere audeat. . . .[86]

The decree was issued for all of Italy, outside of the city of Rome. Within that territory no priest, regardless of privileges he thought himself to possess, could absolve from reservations contained even doubtfully in the Bull *In Coena Domini*, or established by the bishop and reserved to himself, without special faculties from the Holy See or from the bishop respectively. The only exception made was for the hour of death, as provided in the decrees of the Council of Trent.[87]

The restrictions placed upon the privileges of Regulars by Clement VIII were doubtless very necessary to preserve the penitential dis-

[85] Cf. *Fontes*, n. 177.

[86] Cf. S. C. Ep. et Reg., 9 ian. 1601—*Fontes*, n. 1596.

[87] Sess. XIV, *de poenitentia*, c. 7.

cipline as reformed by the Council of Trent. Had Regular confessors been allowed to continue absolving episcopal reservations, then the coercive powers of the local Ordinaries would have been almost nullified, with grave detriment to the common good. However, Clement himself found that such a sweeping abrogation of privileges was too radical. Therefore in the following year he modified the decree of 1601, so that, as to papal reservations, only those cases which were certainly contained in the Bull *In Coena Domini* and five other sins reserved inside Italy, not including the city of Rome, could not be absolved by reason of special privileges. These five cases were: (a) the violation of immunity as set forth in the Constitutions of Gregory XIV; (b) the violation of the papal cloister of nuns for an evil end;[38] (c) the provoking of, and participating in duels; (d) the laying of violent hands upon clerics; (e) the making of simoniacal contracts, even of a confidential nature, regarding benefices. Outside of Italy and within Rome itself the reservation of the above five cases did not bind, and Regulars could [39] absolve by reason of their privileges. The decree of 1601 in so far as it demanded special faculties in every case to absolve from episcopal reservations was not modified.[40]

[38] Const. *Cum alias,* 24 maii 1591—*Fontes,* n. 172.

[39] Cf. Salmanticenses, *Cursus Theologiae Moralis,* I, tr. 10, c. 2, n. 53; Reiffenstuel, *Ius Canonicum Universum,* lib. V, tit. 39, n. 256.

[40] S. C. Ep. et Reg., 26 nov. 1602: "Cum autem dubia quaedam ac difficultates circa eiusdem Decreti interpretationem atque observationem emersissent, Congregatio . . . speciali mandato . . . Clementis VIII . . . ipsum Decretum moderatur ac declarat, videlicet sub eiusdem prohibitione, illos *tantum* in posterum comprehendi casus, qui in Bulla die Coenae Domini legi consueta continentur. Ac praeterea: violationis immunitatis ecclesiasticae in terminis Constitutionis. . . . Gregorii XIV, quae incipit: *Cum alias nonulli*; violationis clausurae Monialium ad malum finem; provocationum et pugnantium in duello iuxta decretum S. C. Tridentinum, et constitutionem. . . . Gregorii Pp. XIII incipientem: *Ad tollendum*; iniicientium violentas manus in clericos, iuxta canonem: *Si quis suadente,* etc., c. 29, C. XVII, q. 4, ad iuris dispositionem; simoniae realis scienter contractae, atque etiam confidentiae beneficialis. Item omnes casus, quos Ordinarii locorum *sibi reservarunt* vel in posterum reservabunt. In quibus . . . enumeratis casibus *dumtaxat* . . . S. C. . . . mandat dictum decretum in . . . robore permanere. Ac declarat eos. . . . Regulares, qui aliquo ex privilegiis . . . in Decreto expressis suffulti fuerint, posse . . . absolvere a casibus in praesenti declaratione non comprehensis. . . ."—*Fontes,* n. 1616.

The decrees of Clement VIII were declarations of the common law and affected all religious with papal privileges.[41] Since they called for a rather drastic limitation of formerly possessed privileges, they were often disregarded. Some authors, in their attempt to justify the practice of those who continued to absolve from episcopal reservations, made the distinction between reservations *ratione peccati,* and reservations *ratione censurae.* They contended that only the former were included in the prohibitions of the Clementine decrees. Therefore, if the local Ordinary reserved a case by attaching a censure to the perpetration of some specifically named sin, the Regular confessor could absolve both censure and sin by reason of his apostolic privileges. Other authors claimed that customary law was substituted in place of the former privileges, and that therefore Regulars could still absolve from such reservations even though the privileges had been abrogated.[42]

To correct such abuses and to confirm once again the abrogations of Pope Clement VIII, Pope Paul V (1605-1621) ordered the Sacred Congregation of Bishops and Regulars to issue a new decree in 1617:

> Quoniam S. C. . . . nuper accepit quamplures Regulares tantum facultatis, seu privilegii ab Apostolica Sede sibi concessum profiteri, ut etiam a casibus locorum Ordinariis in eorum dioecesibus reservatis, absque alia ipsorum Ordinariorum licentia, poenitentes absolvere minime dubitent, nonnullosque alios in decreto . . . die 9 ian. 1601 . . . et 26 nov. 1602 promulgata, excommunicationes Sedi vel Ordinariis praedictis reservatas, minime comprehensas asserere; . . . Ideo eadem Congregatio de . . . Pauli Pp. V speciali mandato . . . decretum huiusmodi . . . necnon censuras . . . et poenas, in eisque contenta omnia confirmanda . . . confirmat . . .

[41] Cf. Passerinus, *op. cit.,* Q. 187, art. 1, n. 380.

[42] Concina (1687-1756) states the contentions of these authors very well: ". . . cui vero (ita dicunt) conceditur facultas absolvendi a casibus Papae reservatis, simul facultas absolvendi a censuris eidem reservatis: quia peccata, inquiunt, reservantur ratione censurae. Contra, ab Episcopo multi casus reservantur absque censura. Ideo, cui conceditur facultas absolvendi a casibus Episcopo reservatis, non propterea impertitur facultas a censuris absolvendi. Subdit, ibidem Viva, per concessionem facultatis absolvendi a censuris Papae reservatis concedi etiam facultatem absolvendi a censuris Episcopo: quia, inquit, ita fert consuetudo."—*Theologia Christiana* (10 vols., Neapoli, 1773), X, lib. 3, diss. 1, c. 7, q. 6, n. 16.

> ab omnibus . . . inviolabiliter observari, ac insuper ut nulli . . . ab excommunicationibus, vel a casibus eisdem Ordinariis, vel Sedi Apostolicae reservatis . . . absolvere audeant. . . .[43]

The Sacred Congregation noted that many Regular confessors had not ceased absolving from episcopal reservations. They justified their conduct on the score that excommunications established by the bishop were not properly episcopal reservations as determined by the Constitutions of Clement VIII. The decree of Paul V implicitly affirmed that both reserved sins and censures were included in the term "episcopal reservations"; and no Regular confessor was entitled to absolve from episcopal censures without special faculties.

The decree of Pope Paul V is noteworthy in as much as it recognized both sins and censures in the general term *reserved cases*. Before 1617 the term was used loosely to mean almost any kind of reservation.[44] There was much dispute as to its precise limits. After 1617 no doubt could be entertained about its meaning. When, therefore, Pope Alexander VII (1655-1667) used the term *reserved cases* in condemning the proposition that Regulars could, without special faculties, absolve from cases reserved to the bishop, no author could question the fact that both sins and censures were included.[45] Confirmations of the decree of Paul V were given in 1646 by the Sacred Congregation of Bishops and Regulars,[46] and by the Sacred Congregation of the Council in 1662.[47]

Another argument proposed by a few authors for the continuance of papal privileges in absolving from episcopal cases, despite the decrees of Clement VIII and Paul V, was the claim that some Orders had received special confirmation of all its privileges after the Coun-

[43] Cf. S. C. Ep. et Reg., decr., 7 ian. 1617—*Fontes*, n. 1684.

[44] Concerning the evolution of specific distinctions between different reservations, cf. Chelodi, *Ius Poenale* (Tridenti, 1933), pp. 36-37; Moriarty, *op. cit.*, pp. 4-6.

[45] *Prop. damn.:* "Mendicantes possunt absolvere a casibus episcopis reservatis, non obtenta ad id episcoporum facultate." Cf. Denz.-Bann., *op. cit.*, n. 1112.

[46] S. C. Ep. et Reg., *Neapolitana*, 7 dec. 1646—*Fontes*, n. 1781.

[47] Cf. S. C. C., *Suessionen.*, 16 sept. 1662—Pallottini, *op. cit.*, s. v. "Sacramentum Poenitentiae," n. 42.

cil of Trent and that among the privileges confirmed was that of absolving from episcopal cases. Since, according to the contentions of these authors, the decrees of Clement VIII and Paul V were not universal, these newly confirmed privileges were not abrogated. Pope Urban VIII, in 1628, decreed that the confirmation of such privileges after the Council of Trent did not justify the right to absolve in such cases.[48]

Finally, Pope Clement X (1670-1676), in the Constitution *Superna*, of June 21, 1670,[49] summarized and definitely settled all the controversies that had arisen between bishops and Regulars with regard to reserved cases. After reiterating the prohibitions of his predecessors, he added that "those who have the faculty of absolving from all cases reserved to the Holy See cannot, in virtue of this privilege absolve from any cases reserved by the bishop to himself."

> Ex facultatibus per Mare Magnum, aliave privilegia . . . factam eis non esse potestatem absolvendi in casibus Episcopo sibi reservatis. . . . Et habentes facultatem absolvendi ab omnibus casibus Sedi Apostolicae reservatis, non ideo a casibus Episcopo reservatis posse absolvere. . . . Vigore . . . privilegiorum nequaquam licere Regularibus . . . absolvere poenitentes a censuris quoad externum (forum).[50]

The special abrogations of the Constitution *Superna*, which had the force of law throughout the Christian world, were directed against the teachings of Suarez (d. 1617), Alterius (d. 1616), Bartholomew Ugolinus (d. 1610), Aegidius Coninck (d. 1633), and others,[51] who maintained that Regulars could absolve episcopal reser-

[48] St. Alphonsus cites the decree: "Per confirmationes privilegiorum, quas Regulares a Sede Apostolica post S. Tridentinum Concilium obtinuerunt, nequaquam revixisse privilegia prius ab eodem Concilio, ac deinde etiam ipsius Congregationis Decretis sublata, atque extincta . . . absolvendi a casibus Ordinario reservatis; quemadmodum nec indulta absolvendi a casibus contentis in Bulla . . . in die Coenae. . . . Ab aliis casibus et censuris Sedi Apostolicae reservatis absolvendi facultatem extra Italiam minime sublatum fuisse eiusdem S. C. Decretis hac de re editis iussu Clementis VIII—Cf. *Theol. Mor.*, lib. VII, n. 95.

[49] Cf. *Fontes*, n. 246.

[50] Cf. also S. C. C., *Colonien.*, 16 nov. 1720—*Fontes*, n. 3216.

[51] Cf. Salmanticenses, *op. cit.*, I, tr. 10, c. 2, n. 40. St. Alphonsus, *op. cit.*, lib. VII, n. 98.

vations by reason of the full papal jurisdiction which they possessed for absolving from the sins of the faithful. The pope, they maintained, had authority to absolve from episcopal censures and sins; therefore, when he granted them jurisdiction to absolve, he also included the power over episcopal reservations with it. Furthermore, Regulars could absolve from many papal reservations, which were of a higher order; *a fortiori* they could absolve from episcopal reservations which were of an inferior rank. Concina (1687-1756)[52] pointed out the fallacy of such reasoning. It is an unwarranted assumption to conclude that the pope, by granting jurisdiction to absolve from one type of reservation, grants jurisdiction to absolve from all types, even though these reservations be of an inferior type.

The final paragraph of the Constitution *Superna* states that all absolution of reserved cases given by Regulars with Apostolic privileges is for the internal forum only. If the reservation became known to the bishop, the penitent could be forced to conduct himself as still laboring under censure until absolution was obtained in the external forum. This was simply a clarification of the response given by the Sacred Congregation of the Council in 1624, which stated that papal privileges in relation to confession were meant for use solely in the internal forum.[53]

Article 4. Teaching of Canonists and Theologians

A study of the decrees of Clement VIII (1592-1605), Paul V (1605-1621) and Urban VIII (1623-1644), reveals a close kinship throughout. In fact, all the later documents mention the preceding decrees. The matter treated is the same; therefore, when an interpretation of them is made, those points which are obscure in any-one of them must be explained in the light of the clearer texts of the others. It is important to insist upon this similarity in the documents, for some canonists, in considering them apart, have made serious errors. For example, when Pope Paul V in 1617 stated that "no priest may absolve from cases reserved to the *same* Ordinaries,

[52] Cf. *Theologia Christiana*, X, lib. 3, diss. 1, c. 7, q. 6, n. 16.

[53] Cf. S. C. C., *Dubium*, mense nov. 1624—Pallottini, *ibid.*, s. v. "Sacramentum Poenitentiae," n. 154; Reiffenstuel, *op. cit.*, lib. V, tit. 39, n. 258.

or to the Apostolic See," some authors interpreted that statement to mean that all privileges regarding the absolution of sins reserved by the Holy See had been abrogated.[54] This was obviously an error, for Pope Urban VIII, just eleven years later (1628), stated that in all cases, except those contained in the Bull *In Coena Domini,* and the five cases specially reserved in Italy, the privileges of Regulars as to papal reservations were not abrogated by either Clement VIII or Paul V.[55] Furthermore, Clement X in 1670, in the Constitution *Superna,* mentioned the fact that those who had the *faculty of absolving from cases reserved to the Holy See* could not on that account absolve from episcopal reservations.

With regard to absolution from papal reservations, the decrees of the three popes, Clement VIII, Paul V and Urban VIII, limited the jurisdiction which Regulars possessed in virtue of their privileges, only in the territory of Italy, but excluding the city of Rome. Within that country Regulars could not validly absolve from the cases reserved in the Bull *In Coena Domini* nor from the five crimes mentioned in the decree of 1602. Outside of Italy, and within Rome itself, only the cases reserved in the Bull *In Coena Domini* were outside the jurisdiction of the Regular confessors.[56]

Again, Clement VIII spoke of cases which local Ordinaries had reserved to themselves (*sibi reservarunt*). Paul V and Urban VIII used somewhat misleading terms in alluding to the same reservations. Paul V used the phrase *eisdem Ordinariis reservatis*; Urban VIII stated that cases *Ordinario reservati* were no longer within the privileged jurisdiction of Regulars with Apostolic faculties. These later statements, if taken by themselves, could refer either to cases which were reserved by the common law to the bishops, or to conciliar reservations, or to special episcopal reservations. But since these later decrees were directly referred to that of Clement VIII, the

[54] Cf. Viva, *in prop. 12 Alex. VII,* cited by St. Alphonsus, *Theologia Moralis,* lib. VII, n. 96. See also, Bonacina, *Theologia Moralis* (3 vols., Venetiis, 1687), III, disp. 1, q. 22, punct. 2, n. 18; Lega, *Praelectiones de Iudiciis Ecclesiasticis* (4 vols., Romae, 1896-1901), III, n. 112.

[55] Cf. S. C. Ep. et Reg., decr., 17 nov. 1628—Cited by St. Alphonsus, *ibid.,* lib. VII, n. 95.

[56] Cf. Bonacina, *op. cit.,* III, disp. 1, q. 22, punct. 2, n. 20.

meaning of the phrases must be understood in the same sense in which Clement VIII dealt with the reservations. It is obvious that Clement's reference was only to the special episcopal reservations. Therefore it is safe to conclude that both Paul V and Urban VIII also referred to that same type of reservation.[57]

The authors who treat of episcopal reservations generally make a threefold division: the first includes those reservations which the bishops by a particular act in a specific case, or in synod, set apart to be personally dealt with; the second consists of those promulgated in writing by provincial or plenary Councils, and are listed under the title of cases *a nobis reservati*; the last embraces those which are reserved by the common law to all Ordinaries, and are called cases *nobis* or *a iure reservati.*[58] The first type is unquestionably the one alluded to by Pope Clement VIII in his decree when he speaks of cases which bishops have reserved to themselves (*sibi reservarunt*). Most authors who wrote concerning the decree of Clement were in agreement in teaching that if a bishop personally reserved a case to himself, Regular confessors could not absolve without special faculties from the bishop.[59]

There was much dispute concerning the jurisdiction of Regular confessors over the second type, namely, that which was enacted in provincial or plenary Councils, and which was promulgated in writing. Concina [60] stated that in his time the common opinion supported the validity of absolution given by Regulars in such cases. This opinion, however, could not be safely held after Pope Alexander VII (1655-1667) condemned the proposition that Mendicants could absolve from cases reserved by bishops without first obtaining spe-

[57] Cf. Salmanticenses, *Cursus Theologiae Moralis,* I, tr. 10, c. 2, n. 52; Reiffenstuel, *op. cit.,* lib. V, tit. 39, n. 257.

[58] Cf. Concina, *Theologia Christiana,* X, lib. 3, diss. 1, c. 7, q. 6, n. 17; Bucceroni, *Commentaria in Constitutione Apostolicae Sedis* (Romae, 1898), pars II, n. 14; Simeone, *Lezione Di Diritto Canonico* (3. ed., 2 vols., Napoli, 1905), II, 203.

[59] Salmanticenses, *loc. cit.* St. Alphonsus mentions Aversa, Diana, Sanchez, Lezana, Vidal and others as supporting this teaching; Suarez, Rodriquez, and others are cited as opposed; cf. *Theologia Moralis,* lib. VII, n. 98.

[60] *Loc. cit.*

cial faculties.[61] This condemned proposition treated of all reservations enacted by bishops, whether personally or in synod; so long as the bishops were the authors of the reservations, Regulars were forbidden to absolve in virtue of their privileges. St. Alphonsus [62] correctly taught that such a condemnation was sufficient to abrogate any privileges contrary to it, even though the other Apostolic privileges were not affected. A further argument for their abrogation was drawn from the fact that such reservations were implicitly contained in the prohibition of Clement VIII, for, in synod, the bishop was the sole legislator,[63] and any reservation enacted by him had therefore to be regarded as an episcopal reservation.

The third type of reservation had its origin in the common law, or in the special decrees of the Roman Pontiffs, but the absolution from it was committed to the Ordinaries. For example, in the Council of Trent,[64] local Ordinaries were granted the faculty to absolve from papal reservations *in foro conscientiae,* provided that the sin was occult. Such cases came under the third type, and were designated as cases *a iure Ordinario reservati.* Other cases likewise, which were once exclusively reserved to the Holy See, were committed to the local Ordinaries for absolution. Thus, the striking of a cleric, according to the ancient discipline,[65] entailed a censure which was reserved exclusively to the Holy See for its absolution. This discipline was mitigated later on so that Ordinaries could absolve from all such crimes, except that of a *gravis percussio,* a grave injury inflicted upon a cleric.[66] By a constitution of Pope Gregory XIV (1590-1591),[67] the penalties for the crime of abortion were modified so that bishops and their delegates could absolve from the attached excommunication. These were only a few of the reservations of the common law which were committed to local Ordinaries for absolution.

[61] Cf. *Prop. damn.*, 24 sept. 1665—Denz.-Bann., *Enchiridion,* n. 1112.

[62] Cf. *ibid.*, n. 98; lib. VII, n. 599; Pignatelli, *Consultationes Canonicae,* I, *consult.* 292.

[63] This is the explicit legislation incorporated into the present Code; cf. canon 362.

[64] Cf. sess. XXIV, *de ref.*, c. 6.

[65] C. 29, C. XVII, q. 4.

[66] Cf. c. 17, X, *de sententia excommunicationis,* V, 39.

[67] Cf. const. *Sedes Apostolica,* 31 maii 1591—*Fontes,* n. 173.

What power did Regular confessors, in virtue of their papal privileges, have over such reservations? There were two opinions: one maintained that the decree of Pope Paul V [68] abolished all privileges of absolving cases reserved in any way to the local Ordinaries.[69] This opinion had relatively few adherents. The opposite opinion, which became the common teaching of canonists and theologians, maintained that Regular confessors could still absolve the third type of reserved case. The opinion was held by Sanchez, Aversa, Lezana, Diana, Pellizarius (d. 1651), de Peyrinis, La Croix (d. 1714),[70] the Salmanticenses, St. Alphonsus, and a host of other authors.

The principal argument for this opinion was drawn from the fact that Regular confessors had most certainly possessed this privilege in the past, and no proof was available to show for certain that the privilege had ever been abrogated. In the documents which have been cited no text can be found to prove the fact of abrogation.[71] The text alleged by those who hold the opposite opinion, and drawn from the decree of Paul V, was almost certainly not such as to derogate from the privilege. For even though the words "reserved to the same Ordinaries" are used in that decree, the reference is to the decree of Clement VIII, who used the words *"sibi reservarunt."* The meaning, therefore, to be attached to the words of Paul V, must have reference to those cases which the Ordinary has personally reserved to himself, and not to cases reserved by the common law to the Ordinary.

Suarez [72] proposed the opinion that cases reserved by the common law were actually not episcopal reservations, but should properly be called papal cases reserved to the local Ordinary by the common law.[73] The Ordinary, therefore, acted rather as a delegate of the Holy See; more properly, one should have spoken of such cases

[68] S. C. Ep. et Reg., decr., 7 ian. 1617—*Fontes*, n. 1684.

[69] St. Alphonsus mentions Cabassutius (d. 1685), Milante (d. 1749) and Viva (d. 1726) as adhering to this opinion—*Op. cit.*, lib. VII, n. 99.

[70] La Croix stated that the opinion was held by more than thirty authors. Cf. St. Alphonsus, *Theologia Moralis*, lib. VII, n. 99.

[71] Cf. Bonacina, *Theologia Moralis*, III, disp. 1, q. 22, punct. 2, n. 18.

[72] Cf. *De Poenitentia*, disp. XXIX, sect. 3.

[73] This opinion is also proposed by Bucceroni—*Commentaria in Const. Apostolicae Sedis*, pars III, n. 76.

as papal reservations concerning which the power to absolve was delegated by law to local Ordinaries.

The opinion of Suarez has much to commend it. In their origin such cases were truly papal reservations. The words of the Council of Trent in accordance with which local Ordinaries were empowered to absolve papal cases indicate that the bishops acted with delegated authority. For example, in the case of occult heresy the Council stated that the bishop could not delegate the faculty to others but had to act personally. If the bishops had exercised their power of absolution in virtue of ordinary episcopal jurisdiction, they could have delegated the power to any priest. The Council of Trent expressly denied this power to them.

What power could Regular confessors exercise over cases reserved specifically to Ordinaries in such a manner that they could not delegate jurisdiction to others, such as, for example, the case of occult heresy? Authors were divided in their opinions. Most of them, however, with de Peyrinis and Pellizarius,[74] placed these reservations in the same category with cases reserved *a iure* to the local Ordinaries. The reason for hesitation in taking a certain stand in the matter is to be found in the severe restrictions which were placed upon bishops by the Holy See. Did the Holy See wish to remove this type of case from the category of those which Regulars could absolve in virtue of their privilege? From the general principle that privileges should be interpreted broadly,[75] they maintained that the Holy See did not wish to abrogate the privileges of Regulars when it made a special reservation by law to local Ordinaries.[76] All of these authors were agreed, however, that if the local Ordinary did reserve to himself a case of this kind, Regular confessors could not absolve without special faculties from the bishop, or from the Holy See.

It is worthy of note that, when authors spoke of reservations of the Holy See, their reference was always to cases reserved *ratione censurae*. The reason for this is obvious: all reservations of the

[74] Apud Salmanticenses, *op. cit.*, I, tr. 10, c. 2, n. 52; cf. also St. Alphonsus, *op. cit.*, lib. VI, n. 599.

[75] Cf. Reg. 15, R. J., in VI°: "Odia restringi, et favores convenit ampliari." Cf. also Reg. 30, 61, R. J., in VI°.

[76] Cf. St. Alphonsus, *loc. cit.*; Elbel, as cited there by St. Alphonsus.

Holy See, up until the time of the Constitution *Apostolicae Sedis* in 1869,[77] were established *ratione censurae,* with the exception of two sins. These sins were (1) the false accusation of solicitation against a priest, and (2) the receiving of notable gifts from religious.[78] Authors were unanimous in teaching that, outside of these two cases, all reservations were had only because of the reserved censure attached to the sin. If, therefore, the censure was not incurred on account of ignorance, or for some other excusing reason, any confessor could absolve the sin.

With regard to their own subjects, the superiors of religious Orders had very extensive privileges. Superiors were restricted in their jurisdiction only in the cases enumerated in the Constitutions of Sixtus IV [79] and Julius II.[80] They could absolve even from the cases reserved in the Bull *In Coena Domini.* The only cases which they could not absolve without special faculties from the Holy See were the cases of relapsed heretics, schismatics, falsifiers of Apostolic letters, carriers of forbidden weapons to infidels, and conspirators against the Roman Pontiff. Their privileges permitted them to absolve in both the internal and the external forum.

To sum up briefly the privileges of Regular confessors with reference to reserved cases prior to the Constitution *Apostolicae Sedis,* Regular confessors who had obtained the approval of the local Ordinary could absolve the faithful of the diocese from all cases reserved to the Holy See, except the cases included in the Bull *In Coena Domini,* and in Italy, but not including the city of Rome, the five cases reserved by Pope Clement VIII in 1602. They could not absolve the faithful from cases reserved by the Ordinary either in synod or by personal precept. Regular confessors, however, according to the common teaching of canonists and moralists, could absolve the faithful from cases reserved by the common law or by custom to the local Ordinary. All of these faculties were operative only in the internal forum.

[77] Cf. *Fontes,* n. 552.

[78] Cf. D'Annibale, *Summula,* I, n. 340.

[79] Const. *Regimini,* 31 aug. 1474—*Bull. Praed.,* III, 516.

[80] Const. *Exponi nobis,* 27 febr. 1510—*Bull Praed.,* IV, 264.

ARTICLE 5. THE CONSTITUTION *Apostolicae Sedis*

Pope Pius IX (1846-1878) introduced the second great abrogation of privileges of Regulars on October 12, 1869, with the promulgation of the Constitution *Apostolicae Sedis*.[81] The purpose of this constitution was the codification of all *latae sententiae* censures established by the common law. It was an exclusive collection of *latae sententiae* censures; all penalties of this type established previously and not expressly mentioned in it were abrogated. One of the most important features of the constitution was that it abolished finally the Bull *In Coena Domini*.[82]

The Constitution *Apostolicae Sedis* is divided into six sections, four of which are concerned with four types of censures: (1) those which are reserved *speciali modo* to the Holy See; (2) those which are *simpliciter* reserved to the Holy See; (3) those which are *a iure* reserved to local Ordinaries, and (4) those which are not reserved to anyone. The final sections of the constitution deal with suspensions and interdicts reserved either to the Holy See or to local Ordinaries.

Two very important paragraphs of the constitution vitally affect the privileges of Regulars, not only with regard to the absolution accorded to the subjects of the religious superior, but also with regard to the absolution accorded to the faithful in confession by the confessors of a religious Order. The first appears after n. 12 under § 1, which section is entitled: *Excommunicationes latae sententiae speciali modo Romano Pontifici reservatae:*

> . . . pro ea generalem concessionem absolvendi a casibus et censuris, sive excommunicationibus R.P. reservatis nullo pacto sufficere declaramus, revocatis insuper earundem respectu quibuscumque indultis concessis sub quavis forma et quibusvis personis etiam Regularibus cuiuscumque Ordinis, Congregationis . . . etiam speciali mentione dignis et in quavis dignitate constitutis. Absolvere . . . praesumentes sine . . . facultate . . . excommunicationis vinculo R.P. reservatae innodatos se sciant, dummodo non

[81] *Fontes,* n. 552.

[82] This Bull had been in existence for many centuries. Its origin was uncertain, and authors variously traced it to the middle of the thirteenth or to the beginning of the fourteenth centuries.

> agatur de mortis articulo, in quo tamen firma sit quoad absolutos obligatio standi mandatis Ecclesiae si convaluerint.

The second paragraph appears near the end of the document:

> Caeterum decernimus, in novis quibuscumque concessionibus ac privilegiis, quae ab Apostolica Sedi concedi cuivis contigerit, nullo modo ac ratione intelligi unquam debere, aut posse comprehendi facultatem absolvendi a casibus et censuris quibuslibet Romano Pontifici reservatis, nisi de iis formalis, explicita, ac individua mentio facta fuerit: quae vero privilegia aut facultates, sive a Praedecessoribus Nostris, sive etiam a Nobis cuilibet Coetui, Ordini, . . . etsi titulo peculiari praedito, atque etiam speciali mentione digno a quovis unquam tempore huc usque concessa fuerint, ea omnia, easque omnes Nostra hac Constitutione revocatas, suppressas, et abolitas esse volumus, prout reapse revocamus . . . minime refragantibus aut obstantibus privilegiis quibuscumque. . . .

An inspection of these passages reveals the drastic changes made by the Constitution of Pius IX in the penal legislation of the Church. After 1869, local Ordinaries, as well as religious superiors, were deprived of all power over the twelve cases mentioned in the Constitution as reserved in a special manner to the Holy See. Special faculties were needed from the Holy See to absolve these cases even when the crime was occult. Thus the faculties which local Ordinaries had received from the Council of Trent to absolve from occult cases of heresy were abrogated, since the sin of heresy was one of those cases which were reserved in a special manner to the Holy See by the Constitution *Apostolicae Sedis*. Only *in articulo mortis* could a penitent be absolved without this special faculty from the Holy See. Regular Prelates who had heretofore possessed the right to absolve from cases reserved in the Bull *In Coena Domini* were deprived of all power in those cases of which mention was made in the new legislation.[83]

The new law, however, preserved the provisions of the Council of Trent in all those cases which were reserved not in a special manner. The constitution mentions expressly that the faculty, as granted to

[83] Cf. Bucceroni, *Commentaria in Const. Apostolicae Sedis*, pars III, n. 134.

bishops by the Council of Trent [84] was to remain in force, except for the cases which were reserved *speciali modo.*[85]

With regard to the special privileges possessed by religious Orders, the words of abrogation are clear and definite: *minime obstantibus privilegiis quibuscumque.* The abolition of all privileges contrary to the constitution is unquestionable. What were the privileges contrary to the legislation? The text of the constitution reads: "In the new concessions and privileges granted to anyone by the Holy See, the faculty of absolving from cases and *censures reserved in any way to the Holy See* [86] will never be granted, unless a formal, explicit, and special mention of it is made; those privileges or faculties which have been granted by our Predecessors, or even by Ourselves up to the present time, to any Society, Order, etc., We wish to be revoked, as We revoke them indeed; all contrary privileges are abrogated." [87]

This enactment therefore determines (1) that all privileges which superiors of religious Orders possessed in the past to absolve censures which were reserved in a special manner, or even simplicitèr to the Holy See by this Constitution are entirely abrogated; (2) that these superiors cannot absolve from any other cases reserved to the Holy See, regardless of their having obtained the privilege of granting absolution either from public or from occult cases, whether for the internal or the external forum.

The superiors of religious Orders shortly after the Council of Trent,[88] by special privilege of Pope Pius V (1566-1572) received with reference to their subjects in the matter of reserved cases the very same powers which local Ordinaries had received through the law of the Council of Trent.[89] The question was raised whether this privilege of Regulars could still be used with regard to censures

[84] Cf. sess. XXIV, *de ref.*, c. 6.

[85] Const. *Apostolicae Sedis,* 12 oct. 1869, § VI, n. 2, *prope finem*: "Firmam tamen esse volumus absolvendi facultatem a Tridentina Synodo Episcopis concessam Sess. XXIV, c. 6, *de ref.*, in quibuscumque censuris Apostolicae Sedi hac Nostra Constitutione reservatis, iis tantum exceptis, quas eidem Apostolicae Sedi speciali modo reservatas declaravimus."—*Fontes,* n. 552.

[86] Italics are those of the author.

[87] *Ibid.*, § VI, n. 2, *in medio*—*Fontes,* n. 552.

[88] Cf. Pius V, const. *Romani Pontificis,* 21 iul. 1571—*Bull. Praed.*, V, 283.

[89] Cf. sess. XXIV, *de ref.*, c. 6.

reserved *simpliciter* to the Holy See by the Constitution *Apostolicae Sedis*. Since special provision was made in the constitution for bishops with regard to occult cases reserved in this manner, Regular Prelates presumed that their powers should likewise be just as extensive. On December 5, 1873, the question was proposed to the Sacred Penitentiary whether Regular Prelates, in virtue of their privileges, could absolve their subjects in cases reserved *simpliciter* to the Holy See? [90] The Sacred Penitentiary answered in the negative, but added that those Orders or persons who possessed temporary indults could make use of them for the duration for which they were granted. This latter concession was simply a restatement of the provision made by the Holy Office two years previously,[91] namely, that revocations of privileges in the Constitution *Apostolicae Sedis* did not include quinquennial or extraordinary faculties granted for a determined period.

The Holy Office was then asked directly whether Regular Prelates in relation to their own subjects should be included under the name of *bishops* as set forth in the Council of Trent (Sess. XXIV, *de ref.*, c. 6).[92] The Holy Office replied that such prelates were included, but only in relation to their own subjects, and with reference to either those cases which were reserved by the Constitution *Apostolicae Sedis* to local Ordinaries, or the cases which pertained to the internal rule of the Order (even though these cases were reserved to the Holy See), provided that the latter cases were not reserved by the Constitution *Apostolicae Sedis*.[93]

The constitution effected the further abrogation of all privileges possessed by Regular confessors for the absolution of lay people from censures reserved to the Holy See. The abrogating clause is clear: "All privileges granted to any Order . . . at any time up to the present are revoked." Therefore Regular confessors were deprived of all power over cases reserved in any way to the Holy See, whether or not these cases were mentioned in the constitution of 1869.

[90] S. Poenit., 5 dec. 1873—cited by Pennacchi, *Commentaria in Const. Apostolicae Sedis* (Romae, 1883), p. 456.

[91] S. C. S. Off., instr., 1 febr. 1871—*Fontes*, n. 1014.

[92] S. C. S. Off., 22 mart. 1881; cf. Lega, *Praelectiones de Iudiciis Ecclesiasticis*, III, n. 112.

[93] Cf. Bucceroni, *op. cit.*, pars II, n. 46.

The constitution listed only three *latae sententiae* censures reserved to the local Ordinaries. These censures were incurred by (1) clerics in sacred Orders and by Regulars or nuns after their solemn profession, as also their accomplices, when they presumed to contract marriage; (2) persons who had effectively procured abortion, and (3) persons who had knowingly made use of falsified apostolic letters or lent their cooperation in such an offense.

What effect did the abrogating clauses of the Constitution *Apostolicae Sedis* have upon the privileges of Regulars for absolution from such censures? The more recent authors were quite hesitant in maintaining that the constitution did not abrogate these privileges. Piat (1815-1904) held that it was very probable that the rights of Regular confessors over censures reserved by the common law to Ordinaries were revoked.[94] He based his argument on the unqualified character of the abrogating clauses regarding privileges. He admitted, however, that while his opinion enjoyed greater probability of correctness than its opposite, it did not altogether reflect a doctrine which could be propounded with full moral certainty. Lega (1860-1935),[95] Haine (1815-1900) [96] and other authors either simply maintained that the privilege no longer existed, or they did not sufficiently distinguish between the various types of censures reserved to Ordinaries. Some, indeed,[97] made a vague distinction between censures *vere episcopales* and others, but they failed to discuss the rights of Regular confessors in these other reservations.

Those who made a clear-cut distinction, however, between the censures which were truly episcopal cases, and the censures which were reserved *a iure* to local Ordinaries, in greater number maintained that the Constitution *Apostolicae Sedis* did not affect the privileges of Regulars in their regard. Appeltern [98] stated simply that nothing was changed in this matter, for the constitution clearly indicates that only privileges regarding the absolution of cases reserved *to the Holy*

[94] *De Iure Regularium,* II, Q. 410.

[95] Cf. *Praelectiones de Iudiciis Ecclesiasticis,* III, n. 112.

[96] *Theologia Moralis* (4. ed., 4 vols. in 2, Lovanii, 1900), II, 339.

[97] Cf. *e. g.,* Marc, *Institutiones Morales,* I, n. 1280.

[98] *Compendium Praelectionum Iuris Regularis,* p. 614.

See were revoked.[99] Bucceroni (1841-1918) [100] likewise held for the continued possession of this privilege. He stated that it was certainly not abrogated by the enactments of popes Clement VIII, Paul V and Urban VIII, inasmuch as the cases in question were not truly episcopal cases, but papal, whose absolution was in virtue of power delegated by law to local Ordinaries. Furthermore, such cases were not such as were reserved to the Roman Pontiff, the absolution from which could not be granted in virtue of papal privilege. These cases were therefore not touched by the Constitution *Apostolicae Sedis,* and continued in the same status as in the past.

A study of the revocatory clauses of the constitution substantiates the findings of Appeltern and Bucceroni. The explicit abrogations of the constitution affected only those privileges which granted *powers over cases reserved to the Roman Pontiff.*[101] It might be objected that the constitution revoked *all* past privileges in the matter of confessional jurisdiction over reserved cases up to the time of the appearance of the constitution of 1869.[102] But even a casual reading will convince one that the clause here in question must be understood in the light of the earlier clause. The whole paragraph treats exclusively of the abrogation of faculties and privileges regarding censures *reserved to the Roman Pontiff.* The censures reserved by the constitution to local Ordinaries cannot in any sense be considered as censures reserved to the Roman Pontiff, even though their origin lay in the common law.

The conclusion is therefore that the constitution of 1869 had no effect upon the objective probability of the jurisdiction claimed by Regular confessors over censures reserved *a iure* to the local Ordinary. This opinion was held by many theologians and canonists, among whom were Bucceroni (d. 1918),[103] D'Annibale (d. 1892),[104] Génicot

[99] *Loc. cit.,* nota 2.

[100] *Op. cit.,* pars III, n. 76.

[101] § VI, n. 2: ". . . absolvendi a casibus et censuris quibuslibet Romano Pontifici reservatis, nisi. . . ."—*Fontes,* n. 552.

[102] ". . . quae vero privilegia aut facultates . . . cuilibet . . . Ordini . . . unquam tempore huc usque concessae fuerint . . . ea omnia easque omnes . . . revocatas . . . esse volumus."—*Loc. cit.*

[103] *Ibid.,* pars III, n. 134.

[104] *Summula,* I, n. 344, nota (42).

(d. 1900),[105] Appeltern,[106] Lehmkuhl (d. 1917),[107] and many others. Since the *sententia communis* prior to the time of the Constitution *Apostolicae Sedis* maintained that Regular confessors could absolve in such cases, there is no doubt that there was sufficient probability of existence for the privilege after 1869 to make its use lawful and valid. In the words of Cardinal D'Annibale, "since the opinion of those who affirm the continued existence of the privilege seems probable, and even more probable according to St. Alphonsus, there can be no doubt that Regulars can use it safely and licitly." [108]

Article 6. The Privileges of Regulars and the Code

Canon 4 of the present legislation determines the relation of the privileges of Regulars possessed prior to the Code, to the Code of Canon Law. All privileges granted by the Holy See which were still in use and which had not been revoked before 1918 remained untouched, unless the canons of the Code expressly revoked them. It has been explained that the only privileges remaining to Regulars for absolving from cases reserved to the Holy See were those which permitted Regular superiors to absolve their own subjects from papal reserved cases which were not mentioned in the Constitution *Apostolicae Sedis* as reserved *simpliciter* or *speciali modo*.[109] All other privileges which empowered Regulars to absolve from censures reserved to the Holy See were expressly revoked by that constitution.[110]

The privileges of Regular confessors for the absolution from truly episcopal cases were likewise effectively abrogated by the decree of Pope Clement VIII in 1601.[111] Consequently, neither the privileges empowering Regulars to absolve from cases reserved to the Holy See, nor those granting jurisdiction over cases which bishops had reserved to themselves, could be claimed after the Code became law. Their

[105] *Theologia Moralis,* II, n. 607, nota 1.

[106] *Compendium Praelectionum Iuris Regularis,* p. 614.

[107] *Theologia Moralis,* II, n. 835.

[108] "Quia affirmantium sententia probabilis, immo S. Alphonso probabilior videtur, dubitandum non est, quin tuto ac licite (uti) possint."—*Loc. cit.*

[109] S. C. S. Off., 22 mart. 1881—cited by Lega, *op. cit.,* III, n. 112.

[110] Cf. *Fontes,* n. 552.

[111] Cf. *Fontes,* n. 1596.

continued existence was ruled out as a necessary consequence of the principle enunciated in canon 4.

Since Regular confessors no longer possess any power in virtue of papal privilege over truly episcopal cases, it is unnecessary here to enter into a study of present legislation. It may be pointed out, however, that Regular confessors, like all other confessors with diocesan faculties, can absolve their penitents from episcopal reservations *ratione peccati* when (1) the penitent is too ill to leave his home; (2) when spouses are making their confession in preparation for marriage; (3) when the legitimate superior has denied faculties to absolve in a determined reserved case; (4) when, in the prudent judgment of the confessor, the faculty to absolve cannot be sought without grave inconvenience to the penitent, or without danger of violation of the seal of confession; (5) when the penitent has left the territory of the one who has reserved the sin.[112]

The present law on penalties recognizes five types of reservations with regard to censures of common law. Three are reserved to the Holy See, namely, those which are reserved *specialissimo modo, speciali modo,* and *simplicter.*[113] The fourth type consists of those reserved *a iure* to the Ordinary; and the last is reserved to no one in particular *(nemini reservata).* In the censures reserved to the Holy See, simple confessors have no powers whatsoever in ordinary circumstances, unless they receive special faculties from the Holy See. Ordinaries, however, in occult crimes, are empowered to absolve from censures reserved in a simple manner to the Holy See.[114] This faculty can be delegated to others. Thus, for example, if a man by engaging in a duel had incurred the censure of excommunication which is reserved *simpliciter* to the Holy See,[115] he could be absolved from the censure by the Ordinary, provided the case was occult. The bishop could absolve the penitent personally or he could delegate a simple confessor to absolve him. But if the case were a public one, the Ordinary's power would be restricted, and faculties for absolving

[112] Canon 900.

[113] Canon 2245, § 3.

[114] Cf. canon 2237, § 2.

[115] Cf. canon 2351, § 1.

would have to be sought from the Holy See.[116] The provision of the law is simply a restatement of the provision found in the decrees of the Council of Trent,[117] which was modified in the Constitution *Apostolicae Sedis*.[118] There is this difference between the previous legislation and that of the Code: whereas the law of the Council of Trent and that of the constitution of 1869 granted the right to absolve from occult cases reserved to the Holy See *only* to local Ordinaries, the Code[119] grants the same right to all Ordinaries. Under the title of Ordinaries are included both local Ordinaries and major superiors of exempt clerical religious institutes.[120] Therefore the powers which superiors of religious Orders possessed before the constitution of Pius IX have been partly restored to them. They now can absolve their own subjects from censures reserved *simpliciter* to the Holy See in occult cases.

With regard to censures *a iure* reserved to Ordinaries, major religious superiors of exempt clerical religious institutes certainly have the power to absolve, provided that the censures are incurred by their own subjects. These subjects include all professed, novices, and those who live day and night in the religious house as servants, students, convalescents or guests.[121]

It has also been seen that Regular confessors, according to the more probable opinion, still retained the privilege of absolving the faithful from censures reserved *a iure* to the Ordinary. The Code does not make any abrogation of this privilege. It therefore retains the same probability of existence which it possessed before the Code became law. Since most of the authors before the Code taught that the use of the privilege was both licit and safe, one can conclude that its use today is likewise safe and licit.[122]

[116] Cf. canon 2237, § 1, 2°.

[117] Cf. sess. XXIV, *de ref.*, c. 6.

[118] Cf. *supra*, p. 91, note 85.

[119] Canon 2237, § 2.

[120] Cf. canon 198, § 1.

[121] Cf. canons 514, § 1; 875, § 1.

[122] Cf. Noldin-Schönegger, *De Censuris* (31. ed., Oeniponte, 1937), n. 95; Fanfani, *De Iure Regularium* (Taurini-Romae, 1925), n. 365; Prümmer, *Manuale Iuris Canonici* (4. ed., Friburgi-Brisgoviae, 1922), n. 324.

The Code has established nine excommunications reserved to the Ordinary. They affect the following persons: (1) those who enter marriage before a non-Catholic minister contrary to the prescriptions of canon 1063, § 1;[123] (2) Catholics who enter wedlock with the implicit or explicit agreement to bring up one or all of their children outside the Church;[124] (3) Catholics who knowingly presume to offer their children to a non-catholic minister for baptism;[125] (4) Catholic parents or guardians who knowingly hand over their children or wards to be reared and educated in a non-Catholic religion;[126] (5) those who fabricate false relics, or who knowingly sell, distribute, or expose them for public veneration;[127] (6) those who lay violent hands upon clerics inferior to bishops, or upon religious of either sex;[128] (7) those who effectively procure abortion, the mother not being excluded;[129] (8) religious of simple perpetual vows in religious institutes, if they presume to contract a marriage even before a civil magistrate, and also their partners in this sin;[130] (9) apostates from a religious institute, whether men or women.[131]

Besides these excommunications, there are two censures of suspensions reserved to the Ordinary: (1) clerics who, without the permission of the local Ordinary, cite another person enjoying clerical privileges before a civil court, incur suspension *ab officio, ipso facto;*[132] (2) a fugitive religious incurs *ipso facto* a suspension reserved to his own major superior.[133] There is likewise one interdict *ab ingressu ecclesiae* reserved to the Ordinary, namely, that of giving voluntary christian burial to infidels, apostates from the faith,

[123] Canon 2319, § 1, 1°.

[124] Canon 2319, § 1, 2°.

[125] Canon 2319, § 1, 3°.

[126] Canon 2319, § 1, 4°.

[127] Canon 2326.

[128] Canon 2343, § 4.

[129] Canon 2350, § 1.

[130] Canon 2388, § 2.

[131] Canon 2385.

[132] Canon 2341.

[133] Canon 2386.

heretics, schismatics, or other persons to whom Christian burial must be denied according to canon 1240, § 1.[134] All of these cases may be absolved in the internal sacramental forum by Regular confessors in virtue of Apostolic privilege, unless the religious superior makes an explicit restriction of jurisdiction in their regard.

[134] Canon 2339.

CHAPTER V

PRACTICAL APPLICATION OF THE PRIVILEGES OF REGULARS IN RESERVED CASES

In the previous chapter the writer has endeavored to show that the privileges of Regulars to absolve from cases reserved by the common law to local Ordinaries have sufficient probability of existence to permit their licit use in the present legislation. In the application of these privileges by Regular confessors certain practical difficulties may arise which could render the use of the privileges imprudent. In this chapter, then, special consideration will be given to (1) the possibility of the suspension of these papal privileges by local Ordinaries; (2) the application of the powers to absolve in the reserved cases of the *familiares* of the religious Order; (3) the practical rules to be observed in the absolution of reserved cases.

Article 1. Suspension of Papal Jurisdiction by the Local Ordinary

The question of the possible suspension of papal jurisdiction by an inferior authority seems absurd to one who relies upon general principles of jurisdiction and reservation. The legislation of the Code, however, has unleashed a storm of disputes within recent years [1] concerning the possibility of local Ordinaries suspending the jurisdiction of Regular confessors in cases reserved *a iure* to the Ordinary.

For the sake of discussion a practical case may be assumed. According to the common law the crime of abortion, *effectu secuto*, is punished by a censure of excommunication reserved to the Ordinary.[2] In virtue of their apostolic privileges Regular confessors, provided they have the approbation of the local Ordinary for the hearing of confessions, may absolve from such a case in confession. How-

[1] Cf. *Ecclesiastical Review*, LXXXIV (1931), 190-192; LXXXV (1931), 73-82; LXXXVI (1932), 292-305. *Commentarium pro Religiosis*, XIV (1933), 287-294; 363-375; 436-447; XVI (1935), 164-175.

[2] Canon 2350, § 1.

ever, in the instance here to be considered, the local Ordinary has annexed to that crime, which is already reserved to himself as a censure by the common law, another reservation from which he alone can absolve. What powers can Regular confessors exercise in such a reserved case?

It has been shown previously that Regular confessors were deprived of all jurisdiction in absolving from purely episcopal reservations.[3] What is the exact nature of the reservations in the case proposed? Has the case become a purely episcopal case? In that event, there is a true suspension of jurisdiction given by a superior authority, and the Regular confessor cannot absolve until he has received special delegation from the Ordinary. Has it become a mixed case which is partly episcopal and partly papal? If it is, then the jurisdiction of the Regular confessor is likewise effectively suspended since he cannot absolve from any sins until the episcopal reservation is removed. But suppose that the Ordinary has exceeded his competency in reserving to himself a case which is already reserved to him by the common law! In that event the episcopal reservation is null and the Regular confessor can ignore it.

The solution of this question hinges upon the interpretation of canons 898 and 2247, § 1. Canon 898 treats explicitly of the right of Ordinaries to reserve sins which have been previously reserved in any way by the Holy See:

> All (having the right to reserve cases) are to refrain entirely from reserving to themselves those sins which have already been reserved, even by reason of censure, to the Holy See; and as a rule *(regulariter)* from all those sins as well, to which a censure, even if reserved to no one *(nemini reservata)*, has been attached by law.[4]

The literal meaning of the text is clear: Ordinaries are not under any circumstances *(prorsus abstineant)* to reserve to themselves any

[3] Cf. Clemens X, const. *Superna*, 21 iun. 1670; S. C. Ep. et Reg., 9 ian. 1601; S. C. Ep. et Reg., 26 nov. 1602—*Fontes*, nn. 246; 1596; 1616.

[4] Canon 898: "Prorsus ab iis peccatis sibi reservandis omnes abstineant, quae iam sint Sedi Apostolicae etiam ratione censurae reservata, et regulariter ab iis quoque, quibus censura, etsi nemini reservata, a iure imposita sit."

sins which are already reserved to the Holy See, even *ratione censurae.* This canon envisages all types of reservations. It includes the one sin reserved *ratione sui vel peccati* to the Holy See [5] as well as all the sins reserved in any way by reason of the censure attached to them. The first part of the canon certainly includes the cases reserved *specialissimo modo, speciali modo,* or *simpliciter* to the Holy See.[6]

The canon states that Ordinaries shall refrain entirely *(prorsus abstineant)* from reserving such cases. What is the canonical force of the word "*prorsus*"? Authors are divided. Vermeersch admits that any Ordinary presuming to act contrary to this law would be sinning gravely, but he maintains that there is nothing intrinsic to the canon which would invalidate a reservation made contrary to the law.[7] The great majority of canonists and theologians, however, see in the term *prorsus* a force which effectively nullifies any reservation placed upon the same sin by an authority inferior to the Holy See.[8]

Canon 2247, § 1, deals with the right of Ordinaries to place special reservations upon censures which are already reserved by the common law:

> If a censure has been reserved to the Apostolic See, the Ordinary cannot *(nequit)* place another censure reserved to himself upon the same delict.[9]

Here again authors differ in the interpretation of the term "*nequit.*" *Nequit* (which is equivalent to *non potest*) is unquestionably stronger than *prorsus* of canon 898. It almost certainly denotes an incapacitating law.[10] Consequently authors commonly hold that to add a censure to another already reserved by a higher authority would not only be gravely illicit, but invalid as well. Fur-

[5] Canon 894.

[6] Cf. canon 2245, § 3.

[7] *Theologia Moralis* (3 vols., Romae, 1923), III, n. 469, 3°.

[8] Cf. Cappello, *De Poenitentia,* n. 519; Noldin-Schmitt, *Theologia Moralis,* III, n. 359, 2°, b.

[9] Canon 2247, § 1: "Si censura Sedi Apostolicae reservata sit, Ordinarius nequit aliam censuram sibi reservatam in idem delictum ferre."

[10] Cf. canon 11.

thermore, such a reservation would be entirely useless, not only because the same type of reservation is made concerning the same delict; but also, because the case has been entirely withdrawn from the competency of the inferior authority.[11]

The second part of canon 898 is subject to even more dispute. The law states that the Ordinaries "as a rule *(regulariter)* are to refrain entirely from reserving to themselves those sins to which a censure, even if reserved to no one, has been attached by the common law." The term *regulariter* implies a directive prescription. All authors are agreed on this point. It binds the Ordinary to use caution, and to establish a reservation only in extraordinary circumstances in the cases which are *nemini reservatae.*[12]

Not all authors are agreed, however, upon the extent of the law in the second part of canon 898. Explicitly the law refers only to cases in which a censure *nemini reservata* has been attached. Does this part also refer to cases in which a censure reserved *a iure* to the Ordinary has been attached? If one assumes that the legislator evidently wished to make provision regarding all types of reservations of the common law in canon 898, the solution is relatively simple. For, in the first part of the canon provision is made regarding only those cases which are reserved to the Holy See.[13] The only other censures of the common law are those reserved *a iure* to the Ordinary and those reserved to no one, both of which would naturally fall into the second part of the canon. Blat and other authors [14] hold that this part of the canon refers to both types of censures. This opinion seems eminently reasonable unless one were to admit that the legislator has left a *lacuna* in the law. According to these authors, therefore, the local Ordinary can legitimately reserve to himself a case

[11] Cf. canon 893, § 1.

[12] Cf. Cappello, *De Poenitentia,* n. 519; Vitali, "Utrum locorum Ordinarii valeant suspendere privilegium Regularium absolvendi a casibus papalibus Ordinariis reservatis per accidens et via exceptionis."—*AER,* LXXXVI (1932), 292, 293.

[13] The dative case is used: *Sedi Apostolicae.* This excludes from the first part censures reserved *a iure* to the Ordinary.

[14] Cf. Blat, *Commentarium in Codicem Iuris Canonici,* III, 265; "Consultationes"—*Jus Pontificium,* XIII (1933), 302.

which is already reserved to himself by the common law by reason of a censure.

Prümmer (1866-1931), Vitali, and many other authors take the opposite view, namely, that the cases which are reserved to the Ordinary by the common law are not contemplated in the second part of canon 898.[15] Their contentions are based upon a study of pre-Code legislation and upon the general principles of law concerning jurisdiction and reservation.

The sources of canon 898 are the decree of Pope Clement VIII, issued through the Sacred Congregation of Bishops and Regulars,[16] and the Instruction of the Holy Office in 1916.[17] The Sacred Congregation of Bishops and Regulars decreed that "Ordinaries must not reserve to themselves indiscriminately those cases which have a major excommunication attached by the common law, whose absolution is reserved to no one *(nemini reservata),* unless on account of frequent scandal or unless some cases of this kind seem to call for specific reservation.[18] It will be noticed that this decree makes no mention of cases reserved by the common law to Ordinaries, even though many cases of this kind were reserved at that time.

The Holy Office in its Instruction of 1916 made a peculiar innovation by introducing the word *etsi* into the text of the decree of the Sacred Congregation of Bishops and Regulars, so that its wording was exactly that which is now reproduced in canon 898. What purpose did the word *etsi* have in the Instruction of 1916? The authors who hold that censures *a iure* reserved to the Ordinary are not contemplated in the canon state that the word *etsi* was introduced into the text simply to clarify the decree of 1602. The meaning of the law then would be: "even though the censure which attaches to the sin is reserved to no one, still the Ordinary must not reserve such a sin

[15] Cf. Prümmer, *Manuale Theologiae Moralis,* III, n. 421; Vitali, *art. cit.,* pp. 292-298.

[16] S. C. Ep. et Reg., 26 nov. 1602—*Fontes,* n. 1615.

[17] S. C. S. Off., instr., 13 iul. 1916—*Fontes,* n. 1302.

[18] ". . . videant ipsi Ordinarii ne illos casus promiscue reservent quibus adnexa est excommunicatio maior a iure imposita, cuius absolutio nemini reservata sit, nisi forte propter frequens scandalum aut aliam necessariam causam aliqui huiusmodi casus nominatim reservandi viderentur."—*Loc. cit.*

except by way of exception when grave scandal or other real necessity warrants it."

This translation of the canon seems to do violence to the text; the exact opposite rather seems to be the mind of the legislator. The word *etsi* was placed in the law designedly to call to mind the fact that sins which have censures *nemini reservatae* attached to them are also included in the general category of sins which have reserved censures attached, and therefore should not, as a rule, be reserved by the Ordinary to himself in their character of sins. The real meaning of the canon then would be: all other sins which have censures attached to them (namely, those not included in the first part of canon 898), even though *nemini reservatae,* should not, as a rule, be reserved by the bishop to himself in the character of sins.

The authors who deny to Ordinaries the right to reserve to themselves sins which are already reserved *ratione censurae* to the Ordinary by the common law have a more plausible argument drawn from the general principles of jurisdiction and reservation. Reservation is the complete withdrawal *(avocatio)* of jurisdiction over a case from the inferior by a superior authority. The inferior authority is thus deprived of all competency over that case.[19] According to the teaching of Suarez (1548-1617)[20] and Lugo (1583-1660),[21] any case which the Holy See has reserved in any way becomes strictly a papal case. It is entirely withdrawn from the jurisdiction of the local Ordinaries. Once these cases have been withdrawn, the Holy See may delegate jurisdiction over them again to all Ordinaries by common law. The case, however, always remains a papal case and is subject to all the conditions which the Holy See has set down for its absolution. The power of absolution exercised by Ordinaries in such cases, therefore, is more accurately called jurisdiction delegated by law, rather than proper jurisdiction.[22] If the Roman Pontiff should therefore reserve a case *ratione censurae* to Ordinaries, the latter, according to these authors, could not validly reserve that same case to them-

[19] Cf. canon 893, § 1.

[20] *De Poenitentia,* disp. 31, sect. 4, n. 26.

[21] *De Poenitentia,* disp. 20, nn. 149, 151.

[22] Cf. Suarez, *De Censuris,* disp. 7, sect. 2, n. 15; D'Annibale, *Summula,* I, n. 338.

selves *ratione peccati*. Much less could they suspend the faculties of those who have received a power similar to that of the Ordinaries from the same higher tribunal.

This argument is admittedly acceptable. It is a valid conclusion which could not be contradicated if the literal meaning of the law did not make provision for the opposite opinion. In the present legislation, however, the argument proves too much, for censures *nemini reservatae* are likewise truly papal cases in their origin; yet no one will deny that a bishop, in exceptional circumstances, is permitted by the present law to reserve to himself a sin which already has a censure *nemini reservata* attached by the common law. Canon 898 explicitly grants this right.

The same authors who argue the invalidity of episcopal reservations of cases reserved by the common law to Ordinaries lay great stress upon the fact that an added reservation is useless. It may be stated at once that this argument does not militate against the validity of the reservation, but only against its lawfulness.[23] One may question the contention that such reservations would necessarily be useless in every case. Indeed, the contrary may be true more often. The purposes of reservations of sins and censures are widely divergent. A censure is essentially a penalty established for the punishment of persons who transgress the law out of contempt. The reservation of a sin does not connote a punishment; it simply withdraws the case from the simple confessor and entrusts it to the judgment of certain more prudent confessors who are skilled in the application of corrective measures. Such is the teaching of Fagnanus (1598-1678),[24] St. Alphonsus (1696-1787),[25] D'Annibale (1815-1892)[26] and most modern authors.[27] This opinion corresponds well to the

[23] Cf. canon 897. The law states that Ordinaries are to reserve sins for no longer a time than that which proves necessary for eradicating some deeply rooted vice and for building up and reinforcing a relapsed and debilitated ecclesiastical discipline.

[24] Cf. *Commentaria in Quinque Libros Decretalium* (Venetiis, 1697), lib. V, tit. 38, c. 12, n. 90.

[25] *Theologia Moralis*, lib. VI, n. 581.

[26] *Summula*, I, n. 343.

[27] Cf. Merkelbach, *Summa Theologiae Moralis* (3. ed., 3 vols., Parisiis, 1936), III, n. 593.

arrangement of the canons of the Code, wherein the treatise of reserved sins is not placed under that of penalties, but under that of the Sacrament of Penance where it properly belongs.[28]

Since the purpose of reserved censures is so different from that of reserved sins, it is easy to imagine what good could be effected if the local Ordinary did reserve to himself *ratione peccati* a case which has already been reserved to him by the common law *ratione censurae*. However, if the Ordinary reserved the same case *ratione censurae*, that would imply on the part of the inferior that he superimposed his own censure on that of the superior, and the added censure would be obviously useless. In such a case there would obtain what is called by theologians a *mixed reservation*.[29] According to all authors such a mixed reservation is juridically impossible.[30] Such a mixed case does not necessarily obtain when a bishop reserves some given sin *ratione peccati*, even though the same sin has attached to it a censure which by law is reserved to the Ordinary for absolution. The episcopal reservation is of a different nature and has a different purpose from the reservation established by the common law.[31] And while the superior authority has withdrawn the case from the competency of the Ordinary with respect to its attached censure, the Ordinary can still validly reserve the case *ratione peccati*.

From a study of the history and of the text of canon 898, therefore, the opinion of those authors who maintain the invalidity of an episcopal reservation of the sin in cases reserved *a iure* to the Ordinary as censures, seems untenable. However, since many outstanding theologians favor the opinion, it is perhaps of a not altogether improbable validity. It has at least sufficient external authority to give

28 Concerning the exact nature of episcopal reservations, and their purpose, cf. St. Alphonsus, *loc. cit.*

29 A mixed reservation is one which is reserved by both the inferior and the superior authorities in the same way, and in relation to the same sin.

30 Cf. Suarez, *op. cit.*, disp. 31, sect. 4, n. 26; D'Annibale, *op. cit.*, I, n. 339, nota (19).

31 According to most of the authors episcopal reservations are presumed to be *ratione peccati*. Cf. Noldin-Schmitt, *Theologia Moralis*, III, n. 363, 3°; Marc-Gestermann, *Institutiones*, II, n. 1770. Cappello holds that, unless the bishop expressly states that his reservation is *ratione peccati*, it may be presumed to be *ratione censurae—De Poenitentia*, n. 515.

it probability. In virtue of canon 209, absolutions given in virtue of this probable jurisdiction would be valid.

Article 2. *Familiares* of the Religious House and Reserved Cases

Canon 615 incorporates into the common law the privilege of exemption from episcopal jurisdiction. All Regulars, according to the present law, whether men or women (except those nuns who are not subject to Regular superiors), including novices, with all their houses and churches, are exempt from the jurisdiction of the local Ordinary, except in those cases with reference to which the law expressly provides otherwise.[82] Members of Mendicant Orders, moreover, have special privileges whereby they are immune from episcopal reservations, except in three cases: if they presume (1) to preach in churches without previous permission from the local Ordinary, (2) to hear confessions of the laity without his approbation, (3) to expose for public veneration scandalous images.[83] Whatever may be the status of the houses of religious Orders with regard to local exemption,[84] it is certain that all professed Regulars and novices are personally exempt from episcopal reservations except in the instances in which the law permits the local Ordinary to legislate and to punish infractions of his law in their regard.

It follows, therefore, that when a professed Regular or novice commits a sin to which the bishop has attached a *censure* reserved

[82] Canon 615: "Regulares, novitiis non exclusis, sive viri sive mulieres, cum eorum domibus et ecclesiis, exceptis iis monialibus quae Superioribus regularibus non subsunt, ab Ordinarii loci iurisdictione exempti sunt, praeterquam in casibus a iure expressis."

[83] Cf. H. Davis, *Moral and Pastoral Theology* (4 vols., New York: Sheed & Ward, Inc., 1935), III, 439.

[84] There is a dispute among authors as to whether the religious house should be considered territory separate from the diocese, or whether it forms a part of the diocesan territory. A study of pontifical documents indicates local exemption; the more probable opinion holds that Regulars enjoy only personal exemption. Cf. Vermeersch, *Epitome Iuris Canonici* (3 vols., Mechlin-Romae, 1927), I, 618, 619; Coronata, *Institutiones Iuris Canonici,* I, n. 621; O'Brien, *Exemption of Religious in Church Law* (Milwaukee: Bruce Pub. Co., 1942), pp. 93, 94.

to himself, he does not incur the penalty. He can be licitly and validly absolved either by a confessor approved by his own religious superior, or by any priest approved by the local Ordinary. In the latter instance, the diocesan confessor does not need to seek special jurisdiction from his Ordinary, since the case is not reserved. If, however, the religious penitent confesses a sin to a diocesan confessor which is reserved in the diocese *ratione peccati,* this confessor cannot validly absolve the sin, since the local Ordinary has withdrawn his jurisdiction over that sin. The reason for the difference between absolution from reserved sins and reserved censures is found in the concept of the reservations. In a censure which is reserved, the sin is affected only indirectly, so that if the censure is not incurred the sin also is not reserved. In a reserved sin, the sin itself is directly affected, so that immediately upon the commission of the sin the jurisdiction over it is removed.[85]

In the matter of episcopal reservations the condition of lay persons residing within the houses and monasteries of religious Orders has been a matter of dispute among canonists and theologians. Those authors who hold that the houses and churches of religious Orders possess local exemption rightly insist that lay people do not incur censures established by the local Ordinary, provided the sins to which the censures are attached are committed within the religious house or church.[86] They are considered as being outside the territory of the bishop who has made the reservation.

The question involves two principles of law: (1) exemption from episcopal authority by reason of their connection with a religious house which is exempt from episcopal authority; (2) papal privileges wherein Regulars were granted confessional jurisdiction over those lay people who lived under the obedience of the Regular superior.

Even before the advent of the Mendicant Orders the Benedictine and Irish monasteries claimed exemption for all persons, lay and religious, residing within the monastery walls. It is evident that in the Irish monasteries all lay persons connected with the monastery, such as servants, students, or aspirants to the religious life, were

[85] Cf. Cappello, *De Poenitentia,* n. 514; Noldin-Schmitt, *Theologia Moralis,* III, n. 356.

[86] Cf. O'Brien, *loc. cit.*

regarded as being of the monastic household *(de familia)*, and therefore as being subject to the jurisdiction of the abbot.[37]

With the appearance of the religious Orders and their many spiritual bonds with the laity, there was grave need for a definition of the limits of exemption. There was a wide-spread enrollment of countless lay people into the Third Orders. These communicated in the privileges of the First Order Regular. On the other hand, many professed religious were only loosely connected with any definite religious house; consequently, stricter control by episcopal authority was necessary when such religious were outside their houses. Penalties and other remedies were often adopted by the bishops and received to some extent the sanction of the Holy See.[38]

The first constitution of the Roman Pontiffs granting to lay people residing within the monastery immunity from episcopal censures was that granted to the Augustinian Order in 1353 by Pope Innocent VI (1352-1362).[39] Those who lived as servants within the religious houses of the Order were declared to be immune from all excommunications and interdicts promulgated by the local Ordinary. There is little evidence, however, that such privileges were generally granted. One discovers some vestiges of it in the decrees of the Council of Trent,[40] wherein lay people who were *de familia* of monasteries or of religious houses were declared exempt from the jurisdiction, visitation, and correction of the local Ordinaries. The Code [41] grants exemption only for the professed religious, and for novices. Aspirants and all persons living in the religious house are not exempt from episcopal reservations in virtue of the common law.

The rights of religious superiors to hear the confessions of lay persons living in the monastery were vindicated early in the history of religious Orders. Explicit confirmation of this right is found as early as 1244, in a constitution of Pope Innocent IV (1243-1254).[42] It was recognized as common law by the V general Lateran Council

[37] Watkins, *History of Penance*, II, p. 614.

[38] Cf. cc. 1, 7, *de privilegiis*, V, 7, in VI°.

[39] Const. *Religionis favor*, 16 ian. 1353—*Bull. O. E. S. A.*, p. 185.

[40] Cf. sess. XXV, *de regularibus*, c. 11.

[41] Canon 615.

[42] Const. *Qui Deum*, 5 febr. 1244—*Bull. Praed.*, I, 131; Potth., n. 11240.

(1512-1517), which Council restricted the jurisdiction of religious superiors to those lay persons who were actually in the service of the monastery, and for the time during which they were under the obedience of the superior.[43] The Council of Trent placed under the jurisdiction of the religious superiors only those *"who belonged to the household of the monasteries."* [44] In order to clarify that clause of the Council of Trent, the Sacred Congregation of the Council [45] decreed that "without the approbation and permission of the local Ordinary, the Regular Prelates could hear the confessions of only those seculars who were *vere de familia et continui commensales."* Clement X (1670-1676) was somewhat more explicit. He decreed that in monasteries, and even in colleges, where regular discipline was established, the prelates and confessors of the Order could hear the confessions of those lay people who were *de familia et continui commensales,* but they were forbidden to hear the confessions of servants who did not live in the monastery.[46] From these decrees Bordonius (d. 1671)[47] concluded that all students residing at the monastery or college of religious Orders could be absolved in virtue of jurisdiction from the religious superior. Ferraris (died c. 1763) included oblates, *donati,* tertiaries, novices and all seculars, as long as these lived *intra septa monasterii* and under the obedience of the religious superior.[48]

The Code has extended the rights of religious superiors in confessional jurisdiction over lay persons residing in religous houses.[49] In the present discipline the superior of an exempt clerical religious institute has jurisdiction to administer the sacraments to all the professed, novices and all other persons living at the religious house day and night, whether as servants, students, convalescents, or guests. He can grant jurisdiction to any priest, in accordance with the statutes of the institute, to hear their confessions.

[43] Leo X, const. *Dum intra,* 19 dec. 1516—*Fontes,* n. 72.

[44] Sess. XXV, *de regularibus,* c. 11.

[45] 14 aug. 1568. This decree is cited by Bouix, *Tractatus de Iure Regularium,* II, p. 220.

[46] Const. *Superna,* 21 iun. 1670—*Fontes,* n. 246.

[47] Cited by St. Alphonsus in his *Theologia Moralis,* lib. VI, n. 583.

[48] Cf. *Bibliotheca,* s. v. "approbatio," art. 1, n. 68.

[49] Canons 875, § 1; 514, § 1.

Lay persons, therefore, who are included within the provisions of canon 514, enjoy the same rights as the professed members to be absolved in virtue of jurisdiction exercised by the religious superior. Consequently, if these persons have committed sins which are reserved in the diocese in any way, they can approach a priest approved by the religious superior, and can be validly and licitly absolved by him. In this case the confessor is not bound by any restrictions placed upon his jurisdiction by the local Ordinary; he absolves in virtue of the jurisdiction granted him by the religious superior. If, however, the same sin has been reserved by both the local Ordinary and the religious institute, then the confessor cannot absolve without first receiving special faculties. Thus, let it be supposed that a lay person has incurred a censure reserved in the diocese. He now makes a retreat of some days' duration at a clerical religious house, and approaches the confessor approved by the religious superior for absolution. This confessor can absolve him from the sin in virtue of faculties from the superior. The same holds true in cases of reserved sins.

With regard to the privileges of Regular confessors to absolve *familiares* of the religious house from censures reserved to Ordinaries by the common law, no special difficulty is encountered. These confessors, approved by the religious superior, can validly and licitly absolve all those enumerated in canon 514 in such cases, unless the superior has explicitly deprived him of such jurisdiction. As pointed out previously, the use of confessional privileges depends upon the will of the religious superior.[50] In ordinary circumstances it is presumed that the superior delegates to his priests at the time he approves them all the faculties which he has received in virtue of apostolic privileges.

Canon 514, § 1, establishes special conditions which must be verified before a lay person can be considered to fall under the jurisdiction of the religious superior: (1) the lay person must live in the religious house, but not necessarily within the cloister; (2) he must live there day and night *(diu noctuque)*. Moralists commonly interpret the phrase *diu noctuque* as implying an intention to remain in

[50] Cf. *supra*, chap. III, art. 2, p. 48.

the religious house at least a day and a night.[51] It is certainly not necessary for him to have stayed there a whole day before the right to confess to a priest approved by the religious superior is made available to him. Moreover, absolution given him by such a priest would certainly be valid even if he should be called away from the religious house before the twenty-four hours had elapsed after his arrival. So long as he intends to stay a day and a night, he can make use of the rights given him by canon 514 as soon as he arrives at the religious house. All authors are agreed, however, that it is not sufficient to intend to stay only during the daytime or during the night. The canon demands the intention of staying for at least a day and night.

On the other hand, the law does not demand the intention of remaining at the religious house habitually, as Merkelbach seems to maintain.[52] Cappello correctly teaches that the day of twenty-four hours need not be reckoned with mathematical exactitude.[53] If one were to absent himself for a few hours during the day he could still confess to a priest who has jurisdiction solely from the religious superior.

While canon 875, § 1, grants to Regular superiors and their delegates very broad faculties to absolve students, guests and others, one must be cautious not to interpret the faculties too broadly. The faculties imply a new extensive concession granted by the legislator in the present discipline, but a strict literal interpretation of it must be made.[54] Consequently, those authors who extend the law to cover the case of students who have already left the religious house and are *en route* to their homes for vacation seem to go beyond the actual extent of the law. Not only have such students severed their condition of living at the religious house as prescribed by the law, but they are also no longer fulfilling the condition of living at the religious house day and night.[55]

[51] Cf. Cappello, *De Poenitentia,* n. 430; Marc-Gesterman, *Institutiones,* II, n. 1772.

[52] *Summa Theologiae Moralis,* III, n. 518, b.

[53] *De Poenitentia,* n. 431.

[54] Cf. canon 18.

[55] Cf. Cappello, *op. cit.,* n. 432; Noldin-Schmitt, *Theologia Moralis,* III, n. 349, 3°.

Article 3. Rules for the Use of Confessional Privileges in Reserved Cases

The penitential discipline of the Church has been established to safeguard the purity of Catholic belief and morality. Following the admonition of St. Paul to "reprove, entreat and rebuke with all patience and teaching," [56] the pastors of the flock of Christ have the right and the duty to make use of coercive means to that end. Within the diocese the local Ordinary has the grave obligation to establish reservations and penalties necessary to deter the weak from transgressing the law of God and to extirpate deep-rooted vices. Only grave reasons can justify him in establishing such reservations.[57] Therefore, when reservations are made by the local Ordinary, it is presumed that he has acted for the common good of his flock.

Since the salvation of souls is the supreme law of the Church, anything that will interfere with that purpose must be carefully avoided. If there is a conflict between the rights of individuals and the common welfare of souls, individual rights must be suspended. Regular confessors enjoy the right to absolve from censures *a iure* reserved to Ordinaries. If the exercise of these privileges in certain circumstances works harm to the welfare of souls, these privileges may not be used. And if there is danger of abuse arising therefrom, caution must be employed, lest perhaps the legitimate commands of ecclesiastical authority be disregarded and Christian discipline be impaired.

What rules then should be followed in the exercise of Apostolic privileges? It is to be noted first of all that a Regular confessor is not free to use, or not to use, the privilege of absolving a penitent who confesses a sin to which the common law has attached a censure reserved to the Ordinary. The privilege was not granted principally for the private good of the religious priest, but for the good of penitents who come to him in confession. According to the principle laid down in canon 69,[58] no one is compelled to make use of a privilege

[56] II Tim., 4, 2.

[57] Cf. canons 895; 897; 899, § 1; 2214, § 2.

[58] Canon 69: "Nemo cogitur uti privilegio in sui dumtaxat favorem concesso, nisi alio ex capite exsurgat obligatio."

given in his favor, unless an obligation arises from some other source. The obligation arising from this other source is verified when the penitent approaches a Regular confessor with a reserved censure. Between the priest and penitent there arises a quasi-contract whereby the confessor is obliged to give absolution if he has the necessary faculties and the penitent is disposed for absolution.[59] Unless a greater good is to be obtained by delaying absolution for a time, the confessor must absolve. This reasoning is confirmed by the law itself which states that absolution cannot be denied when the penitent has receded from his contumacy, and promises to amend his life.[60] There is no questioning here the licit and valid use of the suppletory principle of canon 209, since the principle laid down in canon 69 affords ample reason for making use of it.

The first rule, then, is that absolution should be given in a case reserved by the common law to the Ordinary, unless a greater good is to be obtained by delaying absolution. What reasons, therefore, would justify the delaying of absolution? Perhaps the primary reason for delaying absolution would obtain in the case of sins that have caused grave scandal by reason of their public nature. Thus, if a Catholic would attempt marriage before a non-Catholic minister under the circumstances contemplated in canon 1063, § 1, he would incur an excommunication reserved *a iure* to the local Ordinary. Such a sin by reason of its public nature could occasion grave scandal among the faithful. The common good, therefore, demands that some public reparation be made for the sin, and many bishops will demand absolution in the external forum. Since the Regular confessor has jurisdiction over the case in the internal forum, he can validly absolve such a delinquent but repentant Catholic who confessed the sin to him. Should he give absolution? Ordinarily he should not, except in a case of urgent necessity. For even though the penitent through such an absolution will be reconciled in the sight of God, he would in most instances still have to conduct himself as if laboring under

[59] Cf. Salmanticenses, *Cursus Theologiae Moralis,* III, tr. 18, c. 1, n. 15; Augustine, *Compendium Iuris Regularis,* I, 163; Noldin-Schmitt, *Theologia Moralis,* I, n. 195, 2°; Coronata, *Institutiones,* I, n. 99, nota 1; Michiels, *Normae Generales,* II, 383; Cicognani, *Canon Law,* p. 805.

[60] Canon 2248, § 2.

censure until he receives absolution in the external forum because of the scandal attached to his crime.[61] It must be borne in mind that the privilege of the Regular confessor is operative only in the internal forum. This has always been the mind of the Church, and is expressed succinctly by Pope Clement X:

> In virtue of apostolic privileges it is never permitted Regulars, even after satisfaction has been made, to absolve their penitents in the external forum. And those absolved in the penitential forum are not to be considered as having been absolved in the judicial or contentious forum. Moreover, those who have fallen under ecclesiastical censures and have been denounced to the bishop, can be compelled to conduct themselves as censured, even though they have been absolved by Regulars.[62]

The second rule, then, is that Regular confessors ordinarily should not absolve in a public case in virtue of their privilege if reconciliation is needed in the external forum. They should go through the normal channels of seeking jurisdiction for the external and internal *fora* from the local Ordinary.[63]

For the sake of exemplifying further the rules for the use of privileges the following specific case may be considered. A doctor has established the practice of therapeutic abortion. According to the common law,[64] each time that he performs such an operation, he incurs an excommunication reserved *a iure* to the Ordinary. He comes to confession to a Regular confessor, who absolves him. Thinking that absolution can be easily obtained, he makes little effort to avoid the evil practice, and returns time and again for absolution. Is the Regular confessor justified in absolving such a case, even if the sin is occult? In this case, granting that the person has promised sincere amendment, there is place for the application of the third rule: the Regular confessor should delay the absolution, or deny it, until he has received the faculty and the mandate from the Ordinary, when it is seen to be for the penitent's own good. The best way to

[61] Cf. canon 2251.

[62] Const. *Superna,* 21 iun 1670—*Fontes,* n. 246.

[63] Cf. Gerster, *Ius Religiosorum* (Taurini: Marietti, 1935), p. 285.

[64] Canon 2350, § 1.

impress upon the penitent the seriousness of his crime is to demand that the penitent wait until faculties are received from the Ordinary.

If it should happen that the local Ordinary has reserved to himself *ratione peccati* a sin to which a censure reserved *a iure* to the Ordinary has been attached, the Regular confessor should never absolve from such a reservation in virtue of his privilege, except in most urgent necessity. While it is admitted that the opinion which denies the right of local Ordinaries to reserve sins already reserved *ratione censurae* to the Ordinary has some external probability, the Regular confessor would act rashly in absolving. This is true for a two-fold reason: (1) because of the slight probability of jurisdiction, and (2) because of the presumption that the Ordinary has made use of this double reservation only in extreme cases, which should therefore be referred to him personally. If, however, the penitent belongs to that number contemplated in canon 514, § 1, the Regular confessor may absolve validly and licitly at all times, since his jurisdiction is not restricted by the local Ordinary, but emanates from the religious superior.

If the Ordinary reserves to himself a sin *ratione censurae* which the common law has already reserved to him *ratione censurae,* the Regular confessor can feel more free in the use of his privilege. There is little doubt that such an episcopal reservation would be of no effect, and the confessor can ignore it.

The fourth rule, then, is that in reservations of the common law, the Regular confessor should never as a rule absolve in virtue of his privilege if the local Ordinary has reserved the same case *ratione peccati.* It is otherwise when the episcopal reservation is *ratione censurae.*

There are certain periods of the year when diocesan confessors have more extensive faculties for absolving from reserved cases than at other times. For example, during the Easter season, pastors have by law the right to absolve from all episcopal cases reserved *ratione peccati;* during the time of a mission, the fathers who conduct the mission have the same faculties.[65] Usually the local Ordinary will delegate during the Easter season the faculties to absolve from

[65] Cf. canon 899, § 3.

censures of the common law reserved to himself. At such times, public and external absolution will seldom be demanded. At these periods of the year the Regular confessor can feel more free in the exercise of his privilege. He might feel himself justified in absolving from public cases, provided that in his prudent judgment absolution in the external forum will not be necessary. At other times of the year, however, when the right to absolve in reserved cases is usually restricted to a few priests of the diocese, the Regular confessor should act prudently and cautiously. When he absolves he should inform the penitent that he is being absolved in virtue of special faculties which the confessor possesses in virtue of a privilege. Such a course will explain to the penitent why another priest of the diocese perhaps cannot absolve the same case; it will allay any wonderment on the part of the penitent, or even the possibly belittling of the need of episcopal jurisdiction. In every case, the confessor should impose a penance relatively graver than the usual sacramental penance.

The final rule is, therefore, that the Regular confessor may feel more free to absolve in virtue of his privilege at those times and in such circumstances in which his absolution will not cause undue wonderment on the part of the people. In every instance he will apply a penance relatively graver that the sole sacramental penance.

CHAPTER VI

PRIVILEGES OF REGULARS IN THE DISPENSATION AND COMMUTATION OF VOWS

ARTICLE 1. GENERAL NORMS

A vow is a promise made to God deliberately and freely regarding the personal execution of some good which is not only possible of achievement but which is also of greater spiritual value than its opposite. The fulfillment of a vow connotes the performance of a duty in consequence of a demand which is inherent in the virtue of religion.[1] From the definition, every vow must contain the following elements in order to be a true vow which binds in conscience: (1) it must be a promise, made sincerely with the intention of obliging oneself to its execution; (2) it must be made with full deliberation, the intellect grasping the object of the promise and acting upon it consciously. Error and ignorance are opposed to this condition. (3) It must be made with full consent, the will acting freely and voluntarily. Force and fear are opposed. (4) It must be made directly to God and primarily for His honor. Secondarily, however, it may be made to honor His saints, or His creatures upon earth. To it is opposed any promise made directly to any person, saint or sinner alike, whose purpose has not primarily in view the honor of God. (5) It must be a promise of a good which is at least relatively better than its opposite.[2] In opposition to it is the offering of an evil or of a useless thing. (6) The good promised must be actually possible of fulfillment in relation to the circumstances and conditions of the promisor. Opposed to this condition is the physical or moral impossibility of executing the good which has been promised.

It is not within the scope of this work to enter into a detailed examination of all the elements which must be verified for the con-

[1] Canon 1307, § 1—Votum, idest promissio deliberata ac libera Deo facta de bono possibili et meliore, ex virtute religionis impleri debet.

[2] Cf. Coronata, *Institutiones*, II, n. 889.

stitution of a true vow.[3] One point, however, is worthy of note. The law itself invalidates an otherwise valid vow when it is elicited by a person out of grave and unjust fear.[4] Thus, the vow to enter a religious community made by a boy because of the threats and importunities of his parents is *ipso iure* invalid, despite the fact that it may have been made deliberately and voluntarily.

Vows may be divided into (1) *public and private,* according as they are or are not received by a legitimate agent in the name of the Church; (2) *solemn* and *simple,* according as they are recognized by the Church as such; (3) *reserved* and *non-reserved,* according as the dispensation from them is or is not reserved to the Holy See; (4) *personal, real,* and *mixed,* according as the object which is the substance of the vow is a personal action of the one who has made the vow, a real material thing, or a combination of both.[5] Thus, the vow to observe chastity constitutes a vow of a subjective character and is personal. The vow to give an altar to a Church constitutes a vow of an objective nature and is real. The vow to donate an altar and to celebrate Holy Mass upon it constitutes a mixed vow.

Once the vow has been validly made, a bond of the natural and divine law is created which obliges the promisor in conscience to fulfill the vow. God has, as it were, a quasi-title to exact the object vowed from the promisor.[6] Therefore, in and of itself, no human power can break that bond which has been created between God and the person who has made the vow. For God is thought to ratify in heaven the promises made to Him by His creatures upon earth. Therefore, too, the substance of the vow may not be changed even by the promisor unless he knows for certain that God permits such a change.

The obligation of the vow belongs to the *cultus latriae.* The

[3] Any text in Moral Theology may be consulted with profit; *e. g.*, Noldin-Schmitt, *Theologia Moralis* (24. ed., 3 vols., Oeniponte, 1936), II, nn. 205-213; Prümmer, *Manuale Theologiae Moralis* (2. ed., 3 vols., Friburgi-Brisgoviae, 1923), II, nn. 392-401; Merkelbach, *Summa Theologiae Moralis* (3. ed., 3 vols., Parisiis, 1936), II, nn. 710-721.

[4] Cf. canon 1307, § 3.

[5] Cf. canon 1308.

[6] Cf. Merkelbach, *op. cit.*, II, n. 710.

violation of it constitutes a sin against the virtue of religion. The gravity of the sin is measured from a twofold source: from the evaluation of the object promised, and from the intention of the promisor. For even though the object of the vow should be considered a seriously important matter, the violation of that vow would not be considered a grave sin, unless the promisor in making the vow intended to oblige himself *sub gravi.*

Since human nature is weak, it not infrequently happens that a person acts blindly and impulsively without considering the ultimate effects of his acts. He makes vows on the spur of the moment without adverting to all the hardships involved in the execution of them. He makes vows, too, which, though valid and licit in every respect, become impossible of fulfillment because of unforseen circumstances beyond his control. At times, his action in making the vow is so foolish and hasty that only spiritual destruction can result from the attempt to carry it into execution. What is the person to do in such circumstances? Christ foresaw the need of establishing upon earth some tribunal which could interpret authentically the will of God in such matters. He left to His Vicar upon earth, the pope, the power to bind and loose, promising that whatsoever he should bind on earth would also be bound in heaven; and what things he should loose on earth would also be loosed in heaven.[7] In consequence of these general powers of binding and loosing the popes have exercised the right to interpret authentically what is the obligating force of vows made by their subjects. When the common good of the Church is at stake, or when it is a question of the salvation of souls, they have seen fit to modify, and even to dispense entirely from the obligations attached to the vows made by individual persons.

Since a vow establishes a quasi-contract between a man and his God, the power to dispense from or to relax the obligations arising from the vow pertains to God. Christ has entrusted that power to the popes; the popes, therefore, in dispensing from vows do not act upon their own authority, but upon the authority of God. Their powers are vicarious, not proper.[8] They dispense, not in their own

[7] Matt. XVI, 19.

[8] Cf. canon 197, § 2.

name, but in the Name of God. Consequently, some reasonable cause must be found before a valid dispensation can be given. Dispensation of vows may be defined, therefore, as a relaxation of the obligations of the vows in particular cases by a superior authority, in virtue of a vicarious jurisdiction, accorded in the Name of God, and for a just cause.[9]

In this work the right of those who have dominative power over the will of others to nullify vows will not be considered; for example, the right of parents to nullify the vows of their children. Neither will there be considered here the right of those who have power over the matter of the vow to suspend the obligations of the vow insofar as these obligations prejudice their acquired rights; for example, the right of the husband or wife to suspend the vow of chastity of his spouse in those things which pertain to the legitimate use of marriage.[10] There will be treated only the right to dispense and to commute vows in virtue of jurisdiction possessed by the popes, and delegated by them to others. The Supreme Pontiff can delegate his powers, even though these are vicarious; they derive from his ordinary powers as vicar of Christ.[11]

By commission of the common law all local Ordinaries have the power to dispense both their own subjects and transients residing in their territory from all vows not reserved to the Holy See.[12] The superiors of exempt clerical religious institutes possess the same authority with respect to their subjects, as defined in canon 514, § 1, as do local Ordinaries.[13] These powers are granted with one limitation. In those vows, the dispensation from which would injure the acquired rights of a third party, no dispensation is possible.[14]

Three conditions must be verified for the valid granting of a dispensation from a vow: (1) jurisdiction over the person who seeks

[9] Cf. Coronata, *Institutiones,* II, p. 226, n. 897.

[10] Cf. canon 1312.

[11] Cf. canons 197, § 2; 199, § 1.

[12] Canon 1313, § 1.

[13] Canon 1313, § 2.

[14] Canon 1313: "Vota non reservata possunt iusta de causa dispensare (loci Ordinarius et superior religionis clericalis exemptae), dummodo ne laedant ius aliis quaesitum. . . ."

dispensation, for dispensations derive from juridical authority, and presuppose competency over the person;[15] (2) the special faculty to dispense from vows granted either in the law or by particular delegation of the Holy See; [16] (3) a just cause. It would be a manifest injury to God if one dispensed without sufficient reason. Since the pope requires a justifying reason before making use of his vicarious powers of dispensing, the same or a greater reason is required in his delegate for the valid exercise of dispensing power.[17] Authors commonly teach that the sufficiency of the dispensing cause is to be determined from an inspection of the nobility of the vow, and from the individual circumstances which render the execution of the vow more or less difficult. They hold that a moderately grave cause is sufficient for a licit and valid dispensation of a vow. Such causes are, for example, the common good of the Church, scandal resulting from frequent violation of the vow, the welfare of the state or the family, great difficulty in the fulfillment of the vow, scruples, continual and certain danger of habitual transgression of the vow because of personal circumstances, the lack of complete freedom in the making of the vow because of force or fear, etc.[18]

The commutation of a vow is the transference of the obligation of the vow to some other good work, by the substitution of another work in place of the original, with the same obligation attached to it.[19] Thus, the vow of fasting for a week could be commuted for a reasonable cause to the recitation of the Rosary every day for a week. The commutation of a vow by any person other than the one who has made the vow requires the power of jurisdiction and the faculty to make a substitution of some other work for the object vowed. The common law [20] permits a person to commute the object of his vow into an equal or better work without submitting his case to a superior authority for commutation. However, for the commutation

[15] Cf. Noldin-Schmitt, *Theologia Moralis,* II, n. 229.

[16] Cf. canon 1313, § 3.

[17] Cf. Prümmer, *Manuale Theologiae Moralis,* II, n. 421, 1°.

[18] Cf. Van Etten, *Compendium Privilegiorum Regularium* (Romae, 1900), p. 85; Noldin-Schmitt, *ibid.,* n. 231.

[19] Cf. Prümmer, *ibid.,* n. 429; Coronata, *ibid.,* n. 898.

[20] Canon 1314.

of the obligation to an inferior or less good work, the one who has made the vow must have a reasonable cause for seeking commutation and submit the case to the legitimate authority.

Moralists, relying upon a response of the Sacred Penitentiary in 1899,[21] generally distinguish three types of commutation: (1) a simple commutation into an equal or a better work which can be effected by the person himself; (2) a dispensation by commuting the vow into a work which is somewhat less good; (3) a commutation by dispensing almost completely from the obligation of the vow. As a rule, the faculty of commuting a vow is granted without any restriction of power to one or more of the above types. Unless the power of commuting is specifically limited by the superior, the delegate is free to commute as he prudently sees fit. In the commutation of vows it is well to recall that one who has the power to dispense from vows has likewise the power to commute them.

It has been stated that the common law permits local Ordinaries and superiors of exempt clerical religious institutes to dispense and commute vows. The pope can withdraw from their jurisdiction certain vows and reserve them to himself. This withdrawal of jurisdiction restricts the competency of these superiors the same as the reservation of cases by reason of censure to the Holy See removes those cases from their competency. Moreover, the pope can grant jurisdiction over vows to any priests, or group of priests, without reference to the local Ordinary.

Regular confessors in the past claimed the right to dispense and commute vows in virtue of Apostolic privileges. In the following articles the writer will investigate the basis of these claims and determine the status of possibly existing privileges in the present Code.

Article 2. Dispensation of Vows

The power of religious superiors over the private vows of their subjects had its origin in the privilege of exemption from the local Ordinary. In virtue of this privilege religious were no longer subject to the bishop of the diocese, and the Regular superior assumed quasi-episcopal powers. These powers, although limited to the subjects un-

[21] Cf. Noldin-Schmitt, *Theologia Moralis*, II, n. 238, nota 2.

der his obedience, were just as extensive in the matter of dispensation from non-reserved vows as were those of the bishops.

Obviously, when one speaks of vows made by subjects of the religious superior, one does not refer to the public vows of Religion, which have always been reserved to the Holy See; rather there is reference to those vows only of a private nature which are usually made with the permission of the superior.

The religious superiors were deprived of power over only five vows of a private nature: (1) the vow of making a pilgrimage to the Holy Lands (*peregrinatio ultra-marina*); (2) the vow to make a pilgrimage to the tombs of the Holy Apostles at Rome (*ad limina*); (3) the vow to make a pilgrimage to the tomb of St. James at Santiago de Compostela; (4) the vow of entering a religious institute (since all such institutes at that time made profession of solemn vows, the vow was that of entering a religious institute of solemn vows); (5) the vow of perfect chastity.[22] These vows were reserved to the Holy See. All others came under the jurisdiction of the Regular superior.

There is little evidence that special privileges were granted to religious superiors with regard to the five specially reserved vows. The writer has discovered only one papal document in which a dispensation of such a reserved vow was permitted to the religious superior; in that instance the dispensation amounted rather to a commutation of the vow. Pope Eugene IV (1431-1447), in 1436, granted to the abbots, rectors, and priors of the Benedictine Congregation of Monte Cassino the faculty to dispense anyone applying for entrance into the monastery, and anyone already received into the monastery, from the vow of entering an Order of a stricter life.[23] An examination of the text of the constitution reveals evidently that the faculty was one of commuting the obligation of the vow which bound the aspirant to adopt a stricter form of life to the obligation of observing a life which was less strict. The substance of the vow as such remained the same.

The privileges of Regular confessors to dispense the private vows of the laity have been seriously impugned by several distinguished

[22] C. 5, *de poenitentiis et remissionibus*, V, 9, in Extravag. com.

[23] Const. *Etsi quaslibet*, 30 iun. 1436—*Comp. Privileg.*, pp. 265, 266.

authors. While the common teaching of canonists and moralists has upheld their right to dispense the vows of the laity, as attested to by St. Alphonsus (1696-1787)[24] and Piat (1815-1904),[25] it must be admitted that the papal documents which granted such rights are not entirely beyond dispute. Concina (1687-1756),[26] while admitting that authors commonly held that Regulars possessed the privileges of dispensing, nevertheless maintained that no author had seriously studied the texts of the documents which supposedly granted the privileges. "The one relies upon the authority of the others," he writes, "and thus they all contrive to defend the error." [27] In recent years Moccheggiani (1839-1905) [28] has seriously questioned the possession of such privileges.

To determine the basis of such claims, a thorough investigation of the documents must be made. Critical studies of the documents have been published recently by Oesterle [29] and Vermeersch (1858-1936) [30] to clear up the main points of dispute.

The first papal grant of faculties to dispense was given to the Congregation of Monte Cassino by Pope Eugene IV in 1436.[31] Permission was granted to the Prelates and to the monks, who were chosen by the superiors for the hearing of the confessions of the faithful, to commute and to dispense in all cases which were reserved to local Ordinaries either by synodal or provincial statutes; except with reference to those vows and cases concerning which the Holy See had to be consulted.[32] Authors commonly, except Concina, Em-

[24] *Theologia Moralis,* lib. III, n. 257.

[25] *Praelectiones Iuris Regularis,* II, Q. 412, 4°.

[26] *Theologia Christiana,* III, lib. 4, diss. 3, c. 11, n. 6.

[27] *Loc. cit.*

[28] Cf. *Iurisprudentia Ecclesiastica* (3 vols., Ad Claras Aquas, 1904-1905), II, nn. 182-195.

[29] "Die Dispensgewalt der Regularen bei einfachen Gelübden der Weltleute" —*Theologie und Glaube,* III (1911), 389-402.

[30] "De facultate confessariorum Regularium dispensandi in saecularium votis"—*Periodica,* V (1913), 56-59.

[31] Const. *Etsi quaslibet,* 30 iun. 1436—*Comp. Privileg.*, p. 131.

[32] "Insuper et vota omnia permutare ac in omnibus et singulis casibus etiam Ordinariis aut per synodales et provinciales constitutiones reservatis cum eis dispensare praeter vota et casus de quibus esset merito Sedes Apostolica consulenda."—*Loc. cit.*

manuel Rodriquez (1548-1617) [33] and Moccheggiani, considered this grant as one which enabled the Regular confessor to dispense the laity from non-reserved vows.

A study of the document reveals these facts: (1) the right to commute vows is clearly indicated; (2) the right to dispense is made obscure by the use of the phrase *"casibus reservatis,"* which can refer to any of the following, namely, sins, censures, irregularities and vows. Usually the word *absolvere* is used with reference to sins and censures; *dispensare,* however, can refer to either irregularities or vows. It must be concluded, therefore, that, although the privilege of dispensing from vows may possibly be contained in the constitution, the certain possession of such a privilege on the part of Regulars cannot be established upon it.

Three years after this grant to the Congregation of Monte Cassino, the same pope granted to the Benedictine Congregation of Valladolid the right to choose three or four confessors from among the priests of the monastery who could then dispense from non-reserved vows and from vows reserved to the bishops.[34] The faculty to dispense from vows is clear:

> Ut tres vel quattuor presbyteri monachi cum eis (fidelibus) et eorum quolibet dispensare super votis etiam episcopo reservatis, et ea commutare, toties, quoties, devotioni eorum videbitur expedire . . .

However, since this privilege was restricted in its use to confessors at the monastery, as Concina [35] correctly points out, and was limited to a few priests only, it was certainly not communicated in by other religious Orders.

When the privileges of the monastery of Valladolid were renewed by Pope Sixtus IV in 1476,[36] the privilege was extended so that all priests chosen by the superiors for the office of confessor could dispense from all vows in which the bishop himself could dispense.

[33] *Resolutiones Quaestionum Regularium* (Lugduni, 1634), Q. 63, art. 3.

[34] Eugenius IV, const. *Cum ad ecclesiam,* 3 ian. 1439—*Comp. Privileg.,* p. 133.

[35] *Theologia Christiana, ibid.,* n. 10.

[36] Cf. const. *Exhibita,* 8 iun. 1476—*Comp. Privileg.,* p. 142.

The use of the faculties to dispense the faithful who should present themselves for confession was restricted, however, to their own monasteries and churches. There is question, therefore, concerning the communicability of this privilege.

St. Francis of Paula (1416-1508) founded the Order of Minims in the Archdiocese of Cosenza. The archbishop, in order to show his liberality to the new Order, granted extensive privileges to it. Among these privileges was the faculty to dispense from all vows which the archbishop himself could dispense. Then, after the Order had spread throughout the south of Europe, Pope Sixtus IV (1471-1484) made it one of the Mendicant Orders, and confirmed its privileges in the Constitution *Sedes Apostolica.*[37] Among the privileges which the pope confirmed and extended to the whole Order was that granted by the Archbishop of Cosenza. The text follows:

> Archiepiscopus facultatem concessit sacerdotibus huiusmodi Congregationis confessiones audiendi et ab omnibus casibus, excommunicationibus, suspensionibus et interdictis, ac insuper quacumque irregularitate eidem Archiepiscopo tam a iure quam ab eo reservatis et praemissis toties, quoties, opus foret et esset, absolvendi, *votaque quaecumque permutandi ac relaxandi,* ac poenitentiam salutarem iniungendi.

There is no questioning here the extension of this privilege to the whole Order of Minims, despite the fact that it was originally only granted in the archdiocese of Cosenza; the confirmation and extension was securely effected by Pope Sixtus IV. Moreover, the constitution of Sixtus IV received new confirmations by Pope Julius II (1503-1513) in 1506 [38] and 1507.[39]

Three serious objections have been raised against this privilege and the new confirmations of Julius II. The first, raised by Ferraris (died c. 1763),[40] stated that this privilege was granted only for the dispensation of the vows of those who were members of the Order, and not for all the faithful. Ferraris averred that he had pre-

[37] 27 maii 1474—*Bull. Rom.*, V, 213.

[38] Const. *Dudum ad sacrum*, 28 iul. 1506—*Bull. Rom.*, V, 422.

[39] Const. *Alias*, 29 maii 1507—*Comp. Privileg.*, p. 148.

[40] *Bibliotheca*, s. v., "Votum," art. 3, n. 77.

viously believed it to be a grant for the dispensation of the vows of the faithful, but was compelled to change his view when he read the document himself. The whole tenor of the constitution, he said, showed that it was meant only for the members of the Order. Therefore it could not be applied to all the faithful. Moccheggiani [41] held the same opinion.

It is of course to be admitted that the constitution of Sixtus IV was somewhat obscure. Nevertheless that obscurity can be dispelled by a study of the documents which have relation to it. In the confirmation of the privileges of the Order of Minims in 1506,[42] Pope Julius II explicitly stated that all confessors of the Order could hear the confessions of all secular and religious persons according to the tenor of the privileges granted by Sixtus IV. The parts which are pertinent to the present study are given below:

> Ac pro potiori cautela omnia et singula in dictis litteris quomodolibet contenta, et quoad hoc, ut Franciscus de Paula et alii Ordinis Ministrorum huiusmodi fratres . . . recipere; necnon confessiones quarumcumque personarum tam religiosarum quam ecclesiasticarum et saecularium ubilibet audire et illis auditis *iuxta formam et tenorem privilegii per praefatum Sixtum praedecessorem Ordini Minorum* huiusmodi ac illius personis et fratribus *dudum concessi* et confirmati ac poenitentiam salutarem illis iniungere.

Oesterle [43] correctly maintains that the reference of Julius II must be to the Constitution *Sedes Apostolica* of Sixtus IV, since it is the only possible one to which reference could have been made. The constitution of Sixtus IV must be understood in the light of that of Julius II. Julius II is explicit in the grant of faculties to hear the confessions of all the faithful, whether religious or laity, "according to the form and the tenor of the privilege granted by Sixtus IV." And since Sixtus IV refers to the power of dispensing from vows, one must conclude that after 1506 at least there was no question concern-

[41] *Iurisprudentia Ecclesiastica,* II, n. 188.

[42] Const. *Dudum ad sacrum,* 28 iul. 1506—*Bull. Rom.,* V, 422.

[43] "Die Dispensgewalt der Regularen bei einfachen Gelübden der Weltleute" —*Theologie und Glaube,* III (1911), 391.

ing the extension of the privilege so as to include the vows of the faithful.

The second objection brought by the opponents of this interpretation was that the constitution of Sixtus IV could not possibly have made any reference simply to the dispensation of the private vows of the laity, because it spoke of dispensing all vows without exception.[44] These authors maintained that such a general grant of dispensing power was contrary to the customary procedure of the Holy See, for from the earliest times five vows of a private nature were specifically reserved to the Roman Pontiff, and these reservations were never relaxed. A study of the constitution of Sixtus IV reveals that actually there was no grant of power to dispense from reserved vows. The pope simply confirmed for the whole Order the grant of the Archbishop of Cosenza, who permitted the confessors of the Order to dispense in all cases in which he (the bishop) himself could dispense. The archbishop could not dispense from reserved vows; consequently, no such power was granted by the pope.[45]

The third objection was derived from the word *relaxandi.* The opponents of the common teaching maintained that all previous grants of privileges used the word *dispensare*; the word *relaxandi* was unique, and therefore could not have had the same meaning as *dispensandi.* They translated it to mean: to *commute,* or *partially relax,* that is, to dispense by relaxing, according to the divisions made by the Sacred Penitentiary in 1899.[46] Oesterle, however, in a critical investigation of the pre-Tridentine literature, finds that the word *relaxare,* according to all canonists and theologians, always had the meaning of dispensing or of entirely removing something.[47] From this one may conclude that the grants of Sixtus IV and of Julius II really empowered Regular confessors to dispense from the non-reserved vows of the laity.

Authors who uphold the privileges of Regular confessors in dis-

[44] Cf. *text* on p. 128.

[45] Cf. Salmanticenses, *Cursus Theologiae Moralis,* III, tr. 17, c. 3, n. 94.

[46] Cf. Noldin-Schmitt, *Theologia Moralis,* II, n. 238, 1°.

[47] "In der theologischen Literatur der vortridentinischen Zeit hat *relaxare* sehr wohl die Bedeutung von *dispensare, remittere, tollere.*"—*Art. cit.,* p. 391, n. 4.

pensing from vows place great stress upon a grant of Pope Innocent VIII (1484-1492), which was given *vivae vocis oraculo* to the Friars Minor in 1487.[48] The confessors of the Order were granted the right to dispense in all vows from which the bishop himself could dispense, except the vow of making a pilgrimage which implied more than a two days' journey.[49] Since all grants which had been made *vivae vocis oraculo,* however, were abolished by popes Gregory XV (1621-1623) [50] and Urban VIII (1623-1644),[51] the opponents maintained that all the privileges which had been thus granted no longer continued to exist.

However, it is likewise true that these privileges were not solely of the character of a *vivae vocis oraculum.* Though originally given *vivae vocis oraculo,* these privileges were later reduced to writing and were confirmed *ex certa scientia* by popes Paul IV (1555-1559),[52] Gregory XIII (1572-1585),[53] and other popes. All authors are agreed that a confirmation *ex certa scientia* is equivalent to a new concession. In consequence, if the possession of the grant could not be established by reason of its condition as a *vivae vocis oraculum,* its possession could still be claimed by reason of its confirmation.[54] But even if no such confirmation had been given, one could still contend for the right to dispense through customary law since the privilege had been in use for more than one hundred years before the abrogation of all *vivae vocis oracula.*

The certainty of the possession of the privilege of dispensing the laity from non-reserved vows is established through at least three other documents, the authenticity and meaning of which are beyond dispute. The opponents seem to have overlooked them. In 1507 Pope Julius II granted to the Benedictine Congregation of Mount

[48] Die 1° S. Agnetis secundo, 1487—*Comp. Privileg.*, p. 146.

[49] "Concessit (Innocentius) quod confessores praedicti possunt dispensare in omnibus votis, in quibus episcopi, exceptis votis peregrinationis ultra duas dietas."—*Loc. cit.*

[50] Const. *Romanus Pontifex,* 2 iul. 1622—*Bull. Rom.,* XII, 706.

[51] Const. *Alias,* 11 apr. 1635—*Bull. Rom.,* XIV, 473.

[52] Cf. const. *Ex clementi,* 1 iul. 1555—*Bull. Rom.,* VI, 490.

[53] Const. *Ex benigna,* 21 mart. 1575. The constitution is cited by Oesterle, *art. cit.,* p. 394.

[54] Cf. Piat, *Praelectiones Iuris Regularis,* II, Q. 156.

Olivet the privilege of dispensing the faithful from all vows from which the bishop himself could dispense.[55] The text is given here:

> Vota per eos (fideles) pro tempore emissa in omnibus et singulis casibus locorum Ordinariis etiam per synodales seu provinciales constitutiones reservatis in alia pietatis opera commutare et desuper *cum eis voventibus dispensare,*[56] exceptis tamen votis et casibus, super quibus esset Sedes praefata merito consulenda.

A similar privilege was granted by the same pope to the Canons Regular of the Lateran in 1512.[57] Pope Leo X (1513-1521) granted the very same privilege in identical words to the Camaldolese Hermits in 1513.[58]

A study of the documents which have been cited reveals beyond a doubt the reasonableness of the common teaching of canonists and theologians that Regular confessors possess the privilege of dispensing the non-reserved vows of the faithful. Piat stated that it would be very difficult to deny that Regulars possessed such power.[59]

Vermeersch[60] drew confirmation for the common teaching from the fact that the Holy See had declared that authors could safely teach the doctrine propounded by St. Alphonsus, unless the contrary was expressly decreed by the Holy See. St. Alphonsus held that Regular confessors could dispense from the non-reserved vows of the faithful, which could therefore be safely used. This argument was not to be lightly passed over, stated Vermeersch; for, even though the privilege should not have had strong probability for its existence, whatever probability it had, along with the teaching of St. Alphonsus, made it safe to invoke the use of the privilege.

By reason of the fact that the Holy See has not granted the privilege of dispensing from non-reserved vows in recent years, some authors have contended that the ancient privileges were abrogated.

[55] *Const. Etsi ad universos,* 4 iun. 1507—*Bull. Rom.,* V, 444.

[56] Italics are those of the writer.

[57] Iulius II, const. *Inter caeteros,* 2 apr. 1512—*Bull. Rom.,* V, 516.

[58] Const. *Etsi a summo,* 4 iul. 1513—*Bull. Rom.,* V, 543.

[59] Cf. *op. cit.,* II, Q. 412, 6°, nota 1; see also Van Etten, *Compendium,* pp. 84, 85; Vermeersch, *De religiosis institutis et personis,* I, n. 519, 3.

[60] "De facultate confessariorum Regularium dispensandi in saecularium votis."—*Periodica,* V (1913), 59.

They stated that the practice of the Holy See has changed. In support of their contentions they cited a constitution of Benedict XIII (1724-1730) [61] and another of Leo XII (1823-1829) [62] wherein the privilege of commuting only, with respect to vows, is found. Therefore, so they claimed, the right of Regulars to dispense from vows has been abrogated by contrary legislation and by non-use. However, the very constitution which these authors cited in proof of their opinion, namely, that of Leo XII, granted to the Society of Jesus the special indult which permitted them to dispense from vows. While it is true that this indult granted this faculty for only twenty years, it did show that the Holy See was not adverse to granting the power to dispense. Furthermore, non-use of the ancient privileges did not imply a cancellation of the privileges granted by the Holy See.

In practice, therefore, it is entirely safe for Regular confessors to dispense the faithful from their non-reserved vows when a sufficient cause is present and circumstances warrant such dispensation,[63] so long as the acquired rights of a third party are not injured thereby. The faculty is operative both within and outside the confessional. However, Prümmer prudently pointed out that in most cases dealt with a commutation of the vow rather than a complete dispensation should be granted.[64]

Article 3. The Commutation of Vows

The commutation of vows is considered to be an integral part of the power of dispensation in their regard. Therefore, from the fact that the right of Regular confessors to dispense from the vows of the faithful has been sufficiently established, one can logically conclude that such confessors have also the right to commute the same vows. He who can exercise the greater power can also exercise that power which is an integral part of it.[65]

To complete the historical survey of dispensation and commuta-

[61] Const. *Pretiosus,* 27 maii 1727—*Bull. Rom.,* XXII, 522.

[62] Const. *Plura inter,* 11 iul. 1826—*Bull. Rom. cont.,* XVI, 449.

[63] Cf. O'Brien, *Exemption of Religious in Church Law,* pp. 177, 178.

[64] *Manuale Theologiae Moralis,* II, n. 426.

[65] Cf. Reg. 35, 53, R. J., in VI°: "Plus semper in se continet quod est minus," and "cui licet quod est plus, licet utique quod est minus."

tion, the writer will investigate a few of the constitutions which explicitly granted to Regular confessors the power to commute vows. One of the first privileges of which there is any record was that granted by Pope Eugene IV (1431-1447) to the Benedictine monastery of Monte Cassino in 1436.[66] The superiors and the monks chosen by the superiors for the office of confessors were granted the faculty to commute all the vows of the faithful, except those vows which were specially reserved to the Holy See:

> Insuper vota omnia permutare . . . praeter vota . . . de quibus esset merito Sedes Apostolica consulenda.[67]

Two years later the same pope granted to the Cistercians of the Regular Observance the same powers, and specifically, the power to commute the vow of making a pilgrimage:

> Necnon peregrinationis, et alia quaecumque per eos emissa vota, quae commode servari non possint, in alia pietatis opera in praedictis, non reservatis Sedi Apostolicae commutare. . . .[68]

It will be noted that the constitution made mention of the cause necessary for effecting a commutation, namely, that the vow could not be conveniently fulfilled. Commutation of the vow necessitated a substitution of some other work of piety.

Within the *Mare Magnum* of privileges the concessions for commuting the vows of the faithful were numerous. Pope Sixtus IV granted explicit powers in this regard to the Order of Minims in 1474,[69] and to the Benedictine Congregation of Valladolid in 1476.[70] Pope Innocent VIII granted similar privileges *vivae vocis oraculo* to the Friars Minor in 1487,[71] which privileges were afterward confirmed *in forma specifica*. Julius II, besides granting the power to dispense from vows, also explicitly granted the power to commute,

[66] Const. *Etsi quaslibet*, 30 iun. 1436—*Comp. Privileg.*, p. 131.

[67] *Loc. cit.*

[68] Eugenius IV, const. *Commissum*, 11 iul. 1438—*Comp. Privileg.*, p. 132.

[69] Const. *Sedes Apostolica*, 27 maii 1474—*Bull. Rom.*, V, 213.

[70] Const. *Exhibita*, 8 iun. 1476—*Comp. Privileg.*, p. 142.

[71] Cf. *Comp. Privileg.*, p. 145.

in his concessions to the Benedictine Congregation of Mount Olivet [72] and to the Canons Regular of the Lateran.[73] Leo X granted similar powers to the Camaldolese Hermits in 1513.[74]

In the very year that the Council of Trent was convened, Pope Paul III (1534-1549), in the Constitution *Cum inter cunctas*,[75] granted to the confessors of the Society of Jesus the privilege of commuting all vows, except the five reserved to the Holy See:

> . . . necnon vota quaecumque per eos pro tempore emissa (ultramarinis, visitationis liminum B. Petri et Pauli Apostolorum de Urbe, ac Sancti Jacobi in Compostella, necnon Religionis et castitatis votis dumtaxat exceptis) in alia pietatis opera commutandi, facultatem concedimus.

On May 3, 1575, Pope Gregory XIII granted to the Jesuits the further privilege of commuting vows even though these had been confirmed by oath.[76] This explicit faculty to commute a vow which had been confirmed by an oath seems to have been a clarification of the nature of oaths. While the common teaching held that oaths did not change the nature of vows, but only gave added firmness, some confessors must have been loath to commute such vows. The explicit concession of the faculty for such cases effectively ended all hesitancy in the matter. In the same constitution the pope denied the right to commute when the acquired rights of other persons were involved.

Pope Benedict XIII gave to the Dominican Order the privilege of commuting both vows and oaths.[77] With the restoration of the Society of Jesus in 1826 Pope Leo XII renewed the ancient privileges of the Order, and specifically granted to Jesuit priests who were chosen for the office of confessor the power to commute all non-reserved vows:

72 Const. *Etsi ad universos*, 4 iun. 1507—*Bull. Rom.*, V, 444.

73 Const. *Inter caeteros*, 2 apr. 1512—*Bull. Rom.*, V, 516.

74 Const. *Etsi a summa*, 4 iul. 1513—*Bull. Rom.*, V, 544.

75 3 iun. 1545—*Comp. Privileg.*, p. 150.

76 Const. *Decet Romanum*, 3 maii 1575—*Comp. Privileg.*, p. 156.

77 Const. *Pretiosus*, 26 maii 1727—*Bull. Rom.*, XXII, 522.

> Vota simplicia commutare, nunquam vero vota castitatis, religionis, trium peregrinationum ad sacra B. Apostolorum limina, ad S. Jacobum in Compostellis, et ad Jerusalem, eaque vota in quibus agitur de praeiudicio vel iure tertii.[78]

From these documents it is quite evident that Regular confessors possessed the privilege of commuting all non-reserved vows, even those which had been confirmed by an oath. The reserved vows were the five consistently mentioned in papal constitutions. Furthermore, vows, the commutation of which would prejudice the acquired rights of other persons, could not be commuted until those persons surrendered their rights. The faculty of commuting vows could be exercised both within and outside the confessional the same as that of dispensing. All that was required for its valid use was that the Regular confessor have previously obtained the approbation for the hearing of the confessions of the faithful from the local Ordinary.

Article 4. Privileges of Regulars to Dispense and Commute Vows in Relation to the Code

The Code, in its legislation on vows, contains no clauses abrogating privileges possessed by religious Orders. In virtue of canon 4, therefore, all the privileges for the commuting and dispensing of the vows of the faithful which Regular confessors possessed at the time of the Code's promulgation remain intact.

The powers of the Regular superiors in dispensing from the private vows of their subjects had become part of the common law long before the Council of Trent. Their faculties were equal to those of bishops. The present legislation recognizes them as the equals of local Ordinaries in relation to the commutation and dispensation of the vows of their own subjects. Superiors of exempt clerical religious institutes, moreover, can dispense all those persons enumerated in canon 514, § 1,[79] from non-reserved vows, provided that there is a

[78] Const. *Plura inter,* 11 iul. 1826—*Bull. Rom. cont.,* XVI, 449.

[79] The persons enumerated in canon 514 are: "professis, novitiis, aliisve in religiosa domo diu noctuque degentibus causa famulatus aut educationis aut hospitii aut infirmae valetudinis."

just cause and the rights of a third party are not thereby injured.[80]

In the new law, therefore, the rights of the Regular superior are more extensive than previously. Not only the professed, the novices, and those who reside at the monastery as servants and partake of the common fare come under the superior's jurisdiction in this regard; he can now dispense and commute the vows of all servants, guests, students and convalescents who live day and night in the religious house. Since the present law [81] recognizes only the two private vows of perfect and perpetual chastity and of entering a religious institute of solemn vows, made unconditionally after completion of the eighteenth year, as reserved to the Holy See, the religious superior has more extensive powers than heretofore. He can dispense and commute in the present legislation from three of the five vows previously reserved, namely, the vow of making a pilgrimage either to the Holy Lands, to the tombs of the Apostles in Rome, or to the tomb of St. James at Santiago de Compostela.

It has been shown in the previous articles that the powers of simple Regular confessors with diocesan faculties for the hearing of the confessions of the faithful were similar to those of the local Ordinaries for the dispensation and commutation of vows. These faculties were not abrogated by the Code. A study of the present legislation is necessary, therefore, to discover what are the powers of the bishops in this regard; and consequently, what are the powers of Regular confessors for the dispensation and commutation of the vows of the faithful.

Canon 1313, § 1, states that local Ordinaries have the faculty to dispense, for a just cause, from the non-reserved vows of their subjects and of all transients within their territory, unless there is a question of the acquired rights of a third party.[82] Local Ordinaries,

[80] Canon 1313, § 3: "Vota non reservata possunt iusta de causa dispensare, dummodo dispensatio ne laedat ius aliis quaesitum: (loci Ordinarius et) superior religionis clericalis exemptae quod attinet ad personas quae can. 514, § 1, enumerantur."

[81] Canon 1309.

[82] "Vota non reservata potest iusta de causa dispensare . . . loci Ordinarius quod attinet ad omnes subditos atque etiam peregrinos."

therefore, have the power to dispense all vows not reserved to the Holy See. The vows which are reserved are all public vows, with the exception of those vows which are made in an institute of diocesan right *(iuris dioecesani)*,[83] and the two private vows which are specially reserved by the common law. The local Ordinary has no power even over the temporary vows of men and women who are professed in a religious institute of Pontifical approval.[84] The law itself makes provision for the automatic cessation of the vows of those religious who are legitimately dismissed while they are in temporary vows.[85] The obligations attached to the reception of major Orders, whether these proceed from an implicit vow or from ecclesiastical law, are likewise outside the jurisdiction of the local Ordinary.

The determination of the powers of the local Ordinary with respect to his subjects and all transients actually within his territory shows what are the powers of Regular confessors. Since the latter were granted privileges to dispense and commute vows the same as bishops, "even those which were reserved in synodal and provincial constitutions,"[86] their powers seem to be just as extensive at the present time as are those of the local Ordinary. There is question, however, concerning the Regular confessors' dispensing power in the public vows made in a religious institute of diocesan right. Since the power to dispense from such vows was given to local Ordinaries by a special concession of Pope Leo XIII,[87] one may question the right of Regulars to dispense. In a practical case, if a person with a vow of chastity made in an institute of diocesan right came to confession to a Regular confessor on the day of his marriage and revealed the vow in confession, what would be the power of the confessor? If he decided not to make use of his probable jurisdiction over the vow, he

[83] Cf. Leo XIII, const. *Conditae a Christo*, 8 dec. 1900—*Fontes*, n. 644. It is well to recall that even in such institutes, if a religious has taken the vow of perfect and perpetual chastity, the vow is reserved to the Holy See. It is similar to a private vow of like nature; cf. Coronata, *Institutiones*, II, p. 229, n. 897.

[84] Cf. Coronata, *loc. cit.*

[85] Cf. canons 647; 648.

[86] Cf. Iulius II, const. *Etsi ad universos*, 4 iun. 1507—*Bull. Rom.*, V, 444.

[87] Cf. const. *Conditae a Christo*—*Fontes*, 644.

could at least dispense from the impediment to marriage in virtue of canons 1044 and 1045, § 3, provided the existence of the vow was not publicly known in the neighborhood. The dispensation from the impediment would not remove the vow of chastity but would make it inoperative during the time that the marriage exists.

Besides the public vows and the two private vows reserved to the Holy See, canon 1313 states that local Ordinaries may not dispense vows in which the acquired rights of third parties are injured. For example, a man makes a vow to give a sum of money to a charitable institution, which promise is accepted by the institution. Later on he discovers that it is difficult to perform what he had promised. Can the local Ordinary dispense from his vow? This is an evident case wherein a dispensation from the vow would injure the acquired right of a third party. Moralists teach that not even the pope could inherently dispense from such a vow, unless the institution belonged to the Church; neither could he nullify its obligations.[88] He could not nullify the obligations since he does not possess dominative power over the faithful in this matter. He could not dispense since the third party has a strict right to the money promised by the person who made the vow, and ratified by the institution. A bond of the natural law is created in this instance from which only the person who ratified the promise can release him. Before his vow can be dispensed, he must seek first a release of his obligation from the interested party, after which the local Ordinary can dispense from the vow.[89]

But if that person had made the vow of giving a certain sum of money and the institution had not yet accepted or ratified the promise, then the obligation is as yet *ex voto simpliciter* and the bishop could dispense. The institution has not been injured since it has as yet no title to the donation. Regular confessors have the power to dispense and commute vows of this kind just as the local Ordinary, even though such vows have been confirmed by oath. For an oath does not change the nature of a vow; it gives it added firmness only

[88] Cf. E. Reilly, *General Norms of Dispensation* (Catholic University of America Canon Law Studies, n. 119; Washington, D. C.: Catholic University of America Press, 1939), p. 53.

[89] Cf. Prümmer, *Manuale Theologiae Moralis,* II, n. 423; Noldin-Schmitt, *Theologia Moralis,* II, n. 232.

by reason of the invocation of the Divine Name in witness thereof.[90] It is evident, therefore, that Regular confessors can dispense and commute such vows in virtue of their privileges.[91]

Canon 1313, § 1, states that local Ordinaries can dispense transients *(peregrini)* residing within their territory. Thus, for example, Mr. Brown who has his domicile in diocese *A* can apply for a dispensation from the vow he has made to the bishop of diocese *B* while he is visiting his friend in that diocese. This provision of the Code is new legislation, although customary law before the Code seems to have sanctioned the power of bishops to dispense in such instances.[92] Regular confessors, on the other hand, since their papal privileges were not restricted to the subjects of the local Ordinary, always enjoyed the faculty of dispensing transients who happened to be within the diocese wherein they had been approved for the hearing of confessions.

In pre-Code legislation a much mooted question among theologians was whether Regular confessors could dispense from reserved vows in cases of very urgent necessity in the same manner as local Ordinaries. Let it be supposed, for example, that a person had made the vow of perfect and perpetual chastity whose dispensation is now reserved to the Holy See. This individual wishes to contract marriage, and reveals the presence of the vow to a Regular confessor on the eve of the wedding. Could the confessor dispense him from his vow if there was no time for recourse to the bishop? St. Alphonsus seemed to favor the opinion that Regular confessors had no power over such vows.[93] The reason assigned for this opinion was that Regular confessors, in virtue of their privileges, are empowered to dispense any vows from which the bishops can dispense by reason of their ordinary or usual jurisdiction, not, however, from those from which the bishops dispense only in virtue of extraordinary powers. Since bishops were permitted to dispense from reserved vows in urgent and extraordinary circumstances only, it follows that Regular confessors, whose priv-

[90] Cf. Reg. 42, 58, 69, R. J., in VI°; canon 1318, § 1.

[91] Canon 1320: "Qui irritare, dispensare, commutare possunt votum, eandem potestatem eademque ratione habent circa iusiurandum promissorium."

[92] Cf. Lehmkuhl, *Theologia Moralis,* I, nn. 260, 620.

[93] *Theologia Moralis,* lib. I, Append. II, n. 109; lib. VI, n. 1128.

ileges did not entitle them to absolve in such circumstance, could not dispense from reserved vows at any time.

St. Alphonsus, however, admitted that the opposite opinion was not improbable. Those who favor the opinion that Regular confessors can dispense in urgent necessity state that the power which the local Ordinary uses is, after all, ordinary power. The power is attached to his office; the reservation is simply a withholding of power over the vow in ordinary circumstances, which rule does not bind in urgent necessity.[94] If the local Ordinaries dispense in virtue of their ordinary powers, then Regular confessors, whose powers are similar to those of the bishops, can likewise dispense from such reserved vows in urgent necessity. This opinion was followed by D'Annibale,[95] Marc,[96] and many others before the Code; Coronata,[97] writing after the Code, holds the same opinion. Prümmer does not seem to favor the opinion that Regular confessors can dispense from such vows made before marriage is entered into; but if marriage has been contracted despite the vow, or the vow was made after the marriage, the Regular confessor may at least partially dispense so that the party can seek the marriage debt.[98]

The practical importance of this probable opinion is seen where a person with a reserved vow of chastity approaches a Regular confessor when it is impossible to delay the marriage until the bishop has been petitioned. On the strength of this probability, the confessor could at least partially dispense so that the person would not be living in a continual occasion of sin, and could ask for the marriage debt.

By way of summary it may be stated that Regular confessors, approved by the local Ordinary for the hearing of the confessions of the faithful, can dispense and commute the vows of the faithful in the same manner as the local Ordinary. While the power to dispense can be used both within and outside of the confessional, it is more in accord with the present practice of the Holy See that the faculties

[94] Canon 81.

[95] *Theologiae Moralis Summula,* III, n. 210, nota 35.

[96] Cf. *Institutiones,* nn. 643; 2191, 5°.

[97] *Institutiones Iuris Canonici,* II, p. 229, n. 897.

[98] Cf. *Manuale Theologiae Moralis,* II, n. 427.

be used only within the confessional. The prudent confessor will dispense rarely from a vow; commutation of a vow is more salutary, since the penitent will thus not lose all the merit of the vow, and will moreover acquire a new merit for his obedience.[99]

[99] Cf. Prümmer, *ibid.*, n. 428.

CHAPTER VII

PRIVILEGES OF REGULARS FOR DISPENSATION FROM IRREGULARITIES

ARTICLE 1. GENERAL NORMS

AN irregularity is a permanent impediment, established by canon law, which renders illicit the reception and the exercise of Holy Orders.[1] An irregularity is: (1) an *impediment* or an obstacle the purpose of which is to safeguard against unworthy aspirants the dignity and the reverence due to the Sacred Ministry of Christ. It is: (2) a *permanent impediment,* since in and of its nature it never ceases. Its removal is effected only by the positive will of the legislator, manifested in the law itself, or by a dispensation granted through the legitimate ecclesiastical authority. This condition of permanence differentiates an irregularity from a simple impediment which can cease with the lapse of time, for example, children of non-Catholic parents, so long as the parents remain in error; married men; those who labor under *infamia facti.*[2] It is: (3) established by canon law, since the source of an irregularity is in the will of the legislator. This distinguishes an irregularity from impediments of the natural and positive divine law, such as the lack of a vocation to the priesthood or the radical incapacity of a woman to receive Holy Orders. It is an institute of the common law, that is, of the universal law of the Catholic Church, for it is an axiom of law that irregularities cannot be established by particular law, by custom, or *ab homine.*[3]

[1] D'Annibale defines an irregularity as an "impedimentum ad ordines suscipiendos, et per consequens, ad eos exercendos, iure canonico introductum."—*Summula,* I, n. 399.

Noldin-Schmitt define it as an "impedimentum perpetuum, lege ecclesiastica statutum, quod susceptionem et exercitium ordinum reddit illicita."—*Theol. Mor.,* III, n. 480.

[2] Cf. canon 987.

[3] C. 18, *de sententia excommunicationis,* V, 11, in VI°. See also canon 983.

An irregularity is: (4) a bar to the licit reception of Holy Orders. It points only to unlawfulness, for an action in contravention of the law does not of itself invalidate the reception of the Sacrament, but renders gravely illicit the reception of the Sacrament. It renders the *reception* of Orders illicit, for the primary purpose of an irregularity is to impede the unfit and unworthy from taking on themselves obligations, the exercise of which will cause grave scandal, and lessen the respect for the sacred ministry. An irregularity is: (5) a bar to the licit *exercise* of Holy Orders already received. For its secondary purpose is to prevent from exercising their Orders those who, after receiving Orders, have rendered themslves unworthy or become unfit by reason of some delict or defect. Under the term *Holy Orders* are included all major and minor Orders, episcopal consecration and first tonsure.[4]

The Code makes a twofold division of irregularities; those which are incurred through some physical or moral blemish, over which the person has little if any control; and those which are incurred through grave personal faults or sins. The first type are called irregularities *ex defectu;* the second, irregularities *ex delicto.*[5] A glance at the specific irregularities will discover the essential difference between the two types.

It is not the purpose of this work to discuss the intimate nature of specific irregularities. It will suffice to point out the fact that the new law has dispelled the confusion among moralists and canonists as to their purpose and nature.[6] Irregularities are not penalties. Their position in the new law under the title of Sacred Ordination is evidence of that fact. While it is true that irregularities are also incurred for the commission of certain serious crimes, they are not meant as penalties, but as deterrents from the reception of obligations which the delinquents cannot worthily carry out.

Certain conditions are necessarily presupposed before anyone can incur an irregularity: (1) the person must be a male who has been baptized. Since women are entirely incapable of receiving Holy

[4] Cf. canons 949; 950.

[5] Cf. canons 984; 985.

[6] Cf. D'Annibale, *Summula,* I, nn. 401-403; Marc, *Institutiones Theologiae Moralis,* II, nn. 1927-1931.

Orders, they cannot incur the irregularities which impede the reception and exercise of those Orders. Irregularities are established by positive ecclesiastical law. Therefore a person who is not subject to that law cannot contract the irregularity,[7] for only by baptism does one become subject to ecclesiastical law. (2) Both the law and the fact of incurrence must be certain. For, if it cannot be ascertained whether a sin which one has committed, or the defect under which one labors, is included under the conditions giving rise to a certain irregularity, the irregularity is not incurred. Likewise, one is not obliged to observe the irregularity if one is not certain that he has committed the sin, or that he labors under the defect, which forms the basis for the irregularity. Thus, if a person could not ascertain whether he is of illegitimate birth, he could receive Holy Orders licitly without dispensation. However, in such a doubt of fact, dispensation should be sought *ad cautelam,* lest, when the fact which underlies the irregularity later becomes known, the person becomes subject also to the effects of that fact, that is, the irregularity itself. Any Ordinary can dispense such irregularities in doubt of fact, provided that they be such from which the Holy See usually dispenses.[8] (3) Before there can be question of an irregularity *ex delicto,* the law presupposes that the delicit was a grave sin committed after the reception of baptism, and externally consummated. There is only one exception as to the prerequisite of baptism. It relates to those who, outside of a case of extreme necessity, have allowed themselves to be baptized by non-Catholics.[9] It does not matter whether the sin by which the irregularity will be incurred is public or occult; nor does ignorance of the fact that an irregularity has been enacted excuse one from incurring it.[10]

Once the irregularity has been incurred, it ceases only through the intervention of the legitimate superior. Some authors admit one exception, namely, the irregularity *ex defectu* which results from a grave physical deformity that can be corrected by surgical operation.[11]

[7] Cf. Canon 12.

[8] Cf. canon 15.

[9] Cf. canon 986. See also Prümmer, *Manuale Theol. Mor.*, III, n. 611.

[10] Cf. canon 988.

[11] Cf. canon 984, 2°.

Authors teach that, once the defect has been successfully removed, the irregularity no longer exists.[12] Likewise, if a person were healed miraculously from such a deformity, he could be advanced to Holy Orders without a dispensation.

In the irregularity which results from illegitimacy of status at birth, the legislator has provided for its cessation automatically when the person becomes legitimated,[13] or when he makes profession of solemn vows in a religious Order.

The proper ecclesiastical authority for the granting of a dispensation from all irregularities is the Roman Pontiff. Since irregularities originate only in the common law, the supreme legislator is the only one who dispenses by his own proper authority. However, provision is made by the law itself for local Ordinaries and major superiors of exempt clerical religious institutes to dispense from certain irregularities.[14] According to the Code, Ordinaries can dispense from all irregularities incurred *ex delicto occulto,* except those which result from the execution of, or cooperation in acts of voluntary homicide and effectively procured abortion, or also the cases which have been introduced for a hearing in a judicial court.[15] The law provides the Ordinary with the faculty to delegate this power of dispensing to others. But he is limited to his own subjects; he cannot dispense transients *(peregrini)* even within his own territory.

The Code, furthermore, permits any simple confessor to dispense

[12] Cf. Prümmer, *ibid.,* n. 612, 1°.

[13] Cf. canons 1051; 1116; 1117; 1138, §§ 1, 2; 1363, § 1. See also P. C. I., 13 iul. 1930, ad III; D. An filii legitimati per subsequens parentum matrimonium habendi sint uti legitimi ad effectum, de quo in canone 1363, § 1. R. Affirmative.—*AAS,* XXII (1930), 365.

[14] Cf. canon 990, § 1, taken in relation with canon 198. Canon 990 does not specifically mention major superiors. However, canon 198 includes them under the name of Ordinaries. They can dispense their own subjects just the same as local Ordinaries.

[15] Canon 990, § 1—Licet Ordinariis per se vel per alium suos subditos dispensare ab irregularitatibus omnibus ex delicto occulto provenientibus, ea excepta de qua in canon 985, 4°, aliave deducta ad forum iudiciale.

Canon 985, 4°—Sunt irregulares ex delicto: qui voluntarium homicidium perpetrarunt aut fetus humani abortum procuraverunt, effectu secuto, omnesque cooperantes.

in the same cases, in urgent necessity, when there is no time to have recourse to the Ordinary, and there is danger of grave damage or infamy. This faculty is restricted to dispensing a penitent in order that he may licitly exercise the Orders he has already received.[16] From this it can be seen that the simple confessor may never dispense a person from an irregularity, even in urgent cases, with a view to enabling him to receive Sacred Orders.

The Roman Pontiffs granted special privileges to Prelates of religious Orders for dispensing from the irregularities of their own subjects. Simple Regular confessors in the past obtained extensive privileges from the Holy See to dispense the faithful from irregularities. The writer will in the immediately following articles investigate these privileges in order to determine what is their status in the present law.

Article 2. Dispensing Powers of Regular Superiors in Irregularities of Their Subjects

The concessions of special privileges to religious Orders for the granting of dispensations from the irregularities of the religious subjects are traceable almost at any point in the long history of the privileges of Regulars. One may speculate why such ample privileges were granted to them, and not to the local Ordinaries. One reason may perhaps be inherent in the fact that religious communities were isolated groups wherein a priest, if he was dispensed from his irregularities, could exercise his ministry without grave scandal to the faithful. This statement bears illustration. Let it be supposed that a man had committed a grave delict while he lived among the faithful and had incurred an irregularity in consequence of it. He then entered the monastery, not only to do penance, but to consecrate himself to God by religious vows. By this act the stigma which lay upon him in the world was mitigated, and the judgment as to his fitness for exercising the sacred ministry was left to the Superiors. It can be seen that a dispensation was granted more readily in such

[16] Canon 990, § 2—Eadem facultas competit cuilibet confessario in casibus occultis urgentioribus in quibus Ordinarius adiri nequeat et periculum immineat gravis damni vel infamiae, sed ad hoc dumtaxat ut poenitens ordines iam susceptos exercere licite valeat.

cases, especially if the penitent was to exercise his Orders only within the monastery. Another case may be proposed. It is that of a man who with a physical defect sufficient to make him irregular entered the monastery. In due time he hoped to be admitted to Sacred Orders, with the understanding that he was to exercise them only within the monastery. Here again one finds a reason for the mitigation of ecclesiastical discipline so as to allow for a dispensation of the irregularity more readily.

It must not be presumed that privileges of this kind were given out of gratitude to the religious Orders for their great work in spreading the Faith. The good of the Church demanded that the dignity of Sacred Orders be safeguarded. It was, therefore, for reasons of utility that special privileges were granted them, such as the reasons given above, or because of the difficulty of communicating with the Holy See, etc.

The first privilege of which there is any record in the history of the religious Orders was that granted to the Prior General of the Order of Carmel in 1229, by Pope Gregory IX (1227-1241).[17] This Pope granted the Prior General the faculty to dispense apostates of the Order who had presumed to receive Sacred Orders while in apostasy, and also to celebrate Holy Mass while they were irregular.

More extensive faculties were granted to the Order of Friars Minor in 1256 by Pope Alexander IV (1254-1261).[18] The Superior General and the Provincials of the Order were given the power to dispense from all irregularities of their subjects, except from such as had to be referred specifically to the Holy See. The privilege was worded thus:

> Cum, sicut asseritis, ex indulto Apostolicae Sedis vobis liceat vestri Ordinis fratres curae vestrae commissos ab excommunicatione absolvere, et cum eis super irregularitatibus dispensare, nisi adeo gravis et enormis fuerit excessus, propter quem merito sit Sedes consulenda praedicta, vobis auctoritate indulgemus, ut fratres dicti Ordinis, quos pro tempore in proprios habueritis confessores, absolutionis et dispensationis beneficium vobis, cum

[17] Const. *Providi,* 5 apr. 1229—Potth., n. 8367; *Comp. Privileg.*, p. 263.

[18] Const. *Ordinis vestri,* 21 iul. 1256—Potth., n. 16492, *Comp. Privileg.*, p. 294.

> expedierit, iuxta indulti praefati tenorem valeant impertiri: ne ii qui inter vos praeesse noscuntur, deterioris conditionis, quam ceteri censentur.

This constitution contains certain noteworthy points. In the first place, this constitution was not the first one to be granted to the Order, for the pope refers to a special grant alleged to have been given previously. The irregularities which could not be dispensed are called *grave and enormous excesses,* which indicates that those for which dispensation could be granted were also irregularities resulting from sins. Thus in all probability they were irregularities *ex delicto.* Certain of these excesses were reserved to the Holy See for dispensation, but nothing in the constitution indicates which crimes specifically were reserved to the Roman Pontiff. The privilege permitted the Religious Superiors to dispense only from the irregularities for the professed members of the Order. The use of the privilege was restricted to the General and the Provincials, except for the case wherein these had fallen into the same irregularities themselves. If in their own persons they had incurred any irregularities, they could choose one of their own confessors who would then dispense them from their irregularities.

Pope Celestine V (1294) was more explicit in the designation of the irregularities reserved to the Holy See, when he granted to the abbots of the monasteries of the Celestines ample faculties to dispense. Among the irregularities specifically reserved were the cases of homicide and of the mutilation of a person's bodily members. These irregularities were reserved by the common law.[19] The constitution is given in its pertinent wording:

> Dispensandi etiam cum fratribus seu monachos ad vestra monasteria et loca convolantibus et ibidem degentibus, super irregularitatibus quibuscumque, etiamsi prius eas fortasse contraxerit, quam praedicta loca et monasteria intravissent, dummodo ex homicidii vel mutilationis causa, irregularitates ipsae minime sint contractae, plenam et liberam vobis, filii abbates, auctoritate Apostolica concedimus potestatem.[20]

[19] Cf. cc. 10, 24, X, *de homicidio voluntario vel casuali,* V, 12; c. 2, X, *de clericis pugnantibus in duello,* V, 14.

[20] Const. *Etsi cunctos,* 27 sept. 1294—Potth., n. 23976; *Comp. Privileg.,* p. 264.

This privilege permitted the abbot to dispense from crimes and irregularities incurred before the religious entered the monastery. It granted the abbots the power to dispense from any irregularities whatsoever as long as they were not specifically reserved to the Holy See. It must be concluded, then, that the abbot could dispense even in public and notorious cases. Here again the grant of power for dispensing was limited to crimes which constituted irregularities *ex delicto.*

In 1436 Pope Eugene IV (1431-1447) granted the abbots of the Congregation of Monte Cassino the right to allow monks of illegitimate status at birth, who had lived laudably in the monastery, to be promoted to Sacred Orders, without the dispensation from the irregularity *ex defectu natalium.*[21]

In a constitution, *Ad decorem,* of 1437, the same Pontiff granted to the Cistercians of the Regular Observance the privilege of dispensing from all irregularities, whether public or occult, except the ones arising from voluntary homicide, mutilation, and bigamy:

> Ac cum quibusvis ex monachis, religiosis, et personis praedictis, super irregularitate, si quam ex quavis causa quomodolibet contraxerint, homicidio voluntario, mutilatione membri, ac bigamia dumtaxat exceptis, ut nihilominus non promoti ad omnes sacros Ordines promoveri, ac ipsi et promoti in illis ministrare possint, dispensare.[22]

The constitution thus granted to the Cistercians accorded more extensive privileges than the one to the Celestines. In the one for the Cistercians, only voluntary homicide was reserved; in the other, all types of homicide, whether voluntary or casual, were reserved. The Cistercian superiors could dispense from irregularities of their subjects, not only to permit the licit exercise of powers already received, but also to permit them to be promoted to Sacred Orders.

There is some question concerning the irregularity which resulted from bigamy. In the ancient discipline two kinds of bigamy were recognized as inducing irregularity: *bigamia successiva,* or the marrying of two wives successively, and *bigamia similitudinaria,* or the

[21] Const. *Etsi quaslibet,* 30 iun. 1436—*Comp. Privileg.,* p. 265.

[22] Cf. *Comp. Privileg.,* p. 6.

attempted marriage of a religious in solemn vows. The former constituted an irregularity *ex defectu;* the latter entailed an irregularity *ex delicto.* It is not certain to which type of bigamy reference was made in the Constitution *Ad decorem;* probably the bigamy *ex delicto* was the one reserved, since the other reserved irregularities with which it was included were irregularities *ex delicto.*

Pope Nicholas V (1447-1455) granted to the Spanish provinces of the Order of Trinitarians the privilege of selecting confessors of their Order, who could dispense both subjects and superiors from irregularities, with a view to permitting them to exercise Orders already received.[23]

At the time of the *Mare Magnum* of privileges almost all Orders received general concessions of privileges to dispense from irregularities. Most of them included the same faculties. It will suffice to quote from one:

> Generali et provincialibus Ministris dicti Ordinis pro tempore existentibus, et illorum Vicariis, dispensandi cum dicti Ordinis Minorum professoribus, defectum natalium ex adulterio, sacrilegio, incestu, et quovis alio nefario et illicito coitu provenientem patientibus, necnon cum his qui ex quavis causa (praeterquam homicidii voluntarii, bigamiae, et mutilationis membrorum) irregulares forent, postquam Ordinem ipsum professi fuerint, ut defectu et irregularitate huiusmodi non obstante, irregulares ipsi ad quoscumque etiam sacros ordines promoveri, et in illis altaris ministerio ministrare, et tam ipsi irregulares quam defectum natalium patientes praedicti, ad quascumque administrationes et officia dicti Ordinis eligi, recipi, et assumi, illaque gerere et exercere libere et licite valeant . . . concedimus.[24]

The constitution just quoted again establishes the fact that at least three irregularities were reserved consistently to the Holy See: voluntary homicide, bigamy, and mutilation of one's bodily members. These three must be looked upon as reservations usually reserved to the Holy See. Consequently, if one Order is given the special privilege of dispensing from them, it must be considered as an extra-

[23] Const. *Exposcit,* anno 1447—*Comp. Privileg.,* p. 8.

[24] Sixtus IV, const. *Regimini,* 31 aug. 1474—*Bull. Praed.,* III, 516.

ordinary privilege not subject to communication between the religious Orders.

There is here the same dispute as to the type of bigamy that was meant in the reservation as there was in the previous constitutions. Possibly *successive bigamy* is the irregularity referred to in this document. The rest of the irregularities from which the General and the Provincials of the Dominican and Franciscan Orders could dispense dealt with irregularities *ex delicto,* with the exception of the *defectus natalium.* The superiors could dispense in all of them, whether they were public, notorious, or occult.

Innocent VIII (1484-1492) [25] granted to the Prior General of the Order of Hermits of St. Augustine the faculty of dispensing his subjects from all irregularities, except voluntary homicide and bigamy. This faculty could be communicated to the Provincials of the Order in such manner that they in turn could sub-delegate it to any confessor as often as they found it necessary to do so.

In 1512 the Canons Regular of St. Augustine received the same privileges as were granted to the Franciscans and Dominicans in 1474 by the Constitution *Regimini.*[26] The same grant was made to the Society of Jesus in 1549 by Paul III (1534-1549).[27]

The Clerics Regular were granted the same privileges as were granted to the Franciscans and Dominicans in 1474. The grant was extended, however, to include all persons living under their obedience, discipline, or direction, with a restriction to the sacramental forum.[28]

In 1560 Pope Pius IV (1559-1565) [29] granted the Benedictine Congregation of Mt. Olivet the privilege of dispensing its monks from all irregularities, except voluntary homicide, bigamy, and mutilation, both in order to promote them to Orders, and also in order to enable them to exercise the Orders already received.

Seven years later Pope St. Pius V (1566-1572) granted an unusual privilege to the Order of Theatines.[30] On the day of their solemn

[25] Const. *Tuis supplicationibus,* 16 febr. 1486—*Bull. O. E. S. A.,* p. 193.
[26] Iulius II, const. *Inter caeteros,* 2 apr. 1512—*Bull. Rom.,* V, 516.
[27] Const. *Licet debitum,* 18 oct. 1549—*Bull. Rom.,* VI, 394.
[28] Gregorius XIV, const. *Illius qui,* 21 sept. 1591—*Bull. Rom.,* IX, 479.
[29] Const. *Votis vestris,* 24 maii 1560—*Bull. Rom.,* VII, 26.
[30] Const. *Ad immarcescibilem,* 13 febr. 1567—*Bull. Rom.,* VII, 538.

profession, or on some day previous to it, the members of the Order could be dispensed from all irregularities, except that resulting from voluntary homicide. This privilege probably should be considered as an unusual one in which other Orders did not communicate.

From a study of these documents one can conclude that all the religious Orders possessed in common all the *ordinary* privileges granted to any one of them. By comparison of documents one finds that the general superiors, and also all provincials and abbots, could dispense from all irregularities *ex delicto,* with the exception of voluntary homicide, bigamy, and possibly the mutilation of one's bodily members. These privileges were granted for both the external and the internal *forum,* and for all cases, whether public, notorious, or occult. They could be used for the purpose of dispensing subjects so that these could receive Sacred Orders as well as exercise the Orders already received *(tam in ordine ad suscipiendos Ordines sacros, quam in ordine ad exercendos Ordines sacros iam susceptos).* It is not certain whether local superiors could exercise the same powers. Very probably such powers were denied them. They could, however, receive delegated powers from their superiors.[81]

In relation to irregularities *ex defectu* the constitutions mention expressly only the *defectus natalium.* It is disputed whether bigamy was also included.

The Council of Trent (1545-1563) established the first general norms for the granting of dispensations from irregularities on the part of bishops. In the XXIV Session bishops were granted the general faculties of dispensing from all irregularities *ex delicto,* except that of voluntary homicide, provided that the irregularities arose from an occult crime, and the case had not been taken before a judicial court.[82] This legislation reduced to the common law the rights of bishops over irregularities, and abrogated all privileges given to them in the previous centuries. It did not, however, abrogate the privileges of Regulars, since the law did not mention them. All faculties which

[81] This delegation of jurisdiction was possible, as can be noted from the grant of Innocent VIII, const. *Tuis Supplicationibus;* cf. *supra,* p. 152.

[82] "Liceat episcopis in irregularitatibus omnibus . . . ex delicto occulto provenientibus, excepta ea, quae oritur ex homicidio voluntario, et exceptis, aliis deductis ad forum contentiosum, dispensare. . . ."—Sess. XXIV, *de ref.,* c. 6.

religious Orders possessed up to the advent of the Code in 1918 were held in virtue of papal privileges; many of them were antecedent to the Council of Trent.

Some years after the Council of Trent, Pius V granted to the Dominican Order the same privileges which were granted to bishops in the Council.[88] The pertinent parts of the constitution are quoted here:

> Quia . . . Concilium . . . Tridentinum concessit episcopis, ut absolvere possent, in foro animae seu conscientiae, ab omnibus irregularitatibus prout Sess. XXIV, c. 6 habetur: Ne prior provincialis, et superiores praelati dicti Ordinis . . . in hac parte deterioris conditionis, quam clerici et saeculares existant, eisdem priori conventuali et superioribus praelatis, ut ipsi per seipsos idem omnino possint in Fratres et Moniales dicti Ordinis sibi subditos, quoad absolvendi et dispensandi huiusmodi . . . concedimus.

Some may argue from this document that the previous privileges of the Roman Pontiffs had been abrogated. This is untrue, however, for nowhere does one find any such abrogation. This privilege had for its purpose the granting to Regular superiors specifically the same faculties as were possessed by the bishops after the Council of Trent. It granted, moreover, new faculties to the local superiors of the Order, and, by way of participated communication, to the local superiors of all the other Orders. Thenceforth the local superiors were permitted to dispense their subjects in the internal forum from all irregularities of an occult nature, except that of voluntary homicide.

In the seventeenth and eighteenth centuries a bitter dispute was waged among canonists and theologians concerning the authenticity and the interpretation of a constitution which is supposed to have been granted by Pope Martin V (1417-1431) to the Benedictine Congregation of Valladolid in the year 1424. It was issued in the form of a *vivae vocis oraculum,* and granted to that monastery the privilege of dispensing *in foro conscientiae* from all irregularities without exception, even from voluntary homicide, mutilation, and prodigious effusion of blood, provided that these latter were not notorious. The grant is cited here:

[88] Cf. const. *Romani Pontificis,* 21 iul. 1571—*Bull. Praed.*, V, 283.

> Priori S. Benedicti Vallis Oleti, et virtute extensionis postea factae (Martinus V), omnibus Prioribus Congregationis Hispaniae, ut in foro conscientiae monachos . . . absolvere; et cum eis super omni irregularitate, etiam in illis casibus, in quibus Papa sibi vicem reservat, in morte videlicet, et in truncatione membrorum, et enormi sanguinis effusione, valeat dispensare, dum tamen aliquid horum trium notorium non sit.[34]

Some authors held that this grant was spurious, since it was the only one which gave such extensive faculties. However, the compiler of the *Compendium Privilegiorum* stated that he found it himself in the monastery at Valladolid, and that he transcribed it faithfully.[35] He stated further that it was found in the *Compendium Minorum* which was edited by Casarubios, and also in the *Compendium Fuliensium*. Others questioned whether the privilege was ever communicated in by others, even though one admitted its authenticity. First, it was granted by way of a *vivae vocis oraculum*. Again, all privileges thus granted were abrogated in 1635 by Pope Urban VIII (1623-1644).[36] Finally, a specific abrogation of all grants given by way of *vivae vocis oracula* to dispense from irregularities was effected in 1732 by Pope Clement XII (1730-1740).[37]

But it may be objected that customary law permitted Regulars to dispense in such cases, despite the abrogation of the privilege. This objection, however, cannot be sustained, since it cannot be said that such an extraordinary privilege was customarily used by all religious Orders. Therefore, it must be held that the privilege no longer existed after its specific abrogation in 1732, despite the fact that the Salmanticenses,[38] and likewise other authors, taught that Regulars could dispense also from occult cases of voluntary homicide by virtue of this grant of Martin V.

There are two other documents which granted the faculty to dispense from the irregularity resulting from voluntary homicide.

[34] Cf. *Comp. Privileg.*, p. 421.

[35] *Loc. cit.*

[36] Const. *Alias*, 11 apr. 1635—*Bull. Rom.*, XIV, 473.

[37] Const. *Romanus Pontifex*, 12 febr. 1732—cited by Vermeersch, *De Religiosis Institutis*, II, n. 171.

[38] Cf. *Theol. Mor.*, I, tr. 10, c. 8, n. 17.

The one, granted by Pope St. Pius V to the Benedictine Congregation of Monte Cassino,[39] permitted the abbot to dispense from the impediment *in foro conscientiae* only, provided that the crime was committed before the person entered the monastery. The use of the faculty was not limited to occult crimes. The other, given by Pope Benedict XIII (1724-1730) to the Superior General of the Domincan Order,[40] permitted the Superior General personally to dispense from the irregularity of voluntary homicide, provided that the crime was not committed within the cloister. Piat [41] taught, however, that this constitution of Benedict XIII was revoked by Pope Clement XII fifteen years after it was issued.[42]

Despite the many abrogations of privileges, St. Alphonsus [43] maintained the opinion that Regular superiors still had the power to dispense from the irregularity which arose from voluntary homicide. His opinion was based upon the grant of the *vivae vocis oraculum* of Pope Martin V to the Benedictine Congregation of Valladolid, and upon the constitution of Benedict XIII. But there is a seeming contradiction in his teaching regarding the constitution of Benedict, for in one connection he quotes it in favor of the privilege of Regulars, but in another passage he admits that it was abrogated by Clement XII.[44]

The Salmanticenses held that the Regular superiors had the faculty to dispense from such an irregularity, provided that the delict was not notorious.[45] Castrapalao (1581-1633) taught the same,[46] basing his opinion entirely upon the grant of Martin V.

The attitude of the Holy See toward the question of the participated communication of such extraordinary privileges among the religious Orders can be seen from a response of the Sacred Congre-

[39] Const. *Dum ad congregationem,* 13 iun. 1571—*Bull. Rom.,* VII, 919.

[40] Const. *Pretiosus,* 25 maii 1727—*Bull. Rom.,* XXII, 522.

[41] *Praelectiones Iuris Regularis,* I, Q. 757, 2°.

[42] Const. *Romanus Pontifex, quem,* 30 maii 1742—cited by St. Alphonsus, *Theol. Moralis,* lib. VII, n. 101.

[43] Cf. *op. cit.,* lib. I, Append. II, n. 105; lib. VII, n. 396.

[44] Cf. *op. cit.,* lib. I, Append. II, n. 96.

[45] Cf. *op. cit.,* III, tr. 18, c. 4, n. 25.

[46] Cf. *Theologia Moralis* (3 vols., Lugduni, 1682), Pars VI, *De Censuris,* disp. 6, punct. 7, n. 2.

gation of the Council issued on April 14, 1865.[47] The Procurator General of the Benedictine Congregation of St. Maurus [48] proposed the following query to the Sacred Congregation, namely, whether the superiors of the Congregation could absolve licitly and validly in both *fora,* and dispense from the irregularities and censures of their monks in the cases of homicide committed in war, in rebellions, and in other quasi-indeliberate uprisings? The response was in the negative.[49]

While it must be admitted that this response did not abrogate any existing privileges obtained by reason of participated communication with other Orders, it did give an indication that this privilege was to be considered as an extraordinary one which was not subject to inter-communication with the other Orders.[50] It is very probable, therefore, that only those Orders which received the privilege of dispensing from the irregularity of voluntary homicide directly from the Holy See were permitted to dispense.

In cases of casual homicide, that is, of non-deliberate manslaughter, (*praeter intentionem occisoris*), there was much greater probability that the privilege of dispensing was communicated in by the other Orders. Regular superiors, therefore, could with great probability dispense even in public cases in virtue of the privileges which they possessed by way of participated communication.[51]

With regard to the irregularity incurred by mutilation of the members of the body, Piat taught that Regulars could not dispense.[52] He based his opinion on the fact that the law itself [53] considered mutilation to be comparable to homicide. Since the latter could not be dispensed in virtue of participated privileges, neither could the other. However, D'Annibale [54] pointed out that this was not true,

[47] This response is cited by Piat, *Praelectiones Iuris Regularis,* I, Q. 775, 2°.

[48] This Congregation shared in the inter-communication of privileges.

[49] Cf. Piat, *loc. cit.*

[50] Cf. Reg. 74, R. J., in VI°. For a thorough discussion of privileges which are not subject to a participated communication, cf. Ellis, "De Communicatione Privilegiorum inter Religiones,"—*Periodica,* XXVII (1938), 157-162.

[51] Cf. St. Alphonsus, *op. cit.,* lib. VII, nn. 393-396.

[52] *Op. cit.,* I, Q. 757, 2°.

[53] Cf. c. *un., de domicidio voluntario,* V, 4, in Clem.

[54] Cf. *Summula,* I, n. 421, nota (1).

since the difference between the two was very great. One who mutilated himself was treated much more mildly than one who committed homicide. Probably, therefore, Regular superiors could dispense from such an irregularity, at least in occult cases. For Pope Pius V,[55] in 1571, granted even to local superiors of the Dominican Order the faculty to dispense *in foro conscientiae* in occult cases from this irregularity. The privilege, therefore, of dispensing in such cases did not have to be considered as an extraordinary privilege, and thus it was probable that it was communicated in by the other Orders.

Pope Sixtus V (1585-1590), because of the wide-spread vice of criminal abortion, reserved to himself the dispensation from the irregularity incurred by those who were guilty of any such crime.[56] In his constitution he identified the crime with that of voluntary homicide. He accordingly decreed that any person who had been involved in the criminal abortion of any human fetus was to be barred from receiving Sacred Orders, or, if he already had received Orders, he was not to exercise them. The dispensation from this impediment was reserved specially to the Holy See. Several years later Pope Gregory XIV (1590-1591) decreed that the irregularity was to be attached only to the abortion of a living human fetus.[57] The reservation was left unchanged.

From these documents it will be seen that no Regular superiors, in virtue of privileges, could dispense from the irregularity incurred by co-operating in the criminal abortion of a living human fetus. No privileges in this matter were granted to any Order.

The foregoing discussion may now be shortly summarized. At the time of the advent of the Code in 1918, the Superiors of religious Orders had the privilege of dispensing in the following cases: (1) they could dispense in all irregularities *ex delicto,* except voluntary homicide, mutilation of one's bodily members, and abortion. This faculty could be used in all cases, whether public or occult. For occult cases of mutilation it was the more probable opinion that they could dispense; for occult cases of *casual* homicide it was a probable

[55] Const. *Romani Pontificis,* 21 iul. 1571—*Bull. Praed.,* V, 283.

[56] Const. *Effraenatam,* 29 oct. 1588—*Fontes,* n. 165.

[57] Const. *Sedes Apostolica,* 31 maii 1591—*Fontes,* n. 173.

opinion that the same faculty was granted to them, but not in cases of *voluntary* homicide. The faculty which Religious superiors possessed could be used, both in order that their subjects might be promoted to Sacred Orders, and also to allow them the exercise of Orders already received. (2) The Superiors of religious Orders could dispense in irregularities *ex defectu* when the case was one of illegitimate status at birth, whether the case was public or occult. It was a probable opinion that they could dispense from the irregularity incurred by bigamy.

Article 3. Dispensing Powers of Regular Confessors in Irregularities

The privileges of Regular confessors to dispense from irregularities were of much later origin than the like privileges which had been granted to the Superiors of the religious Orders. In fact, little evidence can be found in any document of the existence of any such faculties before the period of the inter-communication of privileges among the religious Orders.

The first concession of this kind that the writer has been able to discover is related by the author of the *Compendium Privilegiorum*.[58] He stated that in the Bullarium possessed by the Order of St. Jerome, at the monastery of St. Alexis in Rome, there was recorded the following grant:

> (Concessit Martinus V) ut Prior et confessarii ab eo deputati pro saecularibus ad eorum monasteria quacunque de causa venientibus . . . possint etiam absolvere ab omni sententia excommunicationis . . . et ab omni censura . . . in quibus possunt Episcopi; et dispensare super omni irregularitate contracta occasione huiusmodi excommunicationis, suspensionis, et interdicti, si quam etiam celebrando incurrerint tales personae; et dispensare super quibusvis criminibus, etiam enormibus.

This grant was made *vivae vocis oraculo* by Pope Martin V under date of June 25, 1424, and was attested to by the then Cardinal of the Church of St. Eustachius. The document is not cited by any other author; nor is it quoted by canonists of the later centuries.

[58] Cf. p. 129.

According to the concession the prior and confessors chosen by him for the confessions of the laity could dispense from all irregularities in which the bishop could dispense. Since this grant was made *vivae vocis oraculo,* and was probably never confirmed later on, it must be considered as certainly abrogated by the constitutions of Urban VIII [59] and Clement XII.[60]

Sixtus IV, at the time of the general inter-communications of privileges,[61] granted to the Order of Minims the privileges which had been granted by the Archbishop of Cosenza to the religious houses of the Order in his archdiocese:

> Confessiones audiendi, et ab omnibus casibus, excommunicationibus, suspensionibus, et interdictis, ac insuper, super quacunque irregularitate, eidem Archiepiscopo, tam a iure, quam ab eo, reservatis . . .

This constitution was confirmed by Julius II in 1506.[62] According to this concession all confessors chosen for the confessions of the laity were granted the faculty to dispense in all cases of irregularity from which the Archbishop of Cosenza could dispense. Some authors,[63] however, made the claim that these privileges were granted to be used only for members of the Order. The evident error of such a claim is seen from a study of the constitution of Julius II which confirmed that of Sixtus IV. For in the Bull of Julius II there is explicit mention of the fact that these confessors can hear the "confessions of any persons, whether religious or seculars, and absolve them according to the tenor of the constitution of Sixtus IV." [64] It must be concluded, then, that the confessors of the Order were given the same rights of dispensing irregularities that bishops enjoyed. This

[59] Const. *Alias,* 11 apr. 1635—*Bull. Rom.,* XIV, 473.

[60] Const. *Romanus Pontifex,* 12 febr. 1732—cited by Vermeersch, *De Religiosis Institutis,* II, n. 171.

[61] Cf. const. *Sedes Apostolica,* 27 maii 1474—*Bull. Rom.,* V, 213.

[62] Const. *Dudum ad sacrum,* 28 iul. 1506—*Bull. Rom.,* V, 421.

[63] Cf. Concina, *Theol. Christ.,* III, lib. 4, diss. 3, c. 11, n. 11; Moccheggiani, *Iurisprudentia Eccl.,* II, n. 188.

[64] Cf. *supra,* chap. 6, art. 2. The same arguments and objections that are given in that chapter are brought up by the authors here.

power was in its use restricted, however, to the sacrament of penance. By reason of a general communication in privileges with the other Orders, all confessors appointed by their superiors could use the same privileges. This was the opinion of Piat (1815-1904) [65] and of almost all the other authors. Even Concina (1687-1756), though he maintained the opposite,[66] nevertheless admitted that canonists almost unanimously taught that Regular confessors possessed the privilege for dispensing all the faithful.

Lezana (1586-1659) [67] doubted whether the Minims ever made use of the privilege. If they didn't use it, so he argued, then they lost it. But the Salmanticenses correctly pointed out that privileges of this kind were not lost by non-use.[68] And even though it were granted that the Order of Minims lost it, it is nevertheless true that other Orders which communicated in their privileges could still use it, since they received the privileges through a participated communication *in forma aequiprincipali.*[69]

Pope Paul III granted to the confessors of the Society of Jesus [70] the faculty to absolve and *dispense* from all crimes, excesses, and penalties, even though they were reserved to the Holy See, except those which were listed in the Bull, *In Coena Domini.* Julius III, seven years later,[71] granted them the right to absolve from the sins against the faith and censures attached to such sins; furthermore they could dispense from any other effects resulting from such sins *in foro conscientiae,* as often as it was found necessary:

> Facultatem quoscunque a casibus haeresis, et aliis contra fidem et consequentibus censuris . . . absolvendi, et quatenus opus sit, in foro conscientiae dispensandi, ex certa nostra licentia confirmamus.

[65] *Praelectiones Iuris Regularis,* II, Q. 409, 2°.

[66] Cf. *loc. cit.,* n. 1.

[67] Cited by St. Alphonsus, *op. cit.,* lib. VII, n. 355.

[68] Cf. *Theol. Mor.,* III, tr. 18, c. 2, n. 13.

[69] For the effects of such a participated communication, cf. Reiffenstuel, *op. cit.,* lib. V, tit. 33, n. 69.

[70] Const. *Cum inter cunctas,* 3 iun. 1545—*Comp. Privileg.,* p. 150.

[71] Const. *Sacrae,* anno 1552—*Comp. Privileg.,* p. 152.

While it is admitted that no explicit mention of dispensing from irregularities is made in these documents, such mention seems to be implied in the very use of the word *dispensare* in the context. The word *absolvere* is always used to denote a sacramental absolution from sins, or a juridical absolution from censures and other penalties. The word *dispensare* seems somewhat superfluous if there is no reference to irregularities incurred by reason of the delict, since the reference is only to sins against the faith.[72]

Finally, with the restoration of the Society of Jesus in 1826,[73] explicit privileges to dispense from irregularities were granted:

> Etiam eos qui irregularitatem occultam tam ad suscipiendos ordines quam ad exercendos ordines incurrerint, in foro conscientiae tantum ab hoc impedimento absolvendi . . . (facultatem concedimus).

From this document it is evident that the members of the Society were permitted to dispense in the internal forum from any occult irregularity. This privilege must be understood, however, in the light of the decrees of the Council of Trent; there was not given a blanket permission to dispense from all irregularities, whether *ex delicto* or *ex defectu*. The permission obviously extended to the same irregularities from which the Ordinaries could dispense according to the law of the Council. Therefore, the members of the Society were granted the privilege to dispense in all irregularities *ex delicto* in occult cases, except the irregularities which arose from voluntary homicide and abortion.[74] It could be used in order to permit promotion to Sacred Orders, and also in order to allow the licit exercise of the Orders already received. By way of participated communication the other Orders also shared the possession of this privilege.

From the study of the documents the following conclusions can

[72] Many authors held that these constitutions of Paul III and Julius III included the power to dispense from irregularities *ex delicto;* among these were Henriquez, Soto, and Corduba. Suarez, however, said that the reference was only to dispensation from ecclesiastical penalties properly so-called. Cf. Suarez, *Opera Omnia,* tom. XVI, lib. 9, c. 2, n. 41.

[73] Cf. Leo XII, const. *Plura inter,* 11 iul. 1826—*Bull. Rom. cont.,* XIII, 437.

[74] Cf. Piat, *op. cit.,* II, Q. 409, 2°.

be reached: Regular confessors, if they had the faculties to hear the confessions of the faithful, could dispense the faithful from all irregularities resulting from all crimes, except from the crimes of voluntary homicide and of abortion. This power was for its use restricted to the following conditions: (1) the irregularity had to be occult; (2) the dispensation was effective for the sacramental forum only; (3) the privilege could be used to dispense religious, secular clerics, and lay people; (4) the faculty could be used to dispense with a view to enabling a person to receive Sacred Orders, and also in order that he might exercise the Orders which he had already received.

The authors are quite commonly in agreement with these findings.[75]

Article 4. Privileges of Regulars to Dispense from Irregularities, and the Code

In the preceding chapters it has been pointed out that papal privileges which were still in use at the time of the advent of the Code were left intact, unless express revocation of them was made in the Code law.[76] Furthermore, in virtue of canon 613, § 1, and the response of the Pontifical Commission for the Authentic Interpretation of the Code,[77] the privileges possessed by religious Orders through a participated communication with other Orders before the Code are still in force. Those privileges, therefore, the possession of which could be vindicated either by direct concession or by participated communication, can be used by Regulars today, unless there exists an express revocation in the canons of the Code.

The study of the documents reveals that all powers of Regulars, whether for their own subjects, or for the faithful, in the matter of dispensation from irregularities, were possessed only in virtue of special privileges. There were no provisions made for them by the common law. Through these papal privileges extensive faculties were possessed by the major superiors for the dispensation of their

[75] Cf. St. Alphonsus, *op. cit.*, lib. I, Append. II, n. 104; Génicot, *Theol. Mor.*, II, n. 632; Marc, *Inst. Theol. Mor.*, II, n. 2191, 5°; Lehmkuhl, *Theol. Mor.*, II, n. 835, 2°; Van Etten, *Compendium Privilegiorum Regularium*, p. 81.

[76] Cf. canon 4.

[77] 30 dec. 1937—*AAS*, XXX (1938), 73.

own subjects from irregularities. Among these privileges were the following: to dispense in all public and occult cases resulting in irregularities *ex delicto,* except in the cases of voluntary homicide and of the abortion of a living fetus. In casual homicide, and in the mutilation of one's bodily members, it was a probable opinion that they could absolve in occult cases. This faculty was given them that they might dispense their subjects to enable them to receive Sacred Orders; it could be used also to dispense their subjects in order that the latter might exercise licitly the already received Orders.

In irregularities *ex defectu,* superiors could dispense in all public and occult cases of irregularity resulting from illegitimacy. The power to dispense in irregularities resulting from bigamy was much disputed. The documents seem to treat only the one type of bigamy, namely, that which resulted *ex delicto;* consequently it is only slightly probable that Regular superiors could dispense from bigamy when it existed as an irregularity *ex defectu.*[78] While authors generally claimed that Regular superiors could dispense from all irregularities *ex defectu,* except the one mentioned above, there is no explicit mention of any such privilege regarding irregularities resulting from grave defects of body or mind. The natural law impedes the promotion to Sacred Orders of those who are incapable of duly exercising the ministry because of serious mental and physical defects. And the Holy See will certainly not grant a dispensation to anyone whose service in the sacred functions will create scandal or horror among the faithful. Therefore, despite the fact that the much disputed grant of Pope Martin V could be interpreted as implying the power to dispense in such cases, it must be held as certain that such a power was never intended; nor was it ever communicated in by any other Order.

The validity of such a dispensation, when granted for those who became irregular in consequence of serious mental and physical defects after they had received Sacred Orders, was preponderantly probable.[79] That power, however, connoted the possession of an extraordinary privilege, and could be used only by those who received the privilege directly. For minor defects of mind and body, where

[78] Cf. canon 984, 4°.

[79] Cf. Lehmkuhl, *op. cit.,* II, n. 834, 2°.

there is doubt whether the irregularity has been incurred, the Code makes ample provision for dispensation.[80]

Through papal faculties granted to certain religious Orders, which faculties then were shared in by all the other Orders, Regular confessors possessed powers equal to those of local Ordinaries for occult cases. These powers, however, were restricted for their use to the sacrament of penance. Confessors could dispense from irregularities in order to enable the penitent to be promoted to Sacred Orders, and also in order that the penitent might exercise the Orders already received.

The present legislation [81] does not abrogate any of the privileges possessed by Regulars at the time of the Code. Two things, however, are worthy of note in the present law: (1) today, for the first time, one finds express powers granted to major superiors of exempt clerical religious institutes by the common law.[82] Therefore, at the present time, Regular superiors can dispense by reason of the power granted in the law, as well as in virtue of their privileges. (2) The number of irregularities has been definitely reduced; there are only seven irregularities *ex defectu*,[83] and seven, *ex delicto*.[84] The confusion which existed before the Code concerning the number and the nature of irregularities has been entirely eliminated. Today, a number of impediments which were considered irregularities in previous legislation have been designated as simple impediments.[85]

In virtue of powers granted to them by the common law, major superiors of exempt clerical religious institutes possess the same powers as local Ordinaries. They can dispense personally, or through a delegate, all occult irregularities resulting *ex delicto* of their own subjects, except the ones arising from voluntary homicide and effectively perpetrated abortion, and such cases as have been brought before a judicial court.

At the present time, therefore, there can be no dispute con-

[80] Cf. canon 15.

[81] Cf. canons 983-991.

[82] Cf. canon 990, § 1.

[83] Cf. canon 984.

[84] Cf. canon 985.

[85] Cf. canon 987.

cerning the power of these superiors to dispense cases of casual homicide, for casual homicide, as such, is no longer regarded as an irregularity. Nor is there any doubt concerning the superiors' power of dispensing from the irregularity resulting from mutilation of bodily members. The Code grants superiors expressly the faculty to dispense in occult cases.[86] In all cases of voluntary homicide, whether public or occult, the Holy See reserves to itself the right to dispense. Therefore, unless a Regular superior can point to a privilege of the Roman Pontiff directly granting this power to dispense, he cannot presume to dispense from this irregularity.[87] In public cases where there remains a doubt concerning the existence of Apostolic privileges the superior will use his prudent judgment about recourse to the Holy See. He will know that the common law [88] allows him to dispense from all irregularities from which the Holy See is wont to dispense in urgent cases, when there is no time for recourse without grave detriment resulting to the subject.

In irregularities *ex defectu,* the present law expressly states that the *defectus natalium* is removed by the very act of solemn profession.[89] Therefore, dispensation from the irregularity is no longer necessary. In irregularities resulting from grave mental or physical defects, the Regular superior cannot dispense, and particularly not in cases wherein the Holy See is not wont to grant a dispensation. Generally, an application for the dispensation must be made to the Holy See in order to permit the subject to be promoted to Holy Orders. The competent authority is the Sacred Congregation for Religious.[90] In cases wherein the irregularity has been incurred after Sacred Orders have already been received, and it is certain that the subject has completely recovered, the superior may act on probable jurisdiction from his papal privileges. When he dispenses in such cases, he should always follow the precautions usually demanded by the papal rescripts in similar cases, namely, by requiring the assistance

[86] Cf. canons 990, § 1; 985, 5°.

[87] Cf. Bachofen (Charles Augustine), *Compendium Iuris Regularium,* p. 234.

[88] Canon 81.

[89] Cf. canon 984, 1°.

[90] Cf. Cappello, *De Sacra Ordinatione,* n. 514, 1°.

of a priest at the saying of Holy Mass, by insisting that the Mass be said in private, etc.

The Holy See rarely dispenses from the irregularity which results from bigamy *ex defectu.*[91] Since there is little probability that Regulars ever possessed any privilege in this regard, the dispensation must be sought in every case from the Holy See. Furthermore, the Superior cannot dispense from this irregularity even in an extraordinary and urgent necessity, when there is not sufficient time to have recourse to the Holy See, for, in virtue of canon 81, his powers are restricted to those cases in which the Holy See usually dispenses.

Almost all modern authors are agreed that Regular confessors can dispense the faithful from irregularities under the present legislation in the same manner and to the same extent as in pre-Code times.[92] Regular confessors at the present time therefore can dispense in virtue of their privileges from all irregularities in which the local Ordinary dispenses by reason of the common law. All the faithful, whether seculars or religious, who come to them in confession, can be dispensed from irregularities resulting *ex delicto occulto,* except the cases of voluntary homicide and effectively perpetuated abortion, and whatever cases have been brought before a judicial court.

Under the law of the Code [93] any simple confessor can dispense in all cases in which the bishop can dispense, provided there is an urgent necessity for dispensation, and the bishop cannot be approached in time to stave off the danger of grave damage or infamy to the penitent. This power is restricted, however, to dispensing a penitent *with a view to enabling him to exercise licitly the Orders which he has already received.* The Regular confessor, approved by the Ordinary, can dispense in such cases by reason of the common law.

But in virtue of a papal privilege, the Regular confessor's powers

[91] Cf. Grandclaude, *Ius Canonicum* (3 vols., Parisiis, 1883), III, 526; Cappello, *loc. cit.*

[92] Cf. Prümmer, *Theol. Mor.,* III, n. 613; Schäfer, *De Religiosis* (2. ed., Münster, 1931), n. 446; Cappello, *ibid.,* n. 514, 3°.

[93] Cf. canon 990, § 2.

are much more extensive than those of a simple diocesan confessor.[94] He can dispense in every case, without determining whether there is an urgent necessity. While his powers are for their use restricted to the sacramental forum, they are just as extensive as are those of the Ordinary. And he can dispense from the irregularities, not only to permit the penitent to exercise licitly any Sacred Orders he may already have received, *but also to enable the penitent, who has not yet received Sacred Orders, to be licitly promoted to their reception.*

[94] Schäfer states: "Confessarii (Regulares) ergo habent ex privilegio maiorem facultatem; possunt dispensare in irregularitatibus non solum ad exercitium Ordinum iam susceptorum, sed etiam ad ipsos Ordines suscipiendos."—*De Religiosis,* n. 446.

CONCLUSIONS

THE study of the Apostolic privileges of Regulars regarding absolution and dispensation warrants the following conclusions:

1. Professed members of a religious Order, when on a journey with the permission of their superior, may confess to a priest of their own Order who is suited for the hearing of confessions, even though not approved by the superior. In defect of such a confessor of the Order, any other priest, even though not approved by the local Ordinary, may be chosen, provided that he is likewise suited for such confessions, and the constitutions of the Order do not expressly forbid such a choice.

2. Regular confessors, while hearing confessions within the diocese for which they have been approved, may validly absolve the faithful from censures reserved to the Ordinary by the common law. This faculty is restricted to absolution in the internal sacramental forum.

3. Should the local Ordinary, however, reserve to himself *ratione peccati* a sin whose attached censure is already reserved by the common law to the Ordinary, Regular confessors may not absolve from either sin or censure. They can absolve from both if the reservation of the sin by the local Ordinary is made *ratione censurae*.

4. Regulars, including novices, do not incur reservations imposed by the local Ordinary, except in cases explicitly provided in the law. They can, therefore, be absolved by any diocesan confessor from a sin reserved in the diocese *ratione censurae*. It is probable that the faithful who are mentioned in canon 514, § 1, can be absolved from the same cases by a diocesan confessor, provided that the sin was committed within the religious house.

5. Regular confessors, approved by their superiors, can absolve all the faithful who are mentioned in canon 514, § 1, from sins and censures reserved by the local Ordinary, except the ones which are reserved *ab homine*, even though these faithful incurred the reservations before they assumed the status which now brings them within the classification of the faithful mentioned in that canon.

6. Regular confessors, approved for the hearing of confessions by the local Ordinary, can dispense from all private non-reserved vows of the faithful, both within and outside confession, provided that the acquired rights of interested parties are not injured thereby. This faculty extends also to vows which are confirmed by oath.

7. Major superiors of religious Orders can dispense their own subjects from all irregularities *ex delicto,* whether public or occult, except the cases resulting from voluntary homicide and effectively perpetrated abortion. This faculty may be exercised both to make possible the reception of Holy Orders, and also to make possible the lawful exercise of Orders already received.

8. Regular confessors, approved by the local Ordinary for the hearing of confessions, can dispense their penitents from irregularities *ex delicto occulto,* except the cases resulting from voluntary homicide and effectively perpetrated abortion, and whatever cases have been brought before a judicial court. The use of this faculty is not restricted to the more urgent cases; it may be exercised both to permit the penitent to receive Holy Orders and also to allow the penitent to exercise licitly the Orders already received.

BIBLIOGRAPHY

Sources

Acta Apostolicae Sedis, Romae, 1909—

Acta Sanctae Sedis, 41 vols., Romae, 1865-1908.

Augustinus a Virgine Maria, *Compendium Privilegiorum Omnium Religionum,* Lugduni, 1661.

Bullarium Franciscanum, ed. Sbaralea, 4 vols., Romae, 1759-1768.

Bullarium Ordinis Eremitarum S. Augustini, ed. L. Empoli, Romae, 1628.

Bullarium Ordinis Praedicatorum, ed. Th. Ripoll, 8 vols., Romae, 1729.

Bullarum Diplomatum et Privilegiorum Sanctorum Pontificum Taurinensis editio, 25 vols., Augustae Taurinorum, 1857-1872.

Canones et Decreta Sacrosancti Oecumenici Concilii Tridentini, English translation by Schroeder, St. Louis: Herder, 1941.

Codex Iuris Canonici Pii X Pontificis Maximi iussu digestus Benedicti Papae XV auctoritate promulgatus, Romae: Typis Polyglottis Vaticanis, 1917.

Codicis Iuris Canonici Fontes cura Emi. Petri Card. Gasparri editi, 9 vols., Romae (postea Civitate Vaticana): Typis Polyglottis Vaticanis, 1923-1939. Vols. VII-VIII-IX, ed. cura et studio Emi. Iustiniani Card. Serédi.

Collectanea in Usum Secretariae Sacrae Congregationis Episcoporum et Regularium, ed. Bizzarri, Romae, 1885.

Corpus Iuris Canonici, ed. Lipsiensis secunda post A. Richteri curas instruxit A. Friedberg, 2 vols., Lipsiae, 1879-1881.

Denifle, H., *Chartularium Universitatis Parisiensis,* 5 vols., 1889-1907.

Denzinger-Bannwart-Umberg, *Enchiridion Symbolorum, Definitionum, et Declarationum de Rebus Fidei et Morum,* 22.-23. ed., Friburgi-Brisgoviae: Herder, 1937.

Harduinus, J., *Acta Conciliorum et Epistolae Decretales ac Constitutiones Summorum Pontificum,* 12 vols., Parisiis, 1715.

Jaffé, P., *Regesta Pontificum Romanorum ab condita Ecclesiae ad annum post Christum natum MCXCVIII,* 2. ed., 2 vols., Lipsiae, 1885-1888.

Mansi, J., *Sacrorum Conciliorum Nova et Amplissima Collectio,* 53 vols. in 60, Parisiis, 1901-1927.

Mollat, *Jean XXII: Lettres Communes,* 14 vols., Paris, 1904-1935.

Pallottini, S., *Collectio Omnium Conclusionum et Resolutionum quae in causis propositis apud S. Congr. Cardinalium S. Concilii Tridentini Interpretum prodierunt ab anno 1564 ad annum 1860,* 18 vols., Romae, 1868-1895.

Potthast, A., *Regesta Pontificum Romanorum inde ab anno post Christum natum MCXCVIII ad annum MCCCIV,* 2 vols., Berolini, 1874-1875.

AUTHORS

Acta Sanctorum, ed. Bollandus et Henschenius.

Alphonsus Liguori, St., *Theologia Moralis,* ed. Mansi, 3 vols., Bassani, 1833.

Appeltern, V., *Compendium Praelectionum Iuris Regularis,* adm. R. P. Piati Montani ad Recentissimas Leges Ecclesiasticas Redactum, 2. ed., Parisiis: Casterman, 1913.

Aquinas, Thomas, St., *Summa Theologica,* ed. Leonina, 6 vols., Romae, 1894.

———, *Opuscula Selecta,* 4 vols., Parisiis, 1881.

———, *Commentum in Quattuor Libros Sententiarum,* 2 vols. in 3, Parmae, 1858.

Bachofen (Charles Augustine), *Compendium Iuris Regularium,* New York: Benziger, 1903.

Beda, Venerabilis, *Historia Ecclesiastica Gentis Anglorum,* ed. Plummer, 2 vols., London, 1896.

Benedict XIV, *De Synodo Dioecesana,* ed. Azevedo, Mechliniae, 1823.

Blat, A., *Commentarium Textus Codicis Iuris Canonici,* 6 vols., Romae, 1919-1927.

Bollandistae, *Examen Historicum et Canonicum Libri M. Verhoeven,* Bruxellis, 1847.

Bonacina, M., *Theologia Moralis,* 3 vols., Venetiis, 1687.

Bonaventure, St., *Opera Omnia,* 7 vols., Ad Claras Aquas, 1895.

Bouix, D., *Tractatus de Iure Regularium,* 2 vols., Parisiis, 1883.

Bucceroni, J., *Commentaria in Constitutione "Apostolicae Sedis,"* Romae, 1898.

Busenbaum, *Medulla Theologiae Moralis,* 2 vols., Romae, 1844.

Cappello, *De Poenitentia,* Romae: Marietti, 1938.

———, *De Sacra Ordinatione,* Romae: Marietti, 1935.

Castrapalao, F., *Theologia Moralis,* 6 vols. in 3, Lugduni, 1682.

Chelodi, J., *Ius Poenale,* 3. ed., Tridenti, 1933.

Cicognani, A., *Canon Law,* Authorized English Version by J. O'Hara and F. Brennan, Philadelphia: Dolphin Press, 1935.

Concina, D., *Theologia Christiana,* 10 vols., Neapoli, 1773.

Coronata, Matthaeus, Conte A, *Institutiones Iuris Canonici,* 5 vols.: Vols. I-II, 2. ed., 1939; III-V, 1932-1935, Taurini: Marietti.

D'Annibale, J., *Summula Theologiae Moralis,* 4. ed., 3 vols., Romae, 1896-1897.

Davis, H., *Moral and Pastoral Theology,* 4 vols., New York: Sheed & Ward, 1935.

Fagnanus, P., *Commentaria in Quinque Libros Decretalium,* 4 vols., Venetiis, 1697.

Fanfani, L., *De Iure Regularium,* Taurini: Marietti, 1925.

Ferraris, L., *Bibliotheca Canonica, Iuridica, Moralis, Theologica, necnon Ascetica, Polemica, Rubricistica, Historica,* 9 vols., Romae, 1885-1899.

Génicot, E., *Institutiones Theologiae Moralis,* 5. ed., 2 vols., Lovanii, 1905.

Génicot, E.-Salsmans, I., *Theologia Moralis,* 9. ed., 2 vols., Bruxellis, 1921.

Gennari, C., *Consultazioni Morali, Canoniche, Liturgiche,* 2 vols., Romae, 1902-1904.

Gerster, T., *Ius Religiosorum,* Taurini: Marietti, 1935.

Grandclaude, E., *Ius Canonicum,* 3 vols., Parisiis, 1883.

Gury-Ballerini-Palmieri, *Compendium Theologiae Moralis,* 15. ed., 2 vols., Romae, 1907.

Haddon, A.-Stubbs, W., *Councils and Ecclesiastical Documents Relating to Great Britain and Ireland,* 3 vols. in 4, Oxford, 1869-1873.

Haine, A., *Theologia Moralis,* 4. ed., 4 vols. in 2, Lovanii, 1900.

Knowles, D., *Monastic Orders in England,* Cambridge: University Press, 1940.

Lega, M., *Praelectiones de Iudiciis Ecclesiasticis,* 4 vols., Romae, 1896-1901.

Lehmkuhl, A., *Theologia Moralis,* 12. ed., 2 vols., Friburgi-Brisgoviae, 1914.

Lugo, J., *Opera Omnia,* 7 vols. in 4, Venetiis, 1718.

Lupus, Christianus, *Synodorum Generalium ac Provincialium Decreta et Canones,* 12 vols. in 6, Venetiis, 1723-1729.

———, *Exhibitio Sacrorum Canonum circa Ius Regularium Quoad Praedicationem Divini Verbi, Opuscula Posthuma,* Venetiis, 1729.

Marc, C., *Institutiones Morales,* 13. ed., 2 vols., Romae, 1906.

Marc-Gesterman, *Institutiones Moralis,* 2 vols., Parisiis, 1927.

Merkelbach, B., *Summa Theologiae Moralis,* 3. ed., 3 vols., Parisiis, 1936.

Miaskiewicz, F., *Supplied Jurisdiction According to Canon 209,* Catholic University of America Canon Law Studies, n. 122, Washington, D. C.: Catholic University of America Press, 1940.

Migne, J., *Patrologiae Cursus Completus, Series Latina,* 221 vols., Parisiis, 1858-1864.

Moccheggiani, P., *Iurisprudentia Ecclesiastica,* 3 vols., Ad Claras Aquas, 1904-1905.

Montalembert, C., *The Monks of the West,* 2 vols., Boston, 1872.

Moriarty, F., *Extraordinary Absolution from Censures,* Catholic University of America Canon Law Studies, n. 113, Washington, D. C.: Catholic University of America Press, 1938.

Noldin, H.-Schmitt, A., *Theologia Moralis,* 24. ed., 3 vols., Oeniponte, 1936.

Noldin-Schönegger, A., *De Censuris,* 31. ed., Oeniponte, 1937.

O'Brien, J., *Exemption of Religious in Church Law,* Milwaukee: Bruce Publishing Co., 1943.

Oesterle, G., *Praelectiones Iuris Canonici,* Vol. I, Romae: apud Collegium S. Anselmi, 1931.

Pallavicini, P., *Vera Concilii Tridentini Historia,* 3 vols., Antwerp, 1670.

Passerinus, P., *De Statibus Hominum,* 3 vols., Lucae, 1732.

Pellizarius, F., *Manuale Regularium,* Lugduni, 1665.

Pennacchi, J., *Commentaria in Constitutione "Apostolicae Sedis,"* 2 vols., Romae, 1883.

Petra, V., *Commentaria ad Constitutiones Apostolicas,* 5 vols., Venetiis, 1729.

Piatus Montensis, *Praelectiones Iuris Regularis,* 3. ed., 2 vols., Tornaci: Casterman, 1906.

Pignatelli, J., *Consultationes Canonicae,* 10 vols., Coloniae, 1717-1719.

Prümmer, D., *Manuale Theologiae Moralis,* 2.-3. ed., 3 vols., Friburgi-Brisgoviae, 1923.

———, *Manuale Iuris Canonici* in usum clericorum praesertim eorum qui ad Instituta Religiosa pertinent, 4.-5. ed., Friburgi-Brisgoviae, 1922.

Reiffenstuel, A., *Ius Canonicum Universum,* 7 vols., Parisiis, 1864-1870.

Reilly, E., *The General Norms of Dispensation,* Catholic University of America Canon Law Studies, n. 119, Washington, D. C.: Catholic University of America Press, 1939.

Reilly, T., *Visitation of Religious,* Catholic University of America Canon Law Studies, n. 112, Washington, D. C.: Catholic University of America Press, 1938.

Rodriquez, E., *Quaestiones Regulares,* Lugduni, 1634.

Roelker, E., *Principles of Privileges According to the Code of Canon Law,* Catholic University of America Canon Law Studies, n. 35, Washington, D. C.: Catholic University of America Press, 1926.

Salmanticenses, *Cursus Theologiae Completus,* 20 vols., Bruxellis, 1883.

———, *Cursus Theologiae Moralis,* 3 vols., Venetiis, 1714.

Schäfer, T., *De Religiosis,* Münster, 1931.

Schmalzgrueber, F., *Ius Ecclesiasticum Universum,* 5 vols. in 12, Romae, 1843-1845.

Simeone, G., *Lezioni di Diritto Canonico,* 3. ed., 2 vols., Napoli, 1905.

Suarez, F., *Opera Omnia,* 26 vols., Parisiis, 1856-1866.

Toso, A., *Commentaria Minora* ad Codicem Iuris Canonici, Vol. I, Romae, 1921.

Van Espen, Z., *Ius Ecclesiasticum Universum,* 5 vols., Lovanii, 1753.

Van Hove, A., *De Privilegiis,* Mechlin: H. Dessain, 1939.

Van Etten, G., *Compendium Privilegiorum Regularium,* Romae, 1900.

Vasto, A, B., *De Communicatione Privilegiorum praesertim inter Religiones,* Aquilae, 1936.

Vermeersch, A., *De Religiosis Institutis et Personis: Supplementa et Monumenta,* 2 vols., Romae, 1909.

———, *Theologia Moralis,* 3 vols., Romae, 1923.

———, *Epitome Iuris Canonici,* 3 vols., Mechlin-Romae, 1927.

Watkins, O., *A History of Penance,* 2 vols., London: Longmans, Green & Co., 1920.

Wernz, F., *Ius Decretalium,* 6 vols., Romae, 1905-1913.

Wernz, F.-Vidal, P., *Ius Canonicum,* 7 vols. in 8, Romae, 1923-1938.

Articles

Boudinhon, "La Confession des Religieux,"—*Le Canoniste Contemporain,* XXXVII (1913), 698-703.

Ellis, A., "De Communicatione Privilegiorum inter Religiones,"—*Periodica*, XXVII (1938), 157-162.

Fallon, "Selection of Confessor by Exempt Religious *in itinere*,"—*IER*, LVI (1940), 577-580.

Hilling, H., "Das Dekret, *In Audientia*, über die Absolution der Ordenleute,"—*AKKR*, XCIV (1914), 630-632.

Hüfner, A., "Das Rechtsinstitut der klösterlichen Exemtion,"—*AKKR*, LXXXVI (1906), 629-651.

Larraona, A., "Pontificia Commissio ad Codicem authentice Interpretandum,"—*CpR*, XIX (1938), 247-251.

Oesterle, G., "Clemens VIII, relatio ad librum II, C. I. C., tit. X, c. II, de confessariis et cappellanis,"—*CpR*, XI (1930), 358-363.

———, "Die Dispensgewalt der Regularen bei einfachen Gelübden der Weltleute,"—*Theologie und Glaube*, III (1911), 389-402.

Schiewietz, "Pachomianische Klöster im vierten Jahrhunderte," — *AKKR*, LXXXII (1902), 454.

Tatjer, H., "De Communicatione Privilegiorum inter Religiones,"—*Apollinaris*, V (1932), 458-486.

Van Acken, "Abusus Libertatis Religiosis pro Confessione Concessae,"—*CpR*, VII (1926), 255-260.

Van Hove, A., "De Privilegiis et Indultis ad can. 4,"—*Jus Pont.*, IX (1929), 290-295.

Vitali, I., "Adhuc de Mixtis Reservationibus,"—*AER*, LXXXV (1931), 73-83.

———, "Utrum Locorum Ordinarii Valeant Suspendere Privilegium Regularium Absolvendi a Casibus Papalibus Ordinariis Reservatis per Accidens et Via Exceptionis,"—*AER*, LXXXVI (1932), 292-296.

———, "De Reservationibus Pontificiis a Iure Reservatis Ordinario deque Regularium Privilegio ab Iisdem Absolvendi,"—*CpR*, XIV (1933), 287-294; 363-375; 436-447.

———, "Finis Controversiae circa Casus a Iure Reservatos,"—*CpR*, XVI (1935), 164-175.

Vermeersch, A., "De Facultate Confessariorum Regularium Dispensandi in Saecularium Votis,"—*Periodica*, V (1913), 56-59.

Anonymous, "Cases Reserved by the Code and by the Ordinary,"—*AER*, LXXXIV (1931), 190-192.

———, "Consultationes,"—*Jus Pont.*, XIII (1933), 302.

ABBREVIATIONS

AAS—*Acta Apostolicae Sedis.*
AER—*American Ecclesiastical Review.*
AKKR—*Archiv für Katholisches Kirchenrecht.*
ASS—*Acta Sanctae Sedis.*
Bull. Franc.—*Bullarium Franciscanum.*
Bull. O. E. S. A.—*Bullarium Ordinis Eremitarum S. Augustini.*
Bull. Praed.—*Bullarium Praedicatorum.*
Bull. Rom.—*Bullarum Diplomatum . . . Taurinensis editio.*
Comp. Privileg.—Augustinus a Virgine Maria, *Compendium Privilegiorum* . . .
CpR—*Commentarium pro Religiosis.*
de ref.—*de reformatione.*
Fontes—*Codicis Iuris Canonici Fontes . . . a Petro Card. Gasparri editi.*
IER—*Irish Ecclesiastical Record.*
JE—Jaffé, *Regesta Pontificum Romanorum* (edited by Ewald).
JK—Jaffé, *op. cit.* (edited by Kaltenbrunner).
JL—Jaffé, *op. cit.* (edited by Loewenfeld).
Jus Pont.—*Jus Pontificium.*
MPL—Migne, *Patrologia, Series Latina.*
PCI—*Pontificia Commissio Interpretationis.*
Periodica—*Periodica de Re Canonica, Morali,* etc.
R. J.—*Regula Iuris.*
S. C. C.—*Sacra Congregatio Concilii.*
S. C. Ep. et Reg.—*Sacra Congregatio Episcoporum et Regularium.*
S. C. S. Off.—*Sacra Congregatio Sancti Officii.*

ALPHABETICAL INDEX

INDEX OF PONTIFICAL DOCUMENTS

BIOGRAPHICAL NOTE

RALPH VINCENT SHUHLER was born at Salina, Kansas, January 27, 1913. After receiving his primary education in the public schools at East Greenville, Pennsylvania, he entered the Augustinian Preparatory Seminary at Staten Island, New York, in September, 1931. The following year he was received into the Novitiate of the Order of Hermits of St. Augustine and made temporary vows of Religion on September 11, 1933, at New Hamburg, New York. Completing his philosophical studies at Villanova College, Villanova, Pennsylvania, with the degree of Bachelor of Arts, he entered the theological studium of the Order at Augustinian College, Washington, D. C. He was ordained to the Holy Priesthood at the Shrine of the Immaculate Conception, Washington, D. C., on May 30, 1939. The same year he pursued his theological studies at the Catholic University of America. In September, 1940, he entered the Canon Law School of the University, from which he received the Baccalaureate in Canon Law in June, 1941, and the Licentiate in May, 1942.

CANON LAW STUDIES *

1. Freriks, Rev. Celestine A., C.PP.S., J.C.D., Religious Congregations in Their External Relations, 121 pp., 1916.
2. Galliher, Rev. Daniel M., O.P., J.C.D., Canonical Elections, 117 pp., 1917.
3. Borkowski, Rev. Aurelius L., O.F.M., J.C.D., De Confraternitatibus Ecclesiasticis, 136 pp., 1918.
4. Castillo, Rev. Cayo, J.C.D., Disertacion Historico-Canonica sobre la Potestad del Cabildo en Sede Vacante o Impedida del Vicario Capitular, 99 pp., 1919 (1918).
5. Kubelbeck, Rev. William J., S.T.B., J.C.D., The Sacred Penitentiaria and Its Relation to Faculties of Ordinaries and Priests, 129 pp., 1918.
6. Petrovits, Rev. Joseph, J.C., S.T.D., J.C.D., The New Church Law on Matrimony, X-461 pp., 1919.
7. Hickey, Rev. John J., S.T.B., J.C.D., Irregularities and Simple Impediments in the New Code of Canon Law, 100 pp., 1920.
8. Klekotka, Rev. Peter J., S.T.B., J.C.D., Diocesan Consultors, 179 pp., 1920.
9. Wanenmacher, Rev. Francis, J.C.D., The Evidence in Ecclesiastical Procedure Affecting the Marriage Bond, 1920 (Printed 1935).
10. Golden, Rev. Henry Francis, J.C.D., Parochial Benefices in the New Code, IV-119 pp., 1921 (Printed 1925).
11. Koudelka, Rev. Charles J., J.C.D., Pastors, Their Rights and Duties According to the New Code of Canon Law, 211 pp., 1921.
12. Melo, Rev. Antonius, O.F.M., J.C.D., De Exemptione Regularium, X-188 pp., 1921.
13. Schaaf, Rev. Valentine Theodore, O.F.M., S.T.B., J.C.D., The Cloister, X-180 pp., 1921.
14. Burke, Rev. Thomas Joseph, S.T.D., J.C.D., Competence in Ecclesiastical Tribunals, IV-117 pp., 1922.
15. Leech, Rev. George Leo, J.C.D., A Comparative Study of the Constitution "Apostolicae Sedis" and the "Codex Juris Canonici," 179 pp., 1922.
16. Motry, Rev. Hubert Louis, S.T.D., J.C.D., Diocesan Faculties According to the Code of Canon Law, II-167 pp., 1922.
17. Murphy, Rev. George Lawrence, J.C.D., Delinquencies and Penalties in the Administration and the Reception of the Sacraments, IV-121 pp., 1923.
18. O'Reilly, Rev. John Anthony, S.T.B., J.C.D., Ecclesiastical Sepulture in the New Code of Canon Law, II-129 pp., 1923.

* Below n. 100 only the following numbers are still available: Nn. 3, 4, 9, 25, 34, 57 and 75. Beginning with n. 100 only the following are unavailable: Nn. 100, 101, 102, 104, 105, 107, 108, 109, 111 and 113.

19. Michalicka, Rev. Wenceslas Cyrill, O.S.B., J.C.D., Judicial Procedure in Dismissal of Clerical Exempt Religious, 107 pp., 1923.
20. Dargin, Rev. Edward Vincent, S.T.B., J.C.D., Reserved Cases According to the Code of Canon Law, IV-103 pp., 1924.
21. Godfrey, Rev. John A., S.T.B., J.C.D., The Right of Patronage According to the Code of Canon Law, 153 pp., 1924.
22. Hagedorn, Rev. Francis Edward, J.C.D., General Legislation on Indulgences, II-154 pp., 1924.
23. King, Rev. James Ignatius, J.C.D., The Administration of the Sacraments to Dying Non-Catholics, V-141 pp., 1924.
24. Winslow, Rev. Francis Joseph, O.F.M., J.C.D., Vicars and Prefects Apostolic, IV-149 pp., 1924.
25. Correa, Rev. Jose Servelion, S.T.L., J.C.D., La Potestad Legislativa de la Iglesia Catolica, IV-127 pp., 1925.
26. Dugan, Rev. Henry Francis, A.M., J.C.D., The Judiciary Department of the Diocesan Curia, 87 pp., 1925.
27. Keller, Rev. Charles Frederick, S.T.B., J.C.D., Mass Stipends, 167 pp., 1925.
28. Paschang, Rev. John Linus, J.C.D., The Sacramentals According to the Code of Canon Law, 129 pp., 1925.
29. Piontek, Rev. Cyrillus, O.F.M., S.T.B., J.C.D., De Indulto Exclaustrationis necnon Saecularizationis, XIII-289 pp., 1925.
30. Kearney, Rev. Richard Joseph, S.T.B., J.C.D., Sponsors at Baptism According to the Code of Canon Law, IV-127 pp., 1925.
31. Bartlett, Rev. Chester Joseph, A.M., LL.B., J.C.D., The Tenure of Parochial Property in the United States of America, V-108 pp., 1926.
32. Kilker, Rev. Adrian Jerome, J.C.D., Extreme Unction, V-425 pp., 1926.
33. McCormick, Rev. Robert Emmett, J.C.D., Confessors of Religious, VIII-266 pp., 1926.
34. Miller, Rev. Newton Thomas, J.C.D., Founded Masses According to the Code of Canon Law, VII-93 pp., 1926.
35. Roelker, Rev. Edward G., S.T.D., J.C.D., Principles of Privilege According to the Code of Canon Law, XI-166 pp., 1926.
36. Bakalarczyk, Rev. Richardus, M.I.C., J.U.D., De Novitiatu, VIII-208 pp., 1927.
37. Pizzuti, Rev. Lawrence, O.F.M., J.U.L., De Parochis Religiosis, 1927. (Not Printed.)
38. Bliley, Rev. Nicholas Martin, O.S.B., J.C.D., Altars According to the Code of Canon Law, XIX-132 pp., 1927.
39. Brown, Mr. Brendan Francis, A.B., LL.M., J.U.D., The Canonical Juristic Personality with Special Reference to its Status in the United States of America, V-212 pp., 1927.
40. Cavanaugh, Rev. William Thomas, C.P., J.U.D., The Reservation of the Blessed Sacrament, VIII-101 pp., 1927.

41. Doheny, Rev. William J., C.S.C., A.B., J.U.D., Church Property: Modes of Acquisition, X-118 pp., 1927.
42. Feldhaus, Rev. Aloysius H., C.PP.S., J.C.D., Oratories, IX-141 pp., 1927.
43. Kelly, Rev. James Patrick, A.B., J.C.D., The Jurisdiction of the Simple Confessor, X-208 pp., 1927.
44. Neuberger, Rev. Nicholas J., J.C.D., Canon 6 or the Relation of the Codex Juris Canonici to the Preceding Legislation, V-95 pp., 1927.
45. O'Keefe, Rev. Gerald Michael, J.C.D., Matrimonial Dispensations, Powers of Bishops, Priests, and Confessors, VIII-232 pp., 1927.
46. Quigley, Rev. Joseph A. M., A.B., J.C.D., Condemned Societies, 139 pp., 1927.
47. Zaplotnik, Rev. Johannes Leo, J.C.D., De Vicariis Foraneis, X-142 pp., 1927.
48. Duskie, Rev. John Aloysius, A.B., J.C.D., The Canonical Status of the Orientals in the United States, VIII-196 pp., 1928.
49. Hyland, Rev. Francis Edward, J.C.D., Excommunciation, Its Nature, Historical Development and Effects, VIII-181 pp., 1928.
50. Reinmann, Rev. Gerald Joseph, O.M.C., J.C.D., The Third Order Secular of Saint Francis, 201 pp., 1928.
51. Schenk, Rev. Francis J., J.C.D., The Matrimonial Impediments of Mixed Religion and Disparity of Cult, XVI-318 pp., 1929.
52. Coady, Rev. John Joseph, S.T.D., J.U.D., A.M., The Appointment of Pastors, VIII-150 pp., 1929.
53. Kay, Rev. Thomas Henry, J.C.D., Competence in Matrimonial Procedure, VIII-164 pp., 1929.
54. Turner, Rev. Sidney Joseph, C.P., J.U.D., The Vow of Poverty, XLIX-217 pp., 1929.
55. Kearney, Rev. Raymond A., A.B., S.T.D., J.C.D., The Principles of Delegation, VII-149 pp., 1929.
56. Conran, Rev. Edward James, A.B., J.C.D., The Interdict, V-163 pp., 1930.
57. O'Neill, Rev. William H., J.C.D., Papal Rescripts of Favor, VII-218 pp., 1930.
58. Bastnagel, Rev. Clement Vincent, J.U.D., The Appointment of Parochial Adjutants and Assistants, XV-257 pp., 1930.
59. Ferry, Rev. William A., A.B., J.C.D., Stole Fees, V-136 pp., 1930.
60. Costello, Rev. John Michael, A.B., J.C.D., Domicile and Quasi-Domicile, VII-201 pp., 1930.
61. Kremer, Rev. Michael Nicholas, A.B., S.T.B., J.C.D., Church Support in the United States, VI-136 pp., 1930.
62. Angulo, Rev. Luis, C.M., J.C.D., Legislation de la Iglesia sobre la intencion en la application de la Santa Misa, VII-104 pp., 1931.
63. Frey, Rev. Wolfgang Norbert, O.S.B., A.B., J.C.D., The Act of Religious Profession, VIII-174 pp., 1931.

64. Roberts, Rev. James Brendan, A.B., J.C.D., The Banns of Marriage, XIV-140 pp., 1931.

65. Ryder, Rev. Raymond Aloysius, A.B., J.C.D., Simony, IX-151 pp., 1931.

66. Campagna, Rev. Angelo, Ph.D., J.U.D., Il Vicario Generale del Vescovo, VII-205 pp., 1931.

67. Cox, Rev. Joseph Godfrey, A.B., J.C.D., The Administration of Seminaries, VI-124 pp., 1931.

68. Gregory, Rev. Donald J., J.U.D., The Pauline Privilege, XV-165 pp., 1931.

69. Donohue, Rev. John F., J.C.D., The Impediment of Crime, VII-110 pp., 1931.

70. Dooley, Rev. Eugene A., O.M.I., J.C.D., Church Law on Sacred Relics, IX-143 pp., 1931.

71. Orth, Rev. Clement Raymond, O.M.C., J.C.D., The Approbation of Religious Institutes, 171 pp., 1931.

72. Pernicone, Rev. Joseph M., A.B., J.C.D., The Ecclesiastical Prohibition of Books, XII-267 pp., 1932.

73. Clinton, Rev. Connell, A.B., J.C.D., The Paschal Precept, IX-108 pp., 1932.

74. Donnelly, Rev. Francis B., A.M., S.T.L., J.C.D., The Diocesan Synod, VIII-125 pp., 1932.

75. Torrente, Rev. Camilo, C.M.F., J.C.D., Las Processiones Sagradas, V-145 pp., 1932.

76. Murphy, Rev. Edwin J., C.PP.S., J.C.D., Suspension Ex Informata Conscientia, XI-122 pp., 1932.

77. MacKenzie, Rev. Eric F., A.M., S.T.L., J.C.D., The Delict of Heresy in its Commission, Penalization, Absolution, VII-124 pp., 1932.

78. Lyons, Rev. Avitus E., S.T.B., J.C.D., The Collegiate Tribunal of First Instance, XI-147 pp., 1932.

79. Connolly, Rev. Thomas A., J.C.D., Appeals, XI-195 pp., 1932.

80. Sangmeister, Rev. Joseph V., A.B., J.C.D., Force and Fear as Precluding Matrimonial Consent, V-211 pp., 1932.

81. Jaeger, Rev. Leo A., A.B., J.C.D., The Administration of Vacant and Quasi-Vacant Episcopal Sees in the United States, IX-229 pp., 1932.

82. Rimlinger, Rev. Herbert T., J.C.D., Error Invalidating Matrimonial Consent, VII-79 pp., 1932.

83. Barrett, Rev. John D. M., S.S., J.C.D., A Comparative Study of the Third Plenary Council of Baltimore and the Code, IX-221 pp., 1932.

84. Carberry, Rev. John J., Ph.D., S.T.D., J.C.D., The Juridical Form of Marriage, X-177 pp., 1934.

85. Dolan, Rev. John L., A.B., J.C.D., The Defensor Vinculi, XII-157 pp., 1934.

86. Hannan, Rev. Jerome D., A.M., S.T.D., LL.B., J.C.D., The Canon Law of Wills, IX-517 pp., 1934.

87. LEMIEUX, REV. DELISE A., A.M., J.C.D., The Sentence in Ecclesiastical Procedure, IX-131 pp., 1934.
88. O'ROURKE, REV. JAMES J., A.B., J.C.D., Parish Registers, VII-109 pp., 1934.
89. TIMLIN, REV. BARTHOLOMEW, O.F.M., A.M., J.C.D., Conditional Matrimonial Consent, X-381 pp., 1934.
90. WAHL, REV. FRANCIS X., A.B., J.C.D., The Matrimonial Impediments of Consanguinity and Affinity, VI-125 pp., 1934.
91. WHITE, REV. ROBERT J., A.B., LL.B., S.T.B., J.C.D., Canonical Ante-Nuptial Promises and the Civil Law, VI-152 pp., 1934.
92. HERRERA, REV. ANTONIO PARRA, O.C.D., J.C.D., Legislacion Ecclesiastica sobra el Ayuno y la Abstinencia, XI-191 pp., 1935.
93. KENNEDY, REV. EDWIN J., J.C.D., The Special Matrimonial Process in Cases of Evident Nullity, X-165 pp., 1935.
94. MANNING, REV. JOHN J., A.B., J.C.D., Presumption of Law in Matrimonial Procedure, XI-111 pp., 1935.
95. MOEDER, REV. JOHN M., J.C.D., The Proper Bishop for Ordination and Dimissorial Letters, VII-135 pp., 1935.
96. O'MARA, REV. WILLIAM A., A.B., J.C.D., Canonical Causes for Matrimonial Dispensations, IX-155 pp., 1935.
97. REILLY, REV. PETER, J.C.D., Residence of Pastors, IX-81 pp., 1935.
98. SMITH, REV. MARINER T., O.P., S.T.Lr., J.C.D., The Penal Law for Religious, VII-169 pp., 1935.
99. WHALEN, REV. DONALD W., A.M., J.C.D., The Value of Testimonial Evidence in Matrimonial Procedure, XIII-297 pp., 1935.
100. CLEARY, REV. JOSEPH F., J.C.D., Canonical Limitations on the Alienation of Church Property, VIII-141 pp., 1936.
101. GLYNN, REV. JOHN C., J.C.D., The Promoter of Justice, XX-337 pp., 1936.
102. BRENNAN, REV. JAMES H., S.S., M.A., S.T.B., J.C.D., The Simple Convalidation of Marriage, VI-135 pp., 1937.
103. BRUNINI, REV. JOSEPH BERNARD, J.C.D., The Clerical Obligations of Canons 139 and 142, X-121 pp., 1937.
104. CONNOR, REV. MAURICE, A.B., J.C.D., The Administrative Removal of Pastors, VIII-159 pp., 1937.
105. GUILFOYLE, REV. MERLIN JOSEPH, J.C.D., Custom, XI-144 pp., 1937.
106. HUGHES, REV. JAMES AUSTIN, A.B., A.M., J.C.D., Witnesses in Criminal Trials of Clerics, IX-140 pp., 1937.
107. JANSEN, REV. RAYMOND J., A.B., S.T.L., J.C.D., Canonical Provisions for Catechetical Instruction, VII-153 pp., 1937.
108. KEALY, REV. JOHN JAMES, A.B., J.C.D., The Introductory Libellus in Church Court Procedure, XI-121 pp., 1937.
109. McMANUS, REV. JAMES EDWARD, C.SS.R., J.C.D., The Administration of Temporal Goods in Religious Institutes, XVI-196 pp., 1937.

110. MORIARTY, REV. EUGENE JAMES, J.C.D., Oaths in Ecclesiastical Courts, X-115 pp., 1937.

111. RAINER, REV. ELIGIUS GEORGE, C.SS.R., J.C.D., Suspension of Clerics, XVII-249 pp., 1937.

112. REILLY, REV. THOMAS F., C.SS.R., J.C.D., Visitation of Religious, VI-195 pp., 1938.

113. MORIARTY, REV. FRANCIS E., C.SS.R., J.C.D., The Extraordinary Absolution from Censures, XV-334 pp., 1938.

114. CONNOLLY, REV. NICHOLAS P., J.C.D., The Canonical Erection of Parishes, X-132 pp., 1938.

115. DONOVAN, REV. JAMES JOSEPH, J.C.D., The Pastor's Obligation in Prenuptial Investigation, XII-322 pp., 1938.

116. HARRIGAN, REV. ROBERT J., M.A., S.T.B., J.C.D., The Radical Sanation of Invalid Marriages, VIII-208 pp., 1938.

117. BOFFA, REV. CONRAD HUMBERT, J.C.D., Canonical Provisions for Catholic Schools, VII-211 pp., 1939.

118. PARSONS, REV. ANSCAR JOHN, O.M.Cap., J.C.D., Canonical Elections, XII-236 pp., 1939.

119. REILLY, REV. EDWARD MICHAEL, A.B., J.C.D., The General Norms of Dispensation, XII-156 pp., 1939.

120. RYAN, REV. GERALD ALOYSIUS, A.B., J.C.D., Principles of Episcopal Jurisdiction, XII-172 pp., 1939.

121. BURTON, REV. FRANCIS JAMES, C.S.C., A.B., J.C.D., A Commentary on Canon 1125, X-222 pp., 1940.

122. MIASKIEWICZ, REV. FRANCIS SIGISMUND, J.C.D., Supplied Jurisdiction According to Canon 209, XII-340 pp., 1940.

123. RICE, REV. PATRICK WILLIAM, A.B., J.C.D., Proof of Death in Prenuptial Investigation, VIII-156 pp., 1940.

124. ANGLIN, REV. THOMAS FRANCIS, M.S., J.C.D., The Eucharistic Fast, VIII-183 pp., 1941.

125. COLEMAN, REV. JOHN JEROME, J.C.D., The Minister of Confirmation, VI-153 pp., 1941.

126. DOWNS, REV. JOSEPH EMMANUEL, A.B., J.C.D., The Concept of Clerical Immunity, XI-163 pp., 1941.

127. ESSWEIN, REV. ANTHONY ALBERT, J.C.D., Extrajudicial Penal Powers of Ecclesiastical Superiors, X-144 pp., 1941.

128. FARRELL, REV. BENJAMIN FRANCIS, M.A., S.T.L., J.C.D., The Rights and Duties of the Local Ordinary Regarding Congregations of Women Religious of Pontifical Approval, V-195 pp., 1941.

129. FEENEY, REV. THOMAS JOHN, A.B., S.T.L., J.C.D., Restitutio in Integrum, VI-169 pp., 1941.

130. FINDLAY, REV. STEPHEN WILLIAM, O.S.B., A.B., J.C.D., Canonical Norms Governing the Deposition and Degradation of Clerics, XVII-279 pp., 1941.

131. GOODWINE, REV. JOHN, A.B., S.T.L., J.C.D., The Right of the Church to Acquire Property, VIII-119 pp., 1941.
132. HESTON, REV. EDWARD LOUIS, C.S.C., Ph.D., S.T.D., J.C.D., The Alienation of Church Property in the United States, XII-222 pp., 1941.
133. HOGAN, REV. JAMES JOHN, A.B., S.T.L., J.C.D., Judicial Advocates and Procurators, XIII-200 pp., 1941.
134. KEALY, REV. THOMAS M., A.B., Litt.B., J.C.D., Dowry of Women Religious, IX-152 pp., 1941.
135. KEENE, REV. MICHAEL JAMES, O.S.B., J.C.D., Religious Ordinaries and Canon 198, V-164 pp., 1942.
136. KERIN, REV. CHARLES A., S.S., M.A., S.T.B., J.C.D., The Privation of Christian Burial, XVI-279 pp., 1941.
137. LOUIS, REV. WILLIAM FRANCIS, M.A., J.C.D., Diocesan Archives, X-101 pp., 1941.
138. McDEVITT, REV. GILBERT JOSEPH, A.B., J.C.D., Legitimacy and Legitimation, X-247 pp., 1941.
139. McDONOUGH, REV. THOMAS JOSEPH, A.B., J.C.D., Apostolic Administrators, X-217 pp., 1941.
140. MEIER, REV. CARL ANTHONY, A.B., J.C.D., Penal Administration Procedure Against Negligent Pastors, XI-240 pp., 1941.
141. SCHMIDT, REV. JOHN ROGG, A.B., J.C.D., The Principles of Authentic Interpretation in Canon 17 of the Code of Canon Law, XII-331 pp., 1941.
142. SLAFKOSKY, REV. ANDREW LEONARD, A.B., J.C.D., The Canonical Episcopal Visitation of the Diocese, X-197 pp., 1941.
143. SWOBODA, REV. INNOCENT ROBERT, O.F.M., J.C.D., Ignorance in Relation to the Imputability of Delicts, IX-271 pp., 1941.
144. DUBÉ, REV. ARTHUR JOSEPH, A.B., J.C.D., The General Principles for the Reckoning of Time in Canon Law, VIII-299 pp., 1941.
145. McBRIDE, REV. JAMES T., A.B., J.C.D., Incardination and Excardination of Seculars, XX-585 pp., 1941.
146. KRÓL, REV. JOHN T., J.C.D., The Defendant in Ecclesiastical Trials, XII-207 pp., 1942.
147. COMYNS, REV. JOSEPH J., C.SS.R., A.B., J.C.D., Papal and Episcopal Administration of Church Property, XIV-155 pp., 1942.
148. BARRY, REV. GARRETT FRANCIS, O.M.I., J.C.D., Violation of the Cloister, XII-260 pp,, 1942.
149. BOLDUC, REV. GATIEN, C.S.V., A.B., S.T.L., J.C.D., Lés Études dans les Religions Cléricales, VIII-155 pp., 1942.
150. BOYLE, REV. DAVID JOHN, M.A., J.C.D., The Juridic Effects of Moral Certitude on Pre-Nuptial Guarantees, XII-188 pp., 1942.
151. CANAVAN, REV. WALTER JOSEPH, M.A., LITT.D., J.C.D., The Profession of Faith, XII-143 pp., 1942.
152. DESROCHERS, REV. BRUNO, A.B., PH.L., S.T.B., J.C.D., Le Premier Concile Plénier de Québec et le Code de Droit Canonique, XIV-186 pp., 1942.

153. Dillon, Rev. Robert Edward, A.B., J.C.D., Common Law Marriage, X-148 pp., 1942.
154. Dodwell, Rev. Edward John, Ph.D., S.T.B., J.C.L., The Time and Place for the Celebration of Marriage.
155. Donnellan, Rev. Thomas Andrew, A.B., J.C.D., The Obligation of the Missa pro Populo, VII-131 pp., 1942.
156. Eltz, Rev. Louis Anthony, A.B., J.C.L., Cooperation in Crime.
157. Gass, Rev. Sylvester Francis, M.A., J.C.D., Ecclesiastical Pensions, XI-206 pp., 1942.
158. Guiniven, Rev. John Joseph, C.SS.R., J.C.D., The Precept of Hearing Mass, XIV-188 pp., 1942.
159. Gulczynski, Rev. John Theophilus, J.C.L., The Desecration and Violation of Churches.
160. Hammill, Rev. John Leo, M.A., J.C.D., The Obligations of the Traveler According to Canon 14, VIII-204 pp., 1942.
161. Haydt, Rev. John Joseph, A.B., J.C.D., Reserved Benefices, XI-148 pp., 1942.
162. Huser, Rev. Roger John, O.F.M., A.B., J.C.L., The Crime of Abortion in Canon Law.
163. Kearney, Rev. Francis Patrick, A.B., S.T.L., J.C.L., The Principles of Canon 1127.
164. Linahen, Rev. Leo James, S.T.L., J.C.D., De Absolutione Complicis In Peccato Turpi, 114 pp., 1942.
165. McCloskey, Rev. Joseph Aloysius, A.B., J.C.D., The Subject of Ecclesiastical Law According to Canon 12, XVII-246 pp., 1942.
166. O'Neill, Rev. Francis Joseph, C.SS.R., J.C.D., The Dismissal of Religious in Temporary Vows, XIII-220 pp., 1942.
167. Prince, Rev. John Edward, A.B., S.T.B., J.C.D., The Diocesan Chancellor, X-136 pp., 1942.
168. Riesner, Rev. Albert Joseph, C.SS.R., J.C.D., Apostates and Fugitives from Religious Institutes, IX-168 pp., 1942.
169. Stenger, Rev. Joseph Bernard, J.C.D., The Mortgaging of Church Property, 186 pp., 1942.
170. Waldron, Rev. Joseph Francis, A.B., J.C.D., The Minister of Baptism, XII-197 pp., 1942.
171. Willett, Rev. Robert Albert, J.C.D., The Probative Value of Documents in Ecclesiastical Trials, X-124 pp., 1942.
172. Woeber, Rev. Edward Martin, M.A., J.C.D., The Interpellations, XII-161 pp., 1942.
173. Benko, Rev. Matthew Aloysius, O.S.B., M.A., J.C.L., The Abbot *Nullius.*
174. Christ, Rev. Joseph James, M.A., S.T.L., J.C.L., Dispensation from Vindicative Penalties.
175. Clancy, Rev. Patrick M. J., O.P., A.B., S.T.Lr., J.C.L., The Local Religious Superior.

176. Clarke, Rev. Thomas James, J.C.L., Parish Societies.
177. Connolly, Rev. John Patrick, S.T.L., J.C.L., Synodal Examiners and Parish Priest Consultors.
178. Drumm, Rev. William Martin, A.B., J.C.L., Hospital Chaplains.
179. Flanagan, Rev. Bernard Joseph, A.B., S.T.L., J.C.L., The Canonical Erection of Religious Houses.
180. Kelleher, Rev. Stephen Joseph, A.B., S.T.B., J.C.L., Discussions with non-Catholics: Canonical Legislation.
181. Lewis, Rev. Gordian, C.P., J.C.L., Chapters in Religious Institutes.
182. Marx, Rev. Adolph, J.C.L., The Declaration of Nullity of Marriages Contracted Outside the Church.
183. Matulenas, Rev. Raymond Anthony, O.S.B., A.B., J.C.L., Communication, a Source of Privileges.
184. O'Leary, Rev. Charles Gerard, C.SS.R., Religious Dismissed After Perpetual Profession.
185. Power, Rev. Cornelius Michael, J.C.L., The Blessing of Cemeteries.
186. Shuhler, Rev. Ralph Vincent, O.S.A., J.C.L., Privileges of Religious to Absolve and Dispense.
187. Ziolkowski, Rev. Thaddeus Stanislaus, A.B., J.C.L., The Consecration and Blessing of Churches.

www.ingramcontent.com/pod-product-compliance
Lightning Source LLC
LaVergne TN
LVHW050238080826
844660LV00012B/556

9780813223759